To the children that On Location Education has taught through the years, and to Denise, with whom I'll raise our own young performers — AS

To Marilynn, to Tillie, and to the memory of Frances, George, and Julie — BAP

Acknowledgments

Our deepest appreciation goes to:

the great staff of *CallBack: For Young Performers and Their Families*, who month after month wrote numerous articles and gave valuable input, and did so with loyalty and verve. They are: John Attanas, J. Traven Duboff, Roberta Frost, Devorah Kaitz, Scott Knipe (Music Editor), and Jacqueline Kolmes (Dance Editor);

our contributors, who gave their time and expertise to making *CallBack* come alive: Ibrahim Abdul-Malik, Breanna Benjamin, Terry Berland, Neil Burstein, Ken Bush, Michael Chapin, Risa Cherry, Eileen Eichenstein, Bambi Everson, Ari Gold, Pat Golden, Neil Graeme, Jodi Green, Patricia Griffith, Suzette L. Harvey, Cindy Hsu, Howard Isaacs, Bruce Kluger, Melvyn M. Leifert, Rita Litton, Janine Marcel, Ellen Norman Melamed, Dianora Niccolini, Jean Page, Bill Persky, Elsa Posey, Gerald Lee Ratliff, Barbara Sarbin, Karen Schaeffer, Barbara Elman Schiffman, Frank Schindelheim, Randall Short, Lucy Silver, Alan J. Straus, Nancy Van Leuven, Malcolm-Jamal Warner, Linda Washburn, and Terré West;

and our researcher, Jacquelyn MacDowell.

Special appreciation to the people that made this book happen: Rita Rosenkranz, our literary agent, and Hilary Swinson, our editor at Betterway Publications.

—AS and BAP

Cover Photographs

Clockwise, from top left:

Anthony Michael Hall has been acting for 14 years and has appeared in such feature films as *Six Pack, National Lampoon's Vacation, Sixteen Candles, The Breakfast Club, Weird Science, Out of Bounds, Johnny Be Good,* and *Upworld.* He has also appeared in After School Specials, TV Movies of the Week, and countless commercials. (Photo by Ciro Barbaro)

Michelle Thomas has been acting for six years and has appeared for three seasons on *The Cosby Show* in the role of Justine, Theo's girlfriend. She has also starred in NBC's Movie of the Week, *Dream Date,* with Tempestt Bledsoe and played a lead episodic role in ABC's *A Man Called Hawk.* Michelle acted in the title role of *Betsey Brown* at the American Music Theater Festival in Philadelphia, and has performed in various other theater productions, music videos, and commercials. (Photo by Mychal Watts)

Corey Carrier has been acting for six years. His television experience includes appearances on *The Equalizer, Spenser: For Hire,* and the ABC Movie of the Week. Corey's film credits include *Men Don't Leave, Crazy People, The Witches of Eastwick,* and *My Blue Heaven.* Corey also performs stand-up comedy. (Photo by Michele Laurita)

Caroline Wilde has been acting for two years and has extensive television experience. Currently, she can be seen on ABC's *All My Children* as Erica Kane's daughter, Bianca Montgomery. She has appeared on *Kojak* and *Ryan's Hope* and in numerous commercials. (Photo by Jean Elizabeth Poli)

Christopher Collet has appeared in the films *The Manhattan Project, First Born,* and has guest starred in many television shows and specials including *The Cosby Show, The Equalizer,* and *A Hero in the Family.* Christopher has also performed on Broadway in *The Spoils of War* and *Torch Song Trilogy.* (Photo by Nick Granito)

Sarah Geller has been acting for nine years and has performed in many films and television shows including *Melanie Rose, Funny Farm, Crossroads, Spenser: For Hire, Love, Sidney,* and *William Tell.* She has been seen on *Late Night with David Letterman, The Regis Philbin Show, The Edge of Night,* and *As the World Turns.* (Photo by Manning Gurney)

Troy Winbush has been acting for five years and has appeared in movies such as the upcoming *Bonfire of the Vanities, Running on Empty,* and has co-starred in *The Principal* with Lou Gossett, Jr., James Belushi, and Rae Dawn Chong. His television experience includes the CBS After School Special, *The Gamblers,* and a recurring role as Denny on *The Cosby Show.* (Photo by Manning Gurney)

Alexis Cruz has been acting for six years including co-starring with Anthony Quinn in NBC's Movie Special, *The Old Man and the Sea,* working on *Sesame Street* for two years, *The Guiding Light,* and *The Cosby Show.* Alexis has co-starred in the film *Rooftops,* appeared in *The Pick-Up Artist,* and has acted in numerous commercials. (Photo by Barry Burns)

Foreword

Malcolm-Jamal Warner

Photo by Roger Prigent

Goals. Life, to me, is about setting goals. When I was younger, my goal changed from wanting to be a poet to wanting to play basketball for the Los Angeles Lakers. Along the way I ended up in an acting workshop and my goal changed once again — it was to be in a television series. There was never any hard evidence that I would ever reach any of these goals I had set for myself as a child, but it was driven into me by my parents that I had to strive for something.

I was fortunate to be able to live a "normal" childhood. I went to school, played sports, and participated in the community theater workshop. I also had household chores that had to be done before I was able to go out and play. Acting became something that I loved, but my mother let me know that she would have to pull me out of the workshop if my grades or my household responsibilities began to slip. Mind you, I was only nine years old.

This invaluable lesson on being responsible which my mother gave me carried over into my learning about professionalism in the business (a quality lacking in many young actors). Because I had an extremely grounded foundation as a child, when *The Cosby Show* came about, I was prepared for it. I knew how to compare it to life as a "civilian."

I was disciplined enough to sit with my tutors, many times on weekends, to put in 15 to 30 hours a week so that I could keep up with my studies. I missed out on plenty of parties. I missed out on having other kids in my class — no one to pass notes to, or cut up in class with, or beg, in desperation, to let me copy his homework for fear of a demerit. However, I did have friends, and I spent most of my high school years on the honor roll — both friends and school were important to me — and I thrived as a result of my experience. And guess what? Now I have the time to go to all the parties.

An important part of my life, and of my career as well, is my mom, Pamela Warner. Not only is she my mother, but she also doubles as my manager. She always has been and always will be in my corner. She never was a stage parent, simply being satisfied as "Malcolm-Jamal Warner's Mother," so she became a business person in her own right. She now heads her own management company and, more recently, we've formed our own production company, PMJ Productions. She's my mother, manager, business partner, and best friend. I have the security of knowing that she will always be there to watch my back.

Unfortunately, most young people in the business are groomed to become "stars." They don't get a chance to find out who they are first and they approach the business — and their lives — with insecurities. Sometimes they aren't even in the business because they want to be, but because their parents are living vicariously through them.

Personally, I feel that children need to live their lives before entering show business. They need to be kids. They need to learn about themselves and about the responsibilities they undertake when they commit to a career. They need to feel secure with themselves and they need to know that there are alternatives to acting. Families need to know what the life-style — the long hours, the tedium of production, the interruption of school, the effect on other siblings — can do to their children physically, emotionally, and spiritually.

This is why *The Young Performer's Guide* was written — for young performers and their families. This book should help those who aren't knowledgeable about the business, but who wish to find a way — their way — to begin a career. It offers practical advice on a range of topics pertinent to youngsters. It's written not only by agents and managers and casting directors, but by parents, educators, health practitioners, accountants, lawyers, and many others who are child advocates. There's so much to take into account when putting your child in this business that many opinions are necessary to make the right decision about your family's path down the bumpy road towards a career.

The Young Performer's Guide is here to show you your options as it promotes the needs of the child performer. While no one book can tell everything, this guide is one of the best supplements available to a life-style that already promotes a child's best interests.

Young performers have the power to make their careers a reality. If you're going to be in this business, develop your own talents and find your own style. Be real and stay true to yourself. That's the only way you will enjoy the fruits of your success.

Contents

Introduction

CallBack: For Young Performers and Their Families made its first appearance in December 1987. From the start, *CallBack* was for youngsters seeking to understand the *business* side of show business and wishing to become part of it. Our editorial slant, although primarily geared for young actors, offered insight on the world of young dancers and musicians, too. At the same time, we balanced the needs of performers with those of non-performers, and we delved into a discussion of various behind-the-scenes career alternatives.

CallBack wasn't about show biz teenage gossip. We didn't ask what a young actor's favorite color was, or what he ate for lunch, or who his favorite movie star was. What we were after was the input of industry professionals — agents, managers, casting directors, performers, producers, directors, writers, parents, teachers, dentists, psychologists, accountants, lawyers, union members, photographers, and other child advocates — who could offer their expertise on a range of show business related topics.

Our contributors wrote articles on getting an agent and manager and the differences between them. They discussed writing a résumé, taking a headshot, and making a workable videotape. They delved into accounting methods, legal concerns (such as the "Coogan Law"), and securing rights to shows for community theater productions. They talked about technique, scene study, and audition practices. They offered insight into health issues such as diets, eating disorders, and stress signals. They spoke on the unions' education rules, choosing a good college, and surviving economically during performing dry spells. Each issue of *CallBack* was rounded out by a series of celebrity interviews; in-depth discussions with working professionals who offered to share their thoughts on building an ongoing career.

CallBack, though, wasn't just for the young performer. Our audience was also the *parents* of the young performers. In no other career does a youngster need her parents more than in the dog-eat-dog world of show business. In fact, *CallBack* has showed most parents that their children could balance *two* full-time careers in this business, one as actors, the other as students. How a parent approaches show business is often a deciding factor not only in making a child's career successful, but also in her emotional success and stability, as well as in the overall family unit.

From the pages of *CallBack* comes *The Young Performer's Guide*. *The Young Performer's Guide* is more than an anthology of articles that have appeared over the years in the magazine. It is a comprehensive handbook, designed to place at the reader's fingertips the most valuable information about the intricacies and nuances of show business. It's for the novice whose knowledge is limited; but it's also useful for the established performer who looks to reinforce his or her perceptions of the business.

The Young Performer's Guide is different from most references on young performers. In the first place, no other book for young performers offers a section on their health and maintenance. No other book offers a section on babies and how to break an infant or toddler into the business. And no other book has input from some very well-known performers whose careers are benchmarks for other youngsters.

Many of the articles in this book have been written from the perspective of New York or Los Angeles, the two major production centers of our country. Don't let this be daunting if you live in Chicago, Cheyenne, Minneapolis — or Podunk. The information here transcends where you live. Show business is about how you approach your career, how you feel about yourself as a professional, and how the business perceives you.

The Young Performer's Guide knows that entering show business is a family decision, and we hope that young performers and their families will use this book and consider it an invaluable tool towards building a successful career. We're proud of its role in contributing to the well-being of young performers everywhere.

Alan Simon, Editor-in-Chief
Brian A Padol, Publisher
1990

1
Getting Started

There's a big part of me that's still eight years old. And a big part of me that's forty. But that's because the business demands it of you. They want you to be a child, but simultaneously you must be professional, you must be responsible, and you have to be aware. Those things I've just learned how to do.

Martha Plimpton, featured in Parenthood

✪

Getting started? You've already gotten started! You started even before you bought this book. If you're a parent, you have decided that your child has a chance for a career in show business, and you're looking for some advice on how to help your child in the best way without spending too much money. If you're a young performer, you've decided on your career and want some help, for both you and your parents, to make your dream come true.

If you're that young performer, you already know that you like to perform and you think that you're willing to do the work — pay your dues — to be in show business. You've already performed for an audience.

But if you're a parent, we hope that you've done your homework. Does your child *really* want to be a performer? Has your child done some performing in school? Has your child had any special training for performers?

Most important, has someone who is *not* a friend, relative, or teacher, but who is involved in show business somehow, whose opinion is respected, told you that you (if you're the young performer) or your child has talent and that you ought to pursue a career?

If you've done all that work, you can read this guide and start to put some of its concepts into effect as soon as you can. If you haven't, then you must do that work while you're reading this book.

Performing, whether as an amateur or as a professional career, can be rich and rewarding. But....

But the first time it's not fun, the moment that a young performer really wants to get out of the business — that's the time to get out. Nothing is more important than the normal growing-up process of a child. It may be true that the show must go on, but it is also true and is also more important that the young child go on to become a happy, fulfilled adult.

Please keep our warning in mind — and act on it, if needed — but give your try at show business your best effort.

★

Any guide for the young performer should begin with a discussion of agents and managers. For the young performer who is looking to build a career in show business, representation by a qualified professional is the only way to find paying work.

The way the entertainment business operates is that an agent will get a call from the casting director of a specific project (e.g., a commercial, a Broadway show, a film, etc.), who is looking for a certain type of actor to fit a role. The agent in turn will submit the names and photographs of clients who fit that role's description. If a child is represented by a manager, then that agent would call the child's manager to ask if he or she is available for submission.

So, you may wonder, should a novice have an agent or a manager? What really is the difference between the two jobs? What makes for a good agent or manager? How do you find someone to represent you? What do they look for in a client? What will it cost you to have a professional in your corner? Should a parent try to manage his or her child? These are questions that several seasoned professionals try to answer.

THE ROLE OF THE MANAGER
Breanna Benjamin

There shouldn't even have to be managers in this business, and if the industry hadn't evolved the way it did, there wouldn't be a need for them. That's because 30 years ago agents did the jobs that managers are doing now, since they only had 15 or 20 clients and were able to handle all facets of their careers. This included getting the clients from the audition for the project through the public relations to promote it. Now, because of the nature of the industry, most agents have between 50 and 100 clients, and some have as many as 200, with access to nearly 2,000. Because of the economics of the situation, the client/agent relationship has become, in many cases, booking the job, not guiding the career. That's not necessarily a negative point, for we're all in this industry to make money. But because of this change, the manager has evolved and become a very important part of the scene.

If the industry and its economics don't change, then it's possible that in 15 or 20 years there may not be a need for agents. There will be only managers. This is because actors are feeling lost, not because agents aren't doing a good job. They are! But when you have to spend thousands of dollars for office rent, and pay all your employees, then something has to give. That usually means taking on more clients. What happens then is that agents get a bad rap. Usually, the actors get a bad rap, too, because they're likely to agent-hop. Obviously, they need attention from someone, and that's why managers have developed a more prominent role; they're likely to provide that attention. The manager can take on 15 or 20 clients and help boost both the actors' careers and egos.

There are managers who have 100 clients, though I question how they can call themselves managers. Agents are franchised through the unions — Screen Actors Guild (SAG), American Federation of Television and Radio Artists (AFTRA), and Actors Equity Association (AEA). They operate as employment agencies and, therefore, are state-controlled. Managers aren't bound by state or union regulations.

The regulation of agents hasn't meant that they do better jobs. Control doesn't necessarily mean excitement about doing a job; it just makes the agency pay extra dues here or there.

The unions are always available to answer any questions a manager, franchised or not, asks. The point is that a good manager or agent should take the time to ask the right questions, and not take on any more clients than can be handled.

How a manager works

Management of a young performer varies from client to client. It was always my philosophy that being a manager involved working with a small number of people and giving them individual attention. It's important to have the time to learn what a client needs. You may have four 16-year-olds, but they'll have four distinct personalities and four completely different directions to go in the industry.

If a young person is interested in doing commercials for *fun*, whether she does one a year or a hundred a year, she doesn't need a manager. Agents can and will get her the auditions, whether she has a manager or not. It's the young person who thinks she's going to make show business a career who'll need a manager. It may sound funny to assume that the 10-year-old may already know that this is the career that she wishes to pursue, but some children do know instinctively what they want to be. If it's the child's idea, and *not* the parent's idea, she'll need someone for guidance. She'll need someone to introduce her to agents and to get her into the right training. (I'm a big believer in leaving the pre-teen alone and letting her develop naturally. Teenage years are the time to begin studying!) She'll also need someone to guide her to the right public relations representative, if needed.

One of the other big jobs of the manager is to allow the child to be a child and the parent to be a parent. This helps assure that the parent won't have to step in and become a manager. Parents shouldn't have to manage their children's careers. There are, of course, exceptions to every rule, and some parents can manage their children's careers very well. Be advised, though, that it's a full-time job. And in 99 out of 100 of those cases, the child becomes very confused about the role of her parent and about their relationship. She may wonder: Is this my mother? Is this my father? Is this my boss? Is this my business manager?

It's my opinion that the child needs the emotional support from the parent as the parent. The parent can come into the manager's office and we can cuss and discuss, agree and disagree, and advise that the child do this movie and not do that show. A good manager should talk about various projects with the child and the parent and figure out what works best for the family. They should be encouraged to go home and discuss projects, as a family. The parent should be the child's shoulder to cry on, the reward at the end of the hard day's work, not the one who says, "You should have done this." When the child comes out of the audition, it should be the parent who says, "You want to go for a hot dog?" I've turned down many a prospective client for what I've perceived as an unhealthy relationship between parent and child. If it becomes obvious that it's the parent, and not the child, who wants to do this, I don't want to have any part of it.

Who do I see first?

The age-old question asked by most people has to do with whether they should first go to an agent or to a manager. It's still a very difficult question to answer. There are some very good agents in the industry who could handle a beginner's career, and there are equally good managers. Thus, there's no one definite answer, since it depends on how a particular agent or manager does his or her job. For the child interested solely in commercials, I don't believe that a manager is necessary. That child doesn't need grooming, doesn't need handholding, doesn't need guidance to the next level of her career. She needs a good commercial agent.

Managers aren't supposed to book jobs directly because they don't have employment agency licenses. Today, however, more and more managers are getting their licenses for the simple reason that they can then go ahead and book their clients. But this doesn't mean that managers want to do agents out of their jobs. That would be self-destructive, since this business is like any other team sport in that you need the full team to win, to get the client to the top of the heap. Major child actors have the support of one or the other of these professionals, and in most cases, of both. Some parents may feel that they must make a choice between agent and manager, especially when their children work for scale and large percentages are deducted, along with taxes, from their children's paychecks. That alone shouldn't be the determining factor in deciding which type of representation to go with. Not only are many of these expenses likely to be tax deductible, but considering that without these contacts the child was making nothing, she's still in better shape than if she were on her own.

For example, many managers negotiate with the agent for their commissions to be paid directly to them by the production company. This way, the child isn't taxed on monies that she doesn't ever see. If the child makes $100, and 10% goes to the agent, and 15% to the manager, the child is taxed on the $75 that belongs to her, rather than on her pre-commissioned gross of $100. This is only one of the ways that *the team* works for the young performer.

A good manager saves the client money. There are appointments that she would go on if she had no one to guide her away from the unimportant ones. She'd waste money on photographers without someone to recommend a good one the first time, so she wouldn't have to try three times until she got good pictures. Money gets saved all the time, although most parents usually don't consider the hidden savings.

A good manager advises the actor to keep studying. It's been said that if you're a child actor you'll be a has-been by the time you're an adult. That's not necessarily true, although it has been true in some cases. There have been child stars who, when growing up, didn't realize that they had gotten by on their cuteness, naturalness, and wit. They never stopped to study their craft. Somewhere along the line, the young performer must stop and learn the elements of technique.

I also feel that there need to be more classes for parents. The kids in this industry have special needs and it's important for the parents to learn how to support those needs. The parent must help the child succeed not by pushing her, but by remaining in a neutral corner so as to be the child's refuge.

> *Breanna Benjamin is now a casting director for Breanna Benjamin Casting. She became a manager in 1977, when she founded F.C.O. Management, presently run by Shannon Buettow. Ms. Benjamin's management clients have included such noted performers as Ally Sheedy and Christopher Collet. As a casting director, she casts for feature films, television, and theater.*

PARENTS WHO MANAGE THEIR CHILDREN
J. Traven Duboff

Two of the most demanding jobs in this world are being a parent and being a professional talent manager. Each draws upon a person's patience, endurance, and intelligence. Each is challenging. Each is also very rewarding. In spite of the demands, many people both parent and manage. Further, there are parents who not only make their careers as talent managers, but as managers of their own performing offspring.

We asked several of these parent-managers what kind of person takes on that dual role, why they do it, and how it affects the family and the careers of both the parent and the child. As you'll see, managing one's child is a job reserved for a select group.

Knowledge of the *business* of show business is mandatory in order to manage one's child. Many parent-managers have backgrounds in the business. Some, such as Jean Fox, of Fox/Albert Management grew up in the business. As a little girl, Jean sang jingles in commercials and on stage, and as an adult, she made a career in the jingle market. But, when her daughters, Lauren and Haley, began performing, Jean started her management company. At first it was devoted just to child jingle-singers, but the business has grown over the years to represent all kinds of child clients. Lauren and Haley are just two of the many young performers Jean manages.

Some parents' show business education begins when their children start making the rounds. Mary Seaman was a self-described "suburban housewife" before her kids, Page, David, and Geoffrey, started performing. Three years later, she became their manager. Mary began managing kids with the manager and friend of the family who first suggested that the Seaman kids perform. They formed the now-defunct partnership of Rosenberg and Seaman Talent Management. Currently, Mary runs SEA-MAN Management. Her ex-partner, Joan Rosenberg, runs Rosenberg & Associates and manages her own children, Peter James and Jeannine James.

There are many reasons parents would want to manage their children. James Pulliam, whose daughter, Keshia, is featured on *The Cosby Show*, says, "I saw it as a chance to give her something most daughters can't get from their fathers."

James approaches his daughter's management this way: "Who knows what's best for Keshia better than I, her father?"

To supplement their parental nurturing instincts, the Pulliams work with a professional talent manager, Shirley Grant, of Shirley Grant Management, in Teaneck, New Jersey. The Pulliams began their association with Shirley when Keshia was just a baby. Subsequently, as James' business acumen grew, he assumed responsibility for more of the day-to-day details of Keshia's management. While he and his wife, Denise, maintain control of their daughter's career, they still trust and value Shirley's keen business sense and personal input in their lives.

Sometimes contributing to parents opting to manage their children is the perception that the family's first manager didn't give them proper attention and representation. Cathy Parker's impetus for starting Cathy Parker Talent Management, based in Voorhees, New Jersey, near Philadelphia, was their first manager's poor treatment of the career of her son, John Jay.

"There were some commercial calls, but it was all a waste," Cathy explains. "He did not know what was expected of him in front of a camera, and he was usually sent on the wrong calls. All this confusion led up to my becoming a full-time manager."

Cathy bases her business, which she operates out of her home, on the motto, "I'm a mother first and I've been there." Her effort pays off, for Cathy is listed in the roster of the National Conference of Personal Managers, an organization with highly selective standards of membership.

Another management company started by a dissatisfied parent is Suzelle Enterprises, headed by Sue Schachter, and located in Jamaica Estates, New York. Clients include Mindy Cohn of *The Facts of Life*, Haywood Nelson of *What's Happening Now?*, Troy Beyer of *Rooftops*, and Alex Vincent of *Child's Play*. Sue started her company because she felt "the inadequacies and unkindnesses" directed toward her as a stage mother. "I swore I wouldn't do the same." Her three daughters, Felice, Simone, and Janine, all grew up in front of the camera. Felice and Simone are still acting and modeling. Janine works with Sue and is planning a career in management.

With a manager normally earning a commission of 15% of the performer's earnings, one would think money is an important factor to a parent who chooses to manage his child, but this is not, or should not be, the case. For most child performers, a parent's decision to manage is a financial risk. What if the parent can't manage well? The money invested in headshots, lessons, haircuts, and trips to New York and LA is thrown away unless there are returns, and returns are measured solely in bookings. As for the manager's take, "It's better to pay 15% and book than not to book and keep 15% of nothing," says Michelle Donay, of Michelle Donay Talent Management in New York.

Risks and responsibilities of the parent/manager

A parent must be prepared for many changes that will evolve when managing his child. Becoming a parent-manager usually means a change in the parent's career, in the amount of available leisure time, and even in the family's address. Mary Seaman and her family moved from suburban Westchester to Manhattan when she began managing. The many risks involved may not be worth the effort. These include personal burnout, strains on the rest of the family, and neglect of the other children.

Management is a time- and energy-consuming profession. James Pulliam meets with agents and attorneys daily, traveling to their offices and meeting them at his home. Tom Chestaro, stepfather and manager of actor Anthony Michael Hall, works at home and is frequently on the phone till after seven at night. Managers with several clients have to notify them of sudden changes in audition schedules and any other unexpected events. If a client can't be reached from the office, the manager will be on the phone at home. Jean Fox has a mini-office set up in her apartment for just that purpose.

Juggling these responsibilities is a challenge. All the managers *CallBack* spoke with said it was very, very difficult at first to fulfill their parental and managerial roles. Feeling overwhelmed is not uncommon.

What keeps them going is that all these parent-managers have dual loves — a love for their children and a love for show business. Without such feelings, they would have quickly been out of the business. "There are times," says Haley Fox of her mother, "when it seems that she's being more of a mother to her other kids than to me, and more of a manager to me than to them."

None of the parents would provide details about the process by which their jobs transformed from very, very difficult to manageable. Apparently, being a parent-manager doesn't become any easier; people just become better at it with experience.

In fact, many seem to thrive on the very nature of their work. "It's a very, very exciting business," says Tom Chestaro. "I enjoy working with the producers, the directors, the writers, and the executives. I enjoy learning further about the dynamics of the business."

Lauren Fox, describing her mother's commitment to her profession, says, "She really loves what she does. We make fun of it sometimes because she's so involved. She'll call clients on location and ask if everything is all right. She's really involved."

Every successful parent-manager seems to have an entrepreneurial spirit, as is demonstrated by the new businesses they create. Fox/Albert Management, Rosenberg & Associates, SEA-MAN Management, Cathy Parker Talent Management, and Suzelle Enterprises are evidence of this. Tom Chestaro is now executive in charge of production at Midi City Records and manages Sandra Bullock, James Lorinz, and Anthony La Paglia.

There are many sacrifices to be made by the family in which the parent manages a child. When one parent manages, the other must be willing to adapt to the show business lifestyle. Among other adjustments, there are missed meals and less shared recreation time. If the non-managing parent is familiar with this lifestyle, the transition won't be very difficult. Such was the case with Anthony Michael Hall's mother, Mercedes, who is a singer and long-time performer. For others, though, being the "other parent" is a learning experience. Adjusting to it is easier if the new lifestyle is seen as another way a parent can be there for the child.

For some families, it's best for the non-managing parent to take an active interest in the child's career. Denise Pulliam takes Keshia to and from the set of *The Cosby Show*, and works with her, helping her memorize lines.

Though Mercedes Hall often could not accompany Anthony Michael when he worked out of town, her son was always accompanied by at least one relative.

David Seaman appreciates his dad's help: "He participates as much as he can. Though he's a lawyer and very busy, he spends a lot of time taking us out on calls. It's great having two parents who support you in what you're doing."

Scheduling family time away from business is critical. Around Labor Day, the Foxes go to a favorite resort in upstate New York. The quiet setting helps recharge their batteries for the fall, when school resumes and work picks up. As for the rest of the year, Lauren says, "Every week or two we'll notice that we haven't spent any time together, so we'll decide to go out to dinner."

Selma Rubin, of Selma Rubin Talent Management, Inc. in Queens, New York, is acutely aware of another danger parent-managers face. She warns of the danger of neglect of the other children. "If one child is taking time out from school, and the parent is taking that child on auditions and spending so much time with that child," she warns, "tell me, what's going to happen to the other child?" Selma knows; she's managed children for 25 years. She also observes that emotional damage done to a child can't be measured until years later.

That's why Bill Perlman, of New Talent Management in Bricktown, New Jersey, when asked for advice for parents who want to manage their children, said flatly, "Don't."

One way to avoid neglect is to have all the children in the family perform. This worked for Geoffrey, the Seamans' youngest child. Older siblings Page and David were acting, and Geoffrey decided to try it, too. At eight, he was featured in the film *Pippi Longstocking*. Any manager worth his salt, however, will tell you that the "other" child[ren] must *want* to perform.

This brings us back to the primary concern of any parent who manages: What happens to the children? Their needs must be respected and their interests honored. Asked to describe the experience of having their parents as managers, the kids are upbeat and positive. What others see as the peculiarities of their situation are simply matter-of-fact to them.

The children of parent-managers seem to learn the ins and outs of the business at an earlier age than children whose parents don't manage them. "I've been learning a lot through her," says Page Seaman of her mother. "When I answer the phones or help her out, I get the feel of what she does with me. I see all the work she does — calling agents and clients — so I understand both ropes." That's probably why many of the young people consider behind-the-scenes careers in show business.

Children of parent/managers have as hard — or as easy — a time booking as do other performers. Preparation for auditions is still as necessary and not any easier because the manager has the same last name. Casting directors and agents don't favor them. In fact, there's added responsibility on the parents' shoulders to demonstrate that they don't favor their own children over other clients.

What kids and parents think

Many of the kids we spoke with extolled the benefits of being managed by their parents. They feel their parents, who know them best, give them the most honest criticism. The parent and child work more closely together, and the child gets more out of his or her performing experience.

Lauren Fox explains the dynamics between herself and her mother: "There have been times when she has said, 'You're not ready for this,' and it was true. But if I see a script I want to audition for, I'll say 'I know you may not think I'm ready, but I think I can really do this, and I'd really like to try.' It depends. We'll talk about it. If I really want it, and I really think I can do it, she'll work with me and I'll go up for it. She'd rather I try, and not get the part."

Not all commentary, though, was enthusiastic. While none of the people with whom *CallBack* spoke were unhappy, none were quick to recommend parent-management to others. The young performers wouldn't dwell on negative aspects of being managed by their parents, but were always pointing out the positive ones. One, asked for comments regarding being managed by Mom, responded, "It brings me closer to her in two ways because she's involved in my personal life and professional life. That makes it extra special."

Parents, on the other hand, spoke relatively freely of the difficulties their dual roles created.

The children receive a fair number of comments from people who don't understand their experience. From peers, such comments are simply annoying; from professionals, they can be malicious. Friends' remarks usually take such form as "You must have it so easy — your mom *manages* you!" One high school voice teacher, who should have known better, told a student, "Well, a lot of us just aren't as lucky as you."

What's a child to do in such circumstances? The actress on the receiving end of that barb left her school for another one, a drastic step, perhaps, but one which resulted in her being in a more comfortable environment.

Ultimately, whether being managed by one's parent proves to be a benefit or a detriment depends on how well the parent balances the roles. "Parent first, manager second," is the best rule of thumb.

"Being a good parent," Tom Chestaro states, "is first and foremost. It allows you to focus in on everything else and become a better manager for your child. I guess the greatest compliment you can get from your child is if he willingly comes to you and asks you what you think. That's a sign that you're taking care of business — on a personal level as well as a professional one. That," he says, "is the icing on the cake."

✪

It's not much different managing children on the west coast, as manager/parent Jean Page explains.

A CHILDREN'S MANAGER IN LOS ANGELES
Jean Page

Once the show biz bug bites, it injects all of that marvelous craziness — *SHOW BIZ* — into your blood.

"What'll I do with my life?" I questioned loudly. Christopher was off to the University of California at Santa Barbara and was immediately accelerated to Upper Division Party #404. Susie had braces on her teeth — metal ones at that! — and we all know what *that* does to a career. Kelly had flown the nest to "work" — as a ski instructor in Austria.

Since I had been a practicing marriage and family counselor and a published astrological counselor, I took the most obvious course of action and made the decision to stay in the "biz." Why not share my knowledge and help other kids and their moms learn to fill their cars with wardrobe, McDonald's wrappers, and 7–11 cups? Still, it wasn't a simple step to take.

There are some age-old questions that are posed constantly: "Why do I need a manager?" and "What's the difference between an agent and a manager?" From the LA scene, here's a bit of insight:

California, like New York, requires that an agent be franchised by the state. Therefore, the agent is under state jurisdiction to perform within certain guidelines. Most agents are also franchised by the Screen Actors Guild and have its rules as well to comply with. Managers, on the other hand, answer only to their integrity.

To help guide the manager on ethics in the LA area, we have the National Conference of Personal Managers (NCOPM) and the Conference of Personal Managers-West. The organizations differ in their individual guidelines, but both were established to provide a framework to managers, whether they're experienced or not. Otherwise, it's every man for himself, and not every time does the best man win.

Managing pulls people from under rocks that you never knew existed. Since there are no rules governing managers or the amount of money that they may take from clients, horror stories of rip-offs abound. The parent who is unaware of the scams, and who gets caught up in this business with stars in her eyes and promises of stardom for her kids, is truly the loser.

Managers may work out of their own homes. They usually charge 15% of clients' earnings, but it's not unheard of for them to charge more. Most agents work out of offices, whether for someone else or with their own companies, and their rate is prescribed by law at 10%. The NCOPM, both in LA and in New York, is trying its best to provide information to the uninformed public as to how to go about locating reputable managers, how to get started in show business, and the pitfalls to avoid.

An agent has many clients and is required to give them the utmost attention. Most do what they can, but the uninformed mother may need more handholding than the agent can provide. In LA, for a mom to call an agent and take the agent's valuable time by asking if her munchkin's hair is the right length or where she should take those much needed lessons makes Mom an unpopular person in agent country. The agent's time is spent seeing casting directors and putting out breakdown information gotten from a daily bulletin delivered to the office that supplies data on current industry projects in need of talent. If Mom takes up Agent's time on the phone, Agent has no time to read *Breakdown Services* to determine if there's a perfect job opening for Mom's child.

Several agents in LA recommend that their clients see managers, who are better able to service the needs of unknowing parents and direct them to moves that are best for the child. Most agents agree that working with a manager should provide answers to most novices' questions.

Managers get to do research into such subjects as whose ears wiggle, who can blow bubbles, jump double-Dutch, or boast of an innie, instead of an outie, belly-button. Managers usually have a much smaller client list than agents do, and can give more personal attention to the youngster. A contract is usually signed for a three-year period, allowing the business-orientation process time to develop between the family and the manager.

Managers have the ability to put the whole package together, including steering the client to a publicist or a business manager when needed. In general, the manager guides, directs, and offers suggestions on how to get the career moving. The manager gives personalized attention to the family *and* to the agent who books the job.

It's necessary for the manager to be on top of everything in order to provide his clients with the best opportunities available. The manager follows through on many leads and, with the aid of the agent, gets clients through doors that ordinarily might be closed to them. In California, the manager may not solicit employment; he must make all deals through an agent licensed by the state.

Using my own business as an example, I know I leave no stone unturned when trying to secure work, including having the children make voice-over tapes which I distribute for them. Our company puts out a brochure twice a year that's sent to all producers, directors, and casting agents on the east and west coasts. Once a month, I have a day devoted to young people seeking managerial representation. It's called "Super Saturday." The photos of children who aren't selected immediately for principal work are kept on file for extra work. They're filed alongside those of several hundred babies we have access to. Often, this gives the brother or sister of the principal child the chance to work. Frequently, youngsters get upgraded — this means their parts get larger — and they'll automatically be able to join a union, either AFTRA or SAG.

The few children we feel we might work well with are further screened after taking a video-oriented on-camera class to hone their skills. The ones who remain get their headshots and résumés together and are then exposed to the top children's agents in LA.

This is a full-time business, and mothers bitten by the show biz bug have to be attuned to all aspects of their children's careers. The business is constantly changing due to strikes, new laws, and changing business trends, and there will always be a need for knowledgeable people to help share the experiences. And this manager, in particular, is always looking for new ways to help others fulfill their dreams.

> *Jean Page is a personal manager in Los Angeles and is a member of the National Conference of Personal Managers.*

Lucy Silver, a former agent based in New York, talks about what she looked for in a young client.

SECRETS OF THE AGENT
Lucy Silver

As a former talent agent, I received at least 30 pictures and résumés in the mail every day, and I went through all of them because I never knew when the picture of the next young superstar would be there. For every 30 pictures, I called in about six of the children to my office for an interview, or to do a monologue, or to try a cold reading — a reading that the performer hasn't had a chance to rehearse or prepare in advance.

What made me want to meet with someone based on a photo or résumé was something intangible. Certainly an actor's experiences or credits had something to do with it, but most kids simply don't have major credits. I'd say that it was something behind the eyes in the photo that just told me that this might be an interesting person and it would be worth my while to get to know him or her. Of the six I interviewed, usually I'd find only one with whom I really felt I could work successfully. Those are pretty slim odds. It's a very tough business, and it's important for parents and children to understand that they have to keep pushing to be seen. But they also have to know what they're pushing for.

I could spot — in a minute — the child who didn't want to be doing this work. He was the one who came into my office and didn't talk to me. That child's parent was the one who sat in the waiting room promising the child a reward — or bribe — if he talked nicely to me and ended up being booked on a job.

Just because a child says once, while watching a Saturday morning commercial, "I can do that," doesn't mean that the child really *wants* to do it. I looked for the child who had interest! I looked for the child who was well-adjusted, who did well in school. I liked the child who could focus, who was attentive, who was disciplined. I looked for a child who could read well because that made it easier on him in the long run.

I looked for a child who was inquisitive and who asked a lot of questions. I looked for the child who was interested in something else besides this business. I looked for the child who could "hang it up" at the end of the day or the audition, and become a real child again. I didn't want a "package" that the parents concocted and brought into the office.

I looked for children whose parents were supportive of their lives and their extra-curricular activities. The family is a very important stabilizing influence on the child, especially if the family members are realistic. They must know this is a business, that it is competitive, and that there are decisions to be made. As a family unit they must decide, for example, whether to do a play for which the child will earn $250 a week or a national commercial with the potential for lots of residuals. But the family must choose, *based on the child's wishes*, or else whatever the child does is unlikely to succeed.

Parents shouldn't be pushy. They must have a realistic view of who their child is and must accept the kinds of roles that the agent is submitting the child for. A child who is considered by his parents to be beautiful, may be beautiful *only* in his parents' eyes. The reality to me or the casting director may be that this child is overweight, or buck-toothed, or any of a number of hard truths that the parents find difficult to accept. This doesn't mean the child isn't employable; it only means that he might not be right for the roles the parents envision him in.

Certainly parents should ask questions, and should even make suggestions about what they think their child is right for. But, ultimately, the parent must trust the agent's judgment to speak for them and for their child. As long as they have an honest understanding of the child's talent and what the child can do, and how the child looks, then they're off to a good start.

Lucy Silver is now a manager with Miller/Silver Management, Inc.

TOOLS OF THE TRADE

Your business card: the headshot

Most young performers and their families often question how important it is to have a good headshot. Judging from what you're about to read, the answer is *very*. But what do you do if you need a headshot to get started, but can't afford to pay between $200 and $500 a session for a photographer's services, plus another $200 to $300 dollars for reproductions? The answer may be easier — and cheaper — than you think.

Most children take class photos, both with their class and individually. An individual shot is usually reproduced into wallet-size pictures which the family purchases and gives to grandmother, godfather, and cousin Blanche. Why not have extra copies made to send to agents, managers, casting directors, and local theaters?

With costs in mind, interesting an agent or a manager may be as simple as taking a Polaroid® snapshot of your child. Certainly this is not as professional as having a photographer work with you on a session. If what you're looking for, however, is to meet with potential representation to determine if your child stands a chance in this business, then a snapshot will initially suffice.

Once you're told that your child has what it takes, then the headshot/business card becomes essential. If you don't live in one of the major show business centers, you may find it cheaper to get your first set of pictures made in your own home town. Just make sure, however, that the photographer is familiar with how to shoot *headshots*, and is not offering you a posed portrait.

GETTING A GOOD HEADSHOT
John Attanas and Dianora Niccolini

For any young performer to have a legitimate chance at success in today's crowded marketplace, he or she must possess a number of things. One is talent, another is a desire to work hard, a third is the ability to accept rejection and go out on that next audition with the most positive attitude possible, and a fourth is a good headshot. While the first three are to one degree or another innate, a headshot is something entirely manmade, and, therefore, quality-controllable. As is the case with the other three

Carissa Lee Diana   Photo by Boundary Promotions

Marcus Presley

Photo by Michael Ian

necessities, the right headshot may not by itself be able to make your career, but the wrong one can most certainly break it.

For performers of any age, headshots are the means by which they introduce themselves to agents, producers, and casting directors. When a performer is just starting out and has neither a reputation nor connections in the business, he is totally dependent on headshots to get that agent's door open so he can show the agent what he can do. Getting the right headshot, however, is no easy task. While it's certainly simple to look in a trade publication for a photographer's ad and to set up a photo session, there are many things to consider before you decide where to sit down and pose. Unless you make an effort to educate yourself on the dos and don'ts of headshot photography, you might find yourself stuck with bad pictures and out hundreds of dollars as well.

Finding a photographer

When you start looking for a photographer to take your headshots, a good thing to remember, according to Michael Nathan of Ideal Photos, is that the entertainment business is "one big opinion"; everyone involved has an opinion on just about everything. Nathan, whose company reproduces over 700,000 prints per year, has his own opinion about what performers should do when they're ready to have their pictures taken. Noting that there are many seedy characters out there who will promise the moon to unsuspecting newcomers, Nathan advises that a person take as much time as is necessary to find a *good* photographer, because "you need a good photographer to get good prints." In order to find that good photographer, you must shop around, as you would for a TV or an automobile. This process should include calling photographers you've read or heard about, and making appointments to see their work.

According to Caroline Ross, who is an actress as well as a photographer, a person must "interview the photographer," for if you don't like the photographer's personality, "you're not going to open up and trust them."

Steven Speliotis, a headshot photographer who has also done work for the Brooklyn Academy of Music, the Manhattan Theatre Club, and numerous dance companies, agrees, stating, "The most important thing is the rapport with the photographer"; in order to get a good headshot, the subject must feel that the photographer really cares about him or her.

Of equal importance to rapport is a positive response to the work of the photographer you're considering hiring. A performer should be fairly clear as to how he wishes to present himself, according to Dianora Niccolini, whose subjects have ranged from five months to 95 years of age. She believes that if a photographer's style does not jibe with the image the person wishes to present, the individual should continue shopping around.

Ms. Niccolini further recommends consulting with friends and instructors to get recommendations of good photographers. "If you're new in town, the trade papers are the next best idea," reports Ms. Niccolini. "One of the hardest decisions you'll have to make is determining if the photographer you're about to choose is a fly-by-night.

"The two best ways of assessing the situation," she continued, "are by actually visiting the studio to look at the photographer's portfolio and to get a price list or *prices in writing*. It is in your best interest to make the decision without pressure or unnecessary influence from the photographer. You are purchasing an economically feasible photograph, not the photographer's 'personality'. A reputable photographer will have no problem with your decision to 'think things through' outside of his or her studio."

Once the subject decides, however, that he's found the right photographer, other concerns come into play.

Clothes, make-up, hair style, and the time of day your shoot is going to take place have a great deal to do with how your headshots will turn out. Brian Haviland, who's been doing headshots for 15 years, advises performers to stay away from pale colors.

But Denise Winters, who describes her approach to photography as "different from anyone else's," advises performers to bring their favorite clothes, "because the minute you put on something that you like, it shows in your face."

Steven Speliotis agrees, but adds that a performer shouldn't wear anything that's too distracting, such as large jewelry, which not only has the potential to take away from the visual image, but might also put a "label" on the subject.

Dianora Niccolini advises the performer: "Bring three or four different changes. Do not wear black or white. Colors are great, especially pastels. Prints and designs are OK; plaids are great. Do not cover your neck; do not wear turtlenecks. For a commercial look, wear a shirt and sweater or a striped or plaid shirt. For a dramatic look, men should wear a sports jacket and open collar shirt or a very nice and bulky sweater. Women should wear something sophisticated. For singers, wear what you would wear while performing. For a comic look, bring props and wear something funny or casual. For fashion, wear designer clothes. For a sexy look, wear something that makes you look sexy."

Hair and make-up are of great importance, and many photographers will do make-up for the performer, or, for an additional charge, bring in a make-up artist. There are differing opinions as to how much make-up to use, but most photographers agree that too much is never good. Discuss the matter before the day of the shoot, since it would clearly not be to your advantage to arrive for a session only to learn that you should have brought your own make-up to the studio.

Many photographers recommend that unless you have problem hair, in which case a hairdresser could be brought in, you shouldn't do anything different with your hair from what you normally do. "You want a photograph that's going to look exactly like you do on your best day," says Denise Winters. It should simply be attractive to look at.

Not often considered, but nevertheless vital to the quality of headshots, especially for young people, is the time of day a shoot is to take place. While performers who are no longer in school can frequently be flexible in terms of scheduling, many young people have tight schedules that have to be worked around. After a day of classes, a teenager may be too tired to have good photos taken. Therefore, it's important to ask whether a photographer shoots on weekends or in the evenings. If a shoot must take place after school, Caroline Ross recommends that the subject have something to eat beforehand in order to get energized. If the performer is tired when having his pictures taken, it'll be impossible for him to look as good as he would if he were fresh and awake.

Another concern in selecting a photographer is the size and feel of the studio. Since the attention span of babies and very young children is notoriously brief (which is why many photographers have special rates for children under five), a cramped and cluttered studio would probably not be the best environment in which to have them photographed. For a performer of any age, the right studio for a sitting is one that he finds comfortable; if the studio is cold or hot or stuffy or "aromatic," you can be sure it will show up in the photos.

Getting the look you want

A crucial aspect of headshot photography is ending up with a picture that both looks like the subject and also is a little bit different from everyone else's. "The photograph is a performer's business card," says Christopher Johnson, of David Tochterman Casting, who receives 100 to 150 "business cards" in the mail every week. Although all of the pictures he receives are looked at, only a few are picked from the mass; which photos are chosen depends on what projects the casting agency is working on at the time and on which ones grab the attention of the viewer.

"It becomes a game of chance," says Johnson, who generally doesn't remember performers whose photos have them "smiling and looking pretty." The photos he does remember contain an aspect of that, but also are "a little more interesting."

Dianora Niccolini's advice to the young performers is "Be very clear in your mind about how you wish to present yourself in the photograph. The appropriate image is essential to your career. Unless you can clearly visualize in your mind's eye what aspect of your personality you are going to project, it will not happen. So, first of all you must determine whether or not you are going for a commercial look, a dramatic look, a comic look, or a fashion look. It is possible to go for various looks in one session; however, each look must be clearly defined so that when a casting agent looks at the photograph, he or she will immediately be able to say, 'Oh, this person will be great for the part of ... ' Be aware that not only must a good headshot project a well defined personality, but it must look like you!"

Ms. Niccolini has strong feelings about the collaboration between subject and photographer, too. "You cannot be passive while the pictures are being taken," she warns. "Your photographer will bring his or her camera and talent to the photo session and you must be there with the best expressions and concentrated effort that you can give. There is always the first time for everyone, so go home and practice in front of the mirror. A variety of emotions are required and it must show in the eyes. It has to make a statement about who you are and the energy and talent that you have to offer!"

How else does one get that interesting look? Clearly, the physical attributes of the performer come into play, but then there's the photographer's art; this can be thought of as the means by which the photographer brings out a person's "essence," as Steven Speliotis calls it. In many respects, technical matters play a role. Denise Winters shoots headshots mostly in natural light. Brian Haviland and Steven Speliotis use 2¼" square format film, which is larger than standard 35mm film, and thus holds more "information." However, in this business of many opinions, it's widely accepted that when the right subject meets the right photographer, regardless of the technical specifications, the right headshots will result from a photo session.

The results of your photo session will be shown to you in your contact or proof sheet. "From this," instructs Dianora Niccolini, "you must pick the best shot to reproduce for your headshot. Try to get professional advice from others in the business, such as trusted instructors, casting agents, and other actors and actresses. Ask them to help you pick your pictures. A consensus of opinion is the best way to choose. Your own choice may not always be the most accurate. People tend to be too vain and cannot see beyond their vanity. Your first and foremost goal should be to get work, and the 'good' headshot can open the right doors."

One final item on the headshot shopping list, of concern to all performers, but likely of even greater importance when young people are involved, is cost. Since it's probably the child's parents who will pay the photographer's fee, they'll want to feel assured that they'll get their money's worth. When looking for a photographer, you must remember that price varies as greatly as quality, but that the two don't necessarily rise and fall together. That a photographer is more expensive than some competitors does not necessarily mean he or she will take better pictures, nor will a less expensive photographer necessarily take bad pictures. Most photographers agree that someone seeking headshots should not try to do it without a reasonable budget for it.

For the initial session, not including the cost of reproductions, you should plan to pay in the range from a low of $100 to as much as $600.

The money spent on photos is money invested in a career; before you invest, consider carefully whether you feel comfortable with the photographer and like his or her work. If your answer to both questions is yes, that's the photographer to go with, no matter what the cost. While the headshots that result from the shoot will not on their own get you a job or make you a star, they may help to get you either an appointment with an agent or an audition.

That's the point at which you can begin to show people that you're a performer, not just another face.

✪

HOW TO WRITE A RÉSUMÉ
J. Traven Duboff

An actor's résumé is a business card to be presented to agents, managers, and casting directors. It must convey a substantial message in a limited space. If you need to prepare a résumé for yourself or your child, and you're losing sleep over it, the following tips should help.

There are no right or wrong ways to prepare a résumé. Each résumé is as individual as the person it describes. Your résumé will be read by many different people, and it's important that it makes each person reading it want to see you. "Catch me with it," says Breanna Benjamin of Breanna Benjamin Casting. There are a number of ways to do this.

Your résumé should be attached to the back of your 8"x10" headshot, so it's important to use the limited space available wisely. The résumé needs to be concise and convey a strong message. Chances are that the person reading your résumé is reading several others as well. Several hundred résumés can pass through an office each week and points generally are not awarded for length.

Start with the basics. At the top of the résumé appears the address and phone number of the agent or manager who represents you. Under that appears your name — in CAPITALS — and under that is your union affiliation, if any. Beneath your name, to one side, are your vital statistics (height, weight, hair and eye colors, age range, social security number). Your agent's or manager's name, address, and telephone number are on the other. If you are not represented by an agent or manager, place your name at the top, with union affiliations, and then the vital statistics below. This is standard and will vary little from one résumé to the next.

The next part of the résumé usually contains your credits in theater, film, television, video, and commercials. Here format dissolves into what suits your needs. One rule of thumb from Michele Donay of Michele Donay Talent Management is "Less is more." If you have worked in all four media and want to continue to do so, list only one or two major credits in each. The exception to this is commercials, of which you list none. If you have worked in all four media and want to continue only, for example, in film, list only your film credits. The sequence in which you list the media depends on your strengths and on what you want to pursue.

Two notes on style: It's usually important to list your roles with theater, film, or television credits. Some people like to see names of directors and production companies as well. It's best to write "list available upon request," or some similar phrase under the heading for commercials credits. Lists of commercials both muddle the résumé's appearance and can keep you from an audition. A casting director holding auditions for a product brand who sees your credit for a competitive product brand will disregard your résumé out of fear of conflict.

Other items which may or may not belong in your résumé include training and video and audio tapes. A child actor may need no dramatic training and such a listing on a child's résumé can be as confusing as you hope it is promising. A teenage actor's résumé can benefit from noting training, since it demonstrates that actor's desire and commitment. Training need not be dramatic to be important. Lucy Silver of Miller/Silver Management, Inc. says, "If someone has taken karate for seven years, piano for six years, and plays the violin, I'll know that child has discipline."

If you have a video tape of one of your performances, it may not hurt to include a line at the bottom of the résumé which reads "video tape available upon request." If you feel your résumé is already complete, however, this extra item is probably not necessary. The same holds true if you have vocal or instrumental talent and audio tapes available.

The child actor's résumé, more than any other's, requires creativity. Like that of all small children, their dramatic talent flows freely. At this point, however, you simply don't have a list of professional credits to demonstrate this so you must find another way to say through the résumé, "My child is special." This may be easier than you think.

When asked what she looks for in a child actor's résumé, Aggie Gold of Fresh Faces Management replied, "Nothing. If they're cute, with great dispositions, and get along with strangers, that's enough." A recent snapshot may even be enough to convince an agent or manager to represent your child.

It often helps to include on the résumé a list of skills and unique qualities. If your child can roller-skate and wiggle, he might be more desirable to a prospective agent or manager than a child who can simply roller-skate.

After all this you may still feel that you can't prepare a strong résumé, and you may consider embellishing a bit. Don't! It's important to tell only the truth on a résumé. Lying can only result in your child getting hurt. For example, fabricating film or TV credits can backfire if the manager or casting director reading the résumé knows the movie or show you say your child was in, but didn't see him in it. Fabrication of commercial credits is obvious if you have no union affiliation, since you can't be hired for a commercial without it. It's always possible that the manager or casting director will know people connected to your supposed credits.

Remember, your résumé is not intended to tell your whole story. It is supposed to tell key parts of it that make others want to know the rest. Keeping this in mind may lift some of the anxiety that leads actors to lie on their résumés.

"I don't think people should feel inadequate if they don't have a lot of credits," says Barry Moss, casting director at Hughes/Moss Casting Ltd. "An actor without a headshot or résumé can walk into my office, and if the talent is there, I'll work with him."

Perhaps résumés seem threatening because they ask you to reveal yourself. That's hard for anyone, but it's something any good actor must do. Treat preparing your résumé as you would a performance or a shoot: be yourself and have some fun while doing it. Good luck.

The following examples, provided by Michele Donay Talent Management, show just how much two résumés can differ.

ALEX ACTOR

**123 Main Street
Anytown, ST 12345**

(101) 555-9876

HEIGHT: 3'3"
WEIGHT: 33 lbs.
HAIR: Strawberry Blonde
EYES: Blue
AGE RANGE: 2 - 4
SS#: 123-45-6789

THEATER:

            THE KING AND I
                KING'S CHILD
                    Center Stage Productions

            FIDDLER ON THE ROOF
                TZEITLE'S SON
                    Center Stage Productions

PRINT:
LIST AVAILABLE UPON REQUEST

SPECIAL SKILLS:
FISHING, SINGING, DANCING, EXTREMELY
VERBAL, BASEBALL, GOOD INTELLECT, CLIMBING,
GOOD WITH ALL ANIMALS

ADRIENNE ACTRESS
234 Broad Street
Bigtown, ST 87654
(678) 555-4536

UNION MEMBER: SAG
HEIGHT: 4'4"
WEIGHT: 64 lbs.
HAIR: Dark Brown
EYES: Brown
AGE RANGE: 7 - 10
SS#: 987-65-4321

TELEVISION:
    LEGWORK
        BLANCA DEVASQUEZ, WCBS-TV, director: Michael
        Zinberg, guest starring role, 10/87
    THE COSBY SHOW
        NINA CHAVEZ, WNBC-TV, supporting role, 11/86
TELEVISION COMMERCIALS: PRINICIPAL ON CAMERA:
            List upon request
THEATER:
    THE WIZ MUNCHKIN
        Kids For Kids Performing Arts Center,
        Smithtown, N.Y.
    FABULOUS FEET
        FEATURED DANCER Hofstra Univ. Playhouse,
        Hempstead, L.I.
    CARNEGIE HALL & CAMI HALL PIANO RECITAL
VIDEO:
    FUNDANCE KIDS
        FEATURED PROMOTION Mulholland Productions
    LUKA
        Suzanne Vega video, Producer: Kim Dempster
        Directors: Candice Rockinger, Mike Patterson
SPECIAL SKILLS AND TALENTS:
DANCE (jazz, tap, ballet), SKATE BOARDING, PIANO,
ROLLER SKATING, SINGING, ICE SKATING, ACROBATICS,
SWIMMING, JUMP ROPE, BICYCLING
    TRAINING:
ACTING: Kids For Kids Performing Arts Center
DANCE: June Claire School of Dance, Ballet: 6 yrs.
Teacher: Denise Santo , Tap: 7 yrs., Jazz: 2 yrs.
    SINGING: Kids For Kids Performing Arts Center
    PIANO: American College of Musicians, 6 years
Private Teacher: Estelle Natiello, auditions at
Stonybrook University and Carnegie Hall
    TAPES:
THE COSBY SHOW, LEGWORK, FUNDANCE KIDS, and
COMMERCIALS available upon request

VIDEO AND THE YOUNG PERFORMER

These are the 1990s, and the video era is certainly upon us. That should come as no great shock to the young viewers of MTV and VH-1 who have watched music videos proliferate over the last several years. Parents of young performers might wonder whether having a good video tape of their child's work can help his or her career.

"If you want your child to work," says producer/director Robert Deubel, "a video is a necessity. It's now become one of the tools of the trade. Just as a college education is important to the development of the young person's mind, so too is the video essential for the development of the young performer's career."

Mr. Deubel, who, with his partners in Concepts Unlimited, Inc., won an Academy Award for his work on the 1972 documentary, *Norman Rockwell's World ... An American Dream*, has seen how "a good quality video can make the difference in a performer's fortunes.

"There's a young actress I know who, from the minute I met her, I could see was an exceptional talent. Still, she couldn't get arrested. No matter how she tried, no agent, manager, or casting director would interview her. After a period of struggling, I advised her to do a video of several characters that she had been working on in acting class."

The actress subsequently put the video together, and submitted it to the very same professionals who for years refused to work with her. One casting director saw the tape, called her in for a screen test on an upcoming film, and now she's one of the two final candidates.

"It was the casting director's words to her which impressed me most," continues Mr. Deubel. "She told her, 'From your picture and résumé, I'd never have called you in. But when you dropped your tape off, I became interested in you!'"

Bob Anthony, an independent casting director, runs Video Casting and Recording Services. For 10 years, Mr. Anthony has been trying to get performers, both young and mature, to realize that the headshot and résumé system may someday be as antiquated as hoop skirts and powdered wigs.

Mr. Anthony keeps stacked in his office, visible to all who walk in, *thousands* of pictures and résumés that have been submitted during the last four years. It's a staggering sight to see piles and piles of actors' faces lining the shelves.

"Most people are overwhelmed when they see these," says Mr. Anthony. "It gives them pause when they realize that most casting directors receive in a year an amount that equals, if not surpasses, what we keep here. The reality is that most of them throw out pictures after a certain point. After all, where can they store them?"

He continues, "A well-produced video tape allows you to show an agent or a manager who might be interested in handling you what you are like in action. Video tape shows who you are. It conveys the real actor or actress in a way that the picture and résumé can't. Ultimately, it will show whether you have the right stuff for this business, for tape doesn't lie."

Denise Dunayer of Fox/Albert Management, Kids and Company, a firm that manages young performers, was asked, "What do managers and agents look for in a video?"

"When a client approaches me and says, 'Please look at my video tape,' I look for the very same things I'd look for if I went to see him in a showcase or viewed him in a commercial. First, I look to see if he has talent. Second, I see what he looks like. Last, but not least, I look at his type."

Bob Anthony concurs. "I say that if you've got the talent, then let's go to video tape. Within seconds of opening your mouth, the director of a film will see talent, look, and type. If one actor is not what the director wants, then it's very simple to press the fast forward button and see the next actor."

When you realize that there are 100,000 actors who are card-carrying members of the performing unions, with another 400,000 people out there looking for that recognition, a good video tape may provide a sane alternative to making the rounds or going on endless cattle-call auditions.

Says Denise Dunayer, "Most agents and managers say to a prospective client, 'Call me when you're in something!' With a well-produced video, you're always in something.

"It's my feeling," adds Ms. Dunayer, "that a video must show your full potential within a production framework. You can have a video of something you actually performed in, a *reel*, as it's called, of actual broadcast clips, or you can put the time, money, and effort into a produced piece that will make you look good and show you off well."

Cautions Robert Deubel, "Don't put commercial work on an acting reel, or vice versa, since different agents and managers handle either commercials or legit. Make your presentation suitable for the area that you're interested in and for the person whose representation you're seeking.

"I think that it's better for a young person to develop as an actor with proper acting technique, not a 'commercial attitude,' but I realize that this isn't always possible within the realities of the business."

Why has having a well-produced video reached its current level of importance as a viable tool of the trade? Robert Deubel has some feelings on this matter, too.

"The use of video tape has been standard on the west coast for years. It didn't catch on here in the east until about six or eight years ago. One of the reasons for its rise to prominence was simple economics. It costs a lot of money to fly talent from coast to coast for a screen test, and the young performer and his or her family simply can't afford to keep shelling out $300 for plane fare every time an opportunity knocks in LA. Additionally, with rents in New York City averaging over $1,000 per month, regular plane trips can further deplete the family's savings."

Bob Anthony feels, "A great tape is definitely easier to get around to the decision makers, especially during hectic periods of the year, such as pilot season in California, when time is limited."

"In the long run," continues Mr. Deubel, "video is a low-cost way of getting yourself known. If your child has talent, there isn't enough money you can put into making the tape superb. The competition is so fierce out there that you must do something to stand out."

Kevin Mulvey is the cameraman and technical consultant for the Spiral Video Workshop, which specializes in all areas of on-camera technique. Mr. Mulvey was manager of Broadcast Operations for ABC-TV. He has many thoughts about what is needed to make a quality video.

"The key word here is 'quality.' Agents, managers, casting people, and the like, are very tired of garbage. What they don't want is a series of standard monologues shot against a plain black or blue background.

"The actor is advised instead to provide a little production value, with an appropriate setting. Nothing elaborate, mind you, but something that conveys space and dimension. The actor should have the right make-up and clothing to convey the period of the piece that he or she is working on. Additionally, care and consideration should be given to lighting and sound levels. Your tape is of no value if you can't be seen or understood."

"Making a video is not an overnight process," insists Mr. Mulvey. "You may decide that your 22nd take is the one that you want to go with. No agent will ever know. Work on it until you've gotten it right. You may have to spend months until you're satisfied."

About the choice of material, Denise Dunayer says, "A good video presentation should be at least three different pieces that you're comfortable with. I recommend first, a comedic piece, second, a dramatic or serio-comic piece, and third, a character piece."

Kevin Mulvey is in complete agreement. "Not only do I recommend that range of characters," he says, "but it might also make sense to use dialects, as needed, to show even broader skills."

The consensus is that a produced tape should be no more than 10 to 12 minutes long. If you're showing your broadcast-quality material, it needs to be as long as the amount of material you have to show. Bob Anthony advises, "Have someone put it together for you in a creative way. Certain commercials, or out-takes, first, others later on. If done properly, it can be quite impressive."

Robert Deubel is adamant that young actors and actresses put time into their choice of material. He says, "Some standard monologues are used so often that when the performer opens his or her mouth, it's likely to turn off the casting director."

Instead of going for the obvious, Mr. Deubel suggests searching books and adapting suitable passages, viewing feature films and piecing together a character's lines, reading case studies on legal or medical events to get actual dialogue, and searching through periodicals like *Reader's Digest* and *The Village Voice* for other original material.

Continues Mr. Deubel, "When all other possibilities are exhausted, I encourage young people to write about their characters, when they were either 10 years younger or 10 years older. Developing your writing talents is by no means a waste of time."

Says Kevin Mulvey, "The point needs to be made that even having an agent or manager to get you into an audition doesn't equal knowing how to handle a screen test. The best way to do that is to have a working knowledge of video. A young performer who knows how to act for the camera, the young performer who knows that video and film tend to add 10 extra pounds to his look, is more likely to have the advantage when auditioning in those media."

We spoke to two young performers who reaffirmed Mr. Mulvey's sentiments about the potential of video. Actor Paul Gubbay says, "It is very important to learn how to play to a camera. You have to be able to bring the audience in with your eyes, as well as know the camera's boundaries."

Kimberly Demarse is an aspiring young actress who emphasized the positive aspects of being video literate. Says Ms. Demarse, "You learn from watching yourself on tape because it makes it easier to critique yourself. It also emphasizes what the director says to you and helps you to change and improve your work."

Denise Dunayer believes, "Making a video tape is sometimes done just to show how good you look on video. You can be great on the stage, but not on video, and it's important for you and your representation to know that. If you're looking to get into movies and television, then tape has to be your medium."

But, goes the consensus, *no* video is better than *any* video. "A bad video is as bad as a bad headshot."

The video should work to your advantage for, as Bob Anthony says, "Tape is sight, sound, and motion. Nothing is as powerful."

THE CASTING DIRECTOR
Terry Berland

I started at the bottom of the corporate casting totem pole. I worked my way up by getting to know actors, by establishing relationships with agents, and by gaining knowledge of my business and trust from the people with whom I work. Never having been an actress, I approach my work as a business, devoid of any ego. Doing my job well means that I'm connecting people — clients and actors — and making their professional lives easier. I get satisfaction from knowing that my work results in a job for someone, and that filling that job gives the casting process a sense of completion and fullness that began with the first audition.

I hope that this article is especially instructive for parents and children about the ways in which *they* can achieve a sense of fulfillment within the commercial business. It starts with the basics.

In the first place, parents and children should have fun when they come to audition for a commercial. They shouldn't feel desperate or needy. No one's ego should be wrapped up in one job. Good actors have many interests; commercials are only a small part of their lives. With children, especially, there is a freshness and an innocence that doesn't always exist among older actors, and it would be a shame to lose those traits for the sake of one job.

It is also important to gain an understanding of the casting process. It begins when I get a character breakdown from the creative team. The creative team is composed of the art director, the writer, and the producer. The breakdown lists such characteristics as the child's age range, personality, and required acting ability.

When I get an idea of the type I'm looking for, I think of which actors would be good for the part and I call their agents to request their presence at the audition. I work only with SAG franchised agents. I do, however, see non-union actors. If an actor is with an agent, or if he has some acting background, or training, then I'll have that person audition. If he is subsequently booked for the job, then I'll get a waiver from SAG. Being part of the union is not, therefore, of utmost importance in determining who gets seen and who doesn't.

I give the agents the character breakdown and the agents, in turn, give me the names of people they think would be suitable for the roles. I go over names with the agent and the people we choose are given appointments to meet with me. Their auditions are put on video tape, and, when everyone has been seen, the creative group, including the director and me, views the tapes to determine who gets a callback. At the callback, the director's role becomes more visible, especially because he needs to see how a young actor will work on the day of the taping. After all, it's the director's job to bring out the actor's performance, and there's the need to see with whom he will ultimately be working.

Before all is said and done, a team of at least eight people has to decide on which performer gets the job. You can only imagine the fun involved in getting eight people to agree on anything, but somehow we do!

What happens once the actor leaves the comfort of the green room, or waiting area, and enters the casting director's domain? *Usually* (everyone works differently), the child will find the casting director in the taping studio with a video camera and monitor. There could be other people in the studio as well, such as the members of the creative team that I mentioned earlier. Usually, however, they won't be there because they're too busy. Their involvement with the audition process first begins when they review the tapes of all the performers.

If the child I'm seeing can read, we'll have cue cards for him or her to follow. If the child can't read, we'll require that he or she act out the commercial in front of the camera. Most times, there's a rehearsal or two, perhaps one or two takes, and ... that's it!

When young children are involved, I have to take more time when they first come into the room. I try to make them feel comfortable. I'll talk to them. I'll calm them down by starting a conversation in which I'll say something silly and make them laugh. They'll say something silly back to me, and we both laugh. Then they're ready to go.

Parents should never insist on coming into the audition studio. Most don't, since the agents are very good about preparing their clients for the audition's dos and don'ts. When a baby is involved, however, we bend our rules and parents are allowed to "assist" their two- or three-year-old. Still, parents should be aware that we'll have to test a baby to see if he or she will go to someone else besides the mother. When children younger than four are involved, we have to book a lot of kids for that spot because of all of the variables of babyhood. For example, the child can become irritable, or sick, or moody. Since there's no controlling a child that young, we have to have back-ups.

Terry Berland has been a casting director for the past 16 years. She now directs all casting activities for International Creative Casting Group on an exclusive basis for BBDO advertising agency, as well as other independent clients.

Dos and Don'ts of the Audition Process

Upon entering the reception area of the green room, sign in. If there are two sheets to sign, sign them both. Most parents tend to sign the conflict sheet, but not the SAG sign-in sheet. The casting director will call actors into the studio based on the latter, and those who don't sign it will risk being (inadvertently!) passed over.

After signing in, take a script. Take your child aside and start going over the lines. Too often what happens is that the same parents and children will be called for the same auditions and they will see the same people in the green room, over and over again. Be less interested in the social aspect of the situation, and attend to the business at hand — the script and its lines. *Make socializing secondary to getting the role.*

Although it was just recommended that you go over the script with your child, you should not over-rehearse. Become familiar with it, but try to maintain spontaneity and freshness.

Make sure your child's hair is combed and prepared before the casting director calls "next." Don't wait until the child is called to begin grooming and preening. And don't wait for the last minute to have a headshot ready for submission. A word to the wise — be prepared!

Don't put makeup on your child. Lipstick, mascara, and rouge are definite don'ts.

Don't bring extra visitors to the audition. They only clutter up the reception area and leave the impression of a cattle call. It is understandable that when parents can't afford to pay baby sitters, they'll bring the second child with them to the audition. If you can make other arrangements, perhaps with a baby sitter, mother's helper, next-door neighbor, or nonworking relative, do so. The sitter and the second child should also be prepared to wait in the lobby.

Please arrive by the appointment time that is given to the child. Casting directors have a schedule to meet. Often, parents will accept more audition calls than can be dealt with realistically in a given day and show up late at my audition. That causes confusion and creates a back-up.

We don't call children for an audition before 3:30 PM, in compliance with SAG regulations. When I call an agent, I'm advised which children come from Westchester and can't leave school early. I'll help by giving the child a later appointment. I try to end the children's session by 5:30 PM to accommodate dinner schedules and other needs of the family.

Those parents from out-of-town aren't always aware of parking problems in Manhattan (or whatever city the audition is in). Some mothers will park a car in a tow-away zone and will then arrive at the audition frantic. That puts unnecessary pressure on them and their children. Know the city's parking regulations. Know how much a garage costs. If it's too expensive, you may decide to take the train in and leave the car home.

Girls should pay particular attention to what they're auditioning for and should be aware of bogus casting directors who may try to get them to compromise themselves for the sake of the audition. Find out from your agent where you're going, who you're seeing, and what the product is that you're pitching. Ask whether it's a SAG or non-SAG shoot. If it's SAG, be aware that if you're held at the audition for more than an hour, you will be paid for your time. Non-SAG usually means the money won't be as good and your treatment may not be first rate.

Often, parents and children venture to the opposite coasts to try their luck at auditioning for commercials. If you're coming to New York, you'll be delighted at the number of auditions you can attend during the day because of the City's proximity to its studios. New York is known for the theatrical talent of its young performers, and we can determine an experienced actor by his or her stage work. In California, the kids have more TV and movie credentials. Know your region, because the industry people will gauge experience differently.

Commercials can be a lot of fun for children if they want to do them. I am, however, a big believer that no parent should force a child into this line of work, whether for money, excitement, or vicarious pleasure. Not getting a job shouldn't be viewed as rejection of the child, and parents shouldn't view the audition process as an acceptance or rejection experience. It should be viewed as fun, with no pressure, for anyone involved.

SUMMER IN THE CITY:
HOW PROFESSIONALS SEE IT

Summertime in New York City. It's usually equated with blistering heat and humidity. For the young performer, however, a summer in the City should be time wisely spent pursuing one's career.

Many young people are out of town, either in summer camps, or with their families on the beach, or in transit to an exotic vacation. Those who remain actually better their odds at being seen by agents, managers, and casting directors. Many business professionals, who may find themselves with time on their hands, actually keep certain hours open to meet new talent.

Whether you're an out-of-towner or a native New Yorker, if you're planning to make the summer the start of a career, there's a wealth of opportunity available for young performers. If you're properly organized and prepared, you'll be positioned to make the long hot summer work to your best advantage.

CallBack spoke with some of New York's top talent representatives and got their viewpoints on the necessities for a successful summer in the City. Included are Adrienne Albert, manager, of Fox/Albert Management; and Abby Bluestone and Tina Pentimone, both agents from Cunningham, Escott, Dipene, and Associates.

Abby Bluestone believes that a healthy dose of realism is necessary as you plan your adventure to the Big Apple. "Clients who intend to come to New York during the summer," observed Ms. Bluestone, "have to be prepared once they're here for the possibility that they might not book even one job. We have clients who visit the City during the summer and get every job they're up for. Then there are those who audition all over the place and don't get a single thing."

"Certainly," she continued, "there are kids who come here and do a lot of commercials, which not only pay for their stay in town over the summer months, but for their college educations as well. There are also kids who come here and are sent out regularly, but who don't book a thing."

Tina Pentimone noted how, in their individual home towns, these children were considered celebrities. On the local level, they always worked. Both the parents and the children assumed that when they came to New York, success was in the bag. But it didn't happen that way.

Said Adrienne Albert, "I don't think that a young actor and his or her family should come to New York with too many unrealistic expectations about work. This is, after all, the Big Apple, and while there *are* people who come to the City and are instant successes, I think they're the exception, not the rule. If you actually say to yourself, 'Well, this is going to be it, I'm going to get New York, I'm going to rule the business this summer,' then I think you're in trouble."

Since the summer is so short, planning becomes key. Plan ahead. Most people who come for the summer have a reason to be here. They don't just show up in June without having contacted talent representation in March or April or May and let them know that they're planning a trip. Don't wait until you get to town to give them a call.

Tina Pentimone expressed her feeling that usually there's a lot of motivation behind a decision to come to the City. "Clients come because they've met a manager who recommended it, or they've already signed with an agency, or they may have freelance work with several agencies. You either want to have a manager who'll get you to all of the agents, who, in turn, will get you to the casting directors, who, in turn, will hire you, or you want a good agent who's well-connected in his or her area and will push to help you get work."

The performers' representatives agreed that it's very important to have representation of some sort and to have somebody working for you who believes in you as an actor. That representation can be gotten before committing to two or three months in the City over the summer. Since it's so expensive to be in New York, a trip or two by the parent to set the groundwork would be useful. Many managers and agents will take on a client for a three month period if the client comes and says, "I'm planning to be here."

When someone calls Adrienne Albert in March or April or May, she feels, "that the person is really serious, that they're not just wishing for something to happen, but that they're helping to *make* something happen for themselves."

But on the subject of whether or not a young actor should use the summer to study the craft of acting, the representatives were divided on the potential benefits. Ms. Albert, for one, expressed the view that, "Young actors and actresses should come prepared to work and they should come prepared to study. We always encourage our clients to study, at whatever their levels are. Whether for a youngster just starting out in the business or a college student in the late teens or early 20s, serious study is important. If William Hurt can take the time to study between pictures, we can all study and benefit from it."

But Ms. Pentimone isn't so sure. "I work in commercials and I have a different viewpoint from professionals who work in the legit areas of television, theater, and film. When very young children work in commercials, casting directors are only interested in their look and in their personalities. I, therefore, don't think that training at an early age, and in the commercial area in particular, is all that important."

There's apparently no one definitive answer as to whether young people should study, nor how old they should be before studying. Said Ms. Bluestone, bluntly, "You either have talent or you don't. If, at the age of 14 or 15, an actor wants to take his or her natural ability and perfect it, then there are a number of fine acting programs they can enter, whether for theater, film, video, or commercial training, and the summer offers the perfect opportunity to hone the craft."

What are the benefits a young person can reap by being in New York during the summer? If you're thinking of making a long-term move to New York, there's no better time to come here and check the City out thoroughly and become a part of and accustomed to its way of life. As far as commercial work is concerned, it's especially busy in New York, much more than, say, in Los Angeles. A lot of California-based people come to New York during the summer because here you can audition for four, five, sometimes six calls a day. It's also much easier to get around. When it's busy here, that's especially beneficial.

"There's another benefit for the beginner who's considering spending summer in New York," added Tina Pentimone. "A fresh face in summer is a novelty for the casting people. They're not seeing the same kids that come to call after call throughout the year. The kids from far away are the new kids, which is probably why they book so much over the summer. They come in, they go out. They come back the following summer and they're fresh faces all over again. New York is the place to be, and, if it's at all possible, a child should be here rather than working in the home town."

But Adrienne Albert has a different opinion. "If children are only concerned with working in legit areas, then it might be more beneficial for them to stay at home and get some good training under their belts before coming to the City to try their luck. I advise participating in school-oriented programs, doing more regional theater, and, in essence, doing one's homework before coming into town.

"In the commercial area, homework is also important. Refer to *The Ross Reports* and prepare your list of agents. Put together a list of managers and casting directors, too. Have your résumé up-to-date and have plenty of 8" x 10" headshots ready to distribute. Prepare and plan as far ahead as possible," she concluded.

The representatives agreed that if you're contemplating a trip to New York City, you can't plan on coming for a week or two.

Abby Bluestone felt that if you're really planning on coming here for the summer, you have to plan on spending some time. "To fly here for a week is ridiculous. We'll send you out on a call and by the time you get a callback, you're already home! It simply isn't worth your while to come here for less than a month. That's the minimum."

Adrienne Albert spoke about the hard realities of the New York lifestyle. "It's very difficult to say what an investment like this will cost you, although much will really depend on how you choose to live. If you're planning on taking acting lessons at a school, then that will cost you x amount. If you're studying with a teacher privately, that will cost you a different amount."

In figuring out a budget, you have to plan your living expenses, your food, your transportation, and your clothing. People tend to forget how hot and humid and debilitating the City can be during the summer and they have to plan to dress for it. Particularly, they need to plan and get the right clothing for their auditions.

Tina Pentimone wanted parents to *make sure* that they appreciated just how "big a deal housing is." Parents must feel very secure about where they and their family are going to live. Some people stay with relatives, while others put themselves up at efficiencies in the midtown area. There are people who rent out rooms, and there are families who'll house a child who's in for the summer studying dance, or theater, or whatever. If you're staying in a hotel, it will cost you. There are a few dorms available to young people. Many families coming in from out of town share apartments, sometimes doubling and tripling up to save money.

Most important to a summer in New York is, as Abby Bluestone expressed, *learning the game*. "Parents and kids have to understand that when they say they are available to us, then they've really got to be available to audition, to go on callbacks, and to check in with us several times a day, Monday through Friday, 9 AM to 6 PM."

July and August can be very busy months in the commercial business. In July, the fall and back-to-school campaigns are in full swing. By August, the industry is gearing up for the Christmas holiday commercials. Know where your child fits in to the overall casting picture. Children change quickly and what they look like at age 10 will be very different from what they look like at age 12. If they're real awkward one year, they may grow out of it the next, and they'll be more or less employable, depending on what's in.

Whether your child is a baby or is a seven-, nine-, or 13-year-old, you'll find that there's no rhyme or reason as to who books and why. Said Tina Pentimone, "I think it's really important that before coming to New York you make sure you're prepared to spend a lot of time auditioning as well as a lot of time being rejected. Be prepared to stick it out. If you go on five auditions a day and get three callbacks a week but don't book a job immediately, so what? Why leave? Hang in there!"

The representatives issued a collective word of warning: If you meet someone who claims to be an agent or a manager and asks you for money to help get your child into the business, then walk the other way — fast. They're not legitimate, and parents and kids should be very careful about rip-off artists out to make a quick buck. By the time you figure it out, it's too late; you've been had.

"Have fun in New York," urged Adrienne Albert. "It's important to mention that while you're here in New York, aside from pursuing the business end of things, young people should take advantage of the cultural side of the City. Going to see other actors' work is as much an education as are your own acting studies. See lots of theater. Stand in line at the TKTS booth on 47th Street and Broadway for half-price tickets. Or plan ahead, especially if you know you'll be in town over the July Fourth weekend, so that you can see the shows that you want."

The overriding philosophy is to be as well-prepared as possible and to have a realistic concept about what you can achieve in a given period of time. You can't fit a whole lifetime into a summer. Rather, you should come with a plan. Study part of the week. Spend your evenings at the theater. Use part of each day to audition and part to target new agents. A plan such as this would make for a very worthwhile summer.

✪

Several years ago, when her only clients were her children, Los Angeles-based manager Jean Page made the move to New York City for the summer — and survived.

ONE HOLLYWOOD MOTHER'S SUMMER IN THE BIG APPLE

"I explained to my kids that it would be fun to explore the East Coast and see all the wonderful sights and historical places. We'd also see what work the kids could get, since the business is always slow on the West Coast in the summertime and reportedly great in New York City."

Upon her arrival in the City, she found a manager who immediately explained the "New York system" and started sending her kids on rounds. New York was an unbelievable change from LA.

"What a system! I loved it," recalled Jean. "Our manager actually asked us to check in with her three times a day! In California if you call your agent more than once a month, it's too often! Three to five interviews a day — we weren't used to that."

When the New York moms found out that her children were booking, she apologetically told them, "My husband is being transferred to New York." But she could still feel the bristles, especially on the set.

"I didn't feel their reaction to be very fair. We've resigned ourselves to the New York child in LA. The New York child is well-trained. I was amazed when I found out about the lessons that New York children had and how very professional they were. The California child, by and large, comes to New York with a California suntan, no accent, and an outdoorsy look — a good all-around sell, in show biz talk.

"The New York child is not the country bumpkin that we were, but is well-studied and well-prepared, and their moms seem to be on top of everything," Jean admitted. Her kids soon found out that the business was not laid back like in LA, but that it hummed at a frantic pace and they had better keep up with it.

The family met more Hollywood kids and moms doing their summer in the City. The word was out, there *was* more work in New York in the summer than in LA. So some of the California moms came east and subleased apartments.

The Pages got a real kick at seeing movies from the West Coast that the kids were in and seeing commercials that they had shot in LA that they had never seen back home on New York TV. It did, however, make them wonder where the residual checks were. "I was told that the commercials were dead and canceled," said Jean, with a touch of cynicism.

And the cultural shock of the move from the wide open spaces of sunny California took its toll on Jean and her children, Susie and Chris, immediately. The sirens all night long and the rumble of the garbage trucks at 4:00 AM really did them in. "I promised Susie that after she and Chris shot their last jobs, we'd leave the City. This seemed to satisfy her."

Every morning, Jean would go to the donut shop across the street and bring the kids their breakfast. Susie eventually made friends with a delightful bag lady who had her home in a cubicle outside Carnegie Hall. She knew the Pages by name and even offered to babysit.

They quickly learned how hot New York could be, especially with that Eastern humidity. The Garden State Parkway was comparable to the Golden State Freeway in LA — crowded — and the shore will always be the shore. But, "Pay beaches? The waves weren't even that good," her son, Chris, remembered.

They were here for business, and so business it was. The family found that the ad agencies and the interviews were fairly close together. What a relief, they thought, from the spread-out auditions of LA. It gave them extra time to stand in line at TKTS, the half-price tickets booth at 47th Street and Broadway, where one can get discount tickets to Broadway shows. An extra added bonus was that the tickets, as well as the trip to the City, were completely tax deductible, because they had documentation to prove that they were actively seeking work. And the Pages had another apparent advantage in that most of the New York kids seemed to be away for the summer. If they weren't gone for the whole summer, they were out of town on Mondays and Fridays — long weekends — and were at interviews only Tuesdays through Thursdays.

They grew more fond of the New York system. Whatever agency asked for the kids first got them. In California only one agent handles your child and if that agent doesn't get the call from the casting director, you don't get the call either. Therefore, the Los Angelinos developed what's known as "the mother's grapevine," which lets them in on whether their representation is good or not. While many of the LA moms balked at the extra 15% they had to pay to the New York managers, Jean's feeling was that "15% of nothing is 15% of nothing." When in the City for only a short period of time, the manager was the only way to go. "Ours was terrific, too," exclaimed Mrs. Page.

After Susie was hired for her first job, the family got a rude awakening to the New York "way." There was no representative from the state on the set to ensure that SAG regulations and state laws were adhered to. Jean couldn't believe that the overabundance of food that's always available on the set in LA wasn't available in New York. And, if the kids worked past 6:00 PM without a waiver, it was acceptable. Chris could even go on location alone, and Mrs. Page found she was discouraged from going at all. Chris loved it, of course, as the set was in New Jersey and he was the hit of all the locals there. (He and his skateboard, that is.)

The non-supervision made her quite nervous. "In LA," Jean explained, "rules are strictly enforced by both the state and by SAG, whichever is more stringent. This normally means the state of California assures that the children will be well protected, even though I accept the responsibility that still resides ultimately with me as the parent." She seemed particularly grateful that New York and LA are now coordinating their efforts, especially through SAG, to try to protect working children.

When Chris and Susie each had a couple of jobs under their belts, the family set sail for the golden shores of California once more. After all was said and done, the kids, and their mother, agreed that they loved the experience and would happily do it all over again.

BEFORE COMING TO NEW YORK ...

Remember: the key word is planning. Whether you live in New York or Los Angeles, Chicago, Dallas, or Atlanta, the work you must do is the same.

First, buy a copy of *The Ross Reports*, published by Television Index, Inc., which lists all New York-based agents, independent casting directors, advertising casting directors, as well as NY and LA prime time and daytime programs (read soap operas).

The Ross Reports can be purchased for $3.50 from the publisher, located at 40-29 27th Street, Long Island City, NY 11101. It is also available at many bookstores in New York and Los Angeles, as well as in several other choice cities, including Boston (Baker's Plays on 100 Chauncy Street), Washington, D.C. (Backstage, Inc., 2101 P Street, N.W.), Chicago (Act 1 Bookstore, Ltd., 2632 N. Lincoln), and San Francisco (Drama Books, 134 Ninth Street).

A careful reading of the periodical will inform you as to whom you should submit a picture and résumé in consideration for potential work. Under agents, for example, you will have to carefully select those agencies that have children's departments and write to them; you wouldn't want to waste time writing to those organizations that boldly state: NO CHILDREN!

As suggested by the experts earlier in the chapter, let the potential representation know that you'll be coming to New York for the summer. Try to make appointments with them, if possible, *before* you settle in for the summer. In this way, when you arrive, you can get off to a quick start. If it's not possible to get here much before June 1, then have your appointment book for the first week filled with meeting after meeting.

How can you contact managers? Well, *The Ross Reports* can't help you with that one. Rather, you should contact the National Conference of Personal Managers (NCOPM), located at 1650 Broadway, New York, NY 10019.

The NCOPM is a highly selective group that doesn't list *all* the managers in New York or Los Angeles; however, they're a good place to start if you want to be *assured* of a manager's legitimacy.

Managers aren't franchised — that is, licensed by a given state. Whereas a manager *usually* exacts a 15% fee for services rendered, managers who aren't on the up and up have been known to take as much as *50%* of a client's income. There have also been instances in which managers have taken a percentage of income from a performer's "bread and butter" job — any non-performance work, such as waiting tables, selling shoes, or per diem teaching.

Be careful. Don't sign your life away for the sake of a few months in the summer. Know your potential representation. Ask questions of the NCOPM, as well as the unions (SAG, AFTRA, AEA). A little research before you arrive could save you from being someone else's lesson of how *not* to go about a summer in the City.

Finally, a word or two about housing. All the rumors you've heard about astronomical rents are true. A generation ago, your rent should have been no more than one-fourth of your income. Nowadays, that formula no longer holds true — it's more like one-third to one-half of your income. Actually, since most of you will be coming from another part of the country, you have to realize that this will actually be a *second* rent, since we can assume that you live elsewhere.

How do you find housing? The best advice we can give is for you to sublet — or take over the lease — of someone else's apartment. Many people leave town for June, July, and August and are very anxious to have someone reliable watch their pets, take in the mail, and water the plants. You can find out about available apartments by getting a copy of *The New York Times* or *The Village Voice* and reading the real estate sections.

Another method is to go to the Actor's Equity Association's (AEA) or Screen Actors Guild's (SAG) bulletin boards, where many actors will leave descriptions of their apartments. This is usually ideal for short-term subletting, especially since many of these folks who are *not* working need people to share the expenses. Usually, you or your child have to be a member of the union to be able to avail yourselves of this service. However, if you know someone in NY who has his union card — perhaps a friend, perhaps a franchised agent or manager — he may be able to do the scouting for you.

Lastly, bed and breakfast organizations are evolving in many major cities; there are several in New York. These are either hosted or unhosted situations, with prices varying according to such things as the area of town in which you choose to live and the size of the apartment. They're easy to find, since many advertise in *New York Magazine*, as well as respectable travel-industry trade publications.

Good luck.

2
Support Systems

My mother has been behind me 100%. I owe her a lot. She's the reason why I'm where I am now. I owe her everything. She's the world to me. I just can't express my feelings towards her because they're so strong.

Troy Winbush, *featured on* The Cosby Show

CONFESSIONS OF AN OFF-SCREEN MOM
Barbara Elman Schiffman

As every proud parent in America knows, Hollywood is always looking for new faces. Ads touting inside tips on breaking into showbiz adorn the pages of *Dramalogue, Show Business*, and even the *Los Angeles Times* classifieds. Slick magazines promise to get your child's photo on agents' desks if you invest your money in some high priced "exposure." These come-ons are meant to lure starstruck parents who hear of children earning big bucks through commercials or notice the growing number of babies through teens starring in TV series.

Showbiz fever struck my family when we least expected, and nine years later we're still deep in its throes. Legend says Lana Turner was approached by a talent agent at Schwab's drugstore, but my six-month old daughter Risa was literally "discovered" in her baby carriage on Hollywood Boulevard, a few blocks from our hillside home. Out for a stroll, Risa's babysitter was stopped by a children's agent who gave the sitter her card and said to "have the mom call me, dear." Although I'd worked in show business for years, every actor I knew has had to pound on agents' doors until they found one who would agree to take them on. Curious and suspicious, I called first thing next morning.

Fortunately, this agent was not a child-napper or new-comer just looking to fatten up her client list. She was well-es-tablished at one of the top children's talent agencies, so my maternal pride soared as she claimed my cherub-cheeked little redhead had, in her expert opinion, "poh-ten-shul." What could I say but "yes" when she asked to represent Risa, although I'd never imagined my infant might be thrust onto the showbiz fast track and ultimately be one of the lucky "working kids" under 18 who earn adult-sized dollars from print ads, commer-cials, and films. (There are over 8,000 Screen Actors Guild members under 18, with about 15% earning top dollar; the rest audition a lot and work occasionally, averaging incomes in the thousands of dollars vs. tens of thousands, from commercials, TV shows, and educational films.)

I, in turn, became yet another off-screen mom waiting not so patiently in casting office lobbies, my fingers double-crossed in hopes my bouncing baby would be "the right one." This lasted three months — through the initial "look-see" agent meeting, several rolls of "natural" snapshots for their already-stuffed baby files, some cattle-calls where cooing (or crying) babies perched wall-to-wall on mothers' shoulders and at last, Risa's first job — an actual Johnson & Johnson toys print ad photo session which paid $60 for an hour's work. But my own career was getting busy so the usual response to my weekly agent "check-in" calls ("nothing today, dear") finally took its toll. I quit phoning, life returned to normal, and the showbiz fastlane sped by minus my darling daughter, her singular success pasted prominently in our scrapbook where it sits today, edges curling.

Six years later, however, Risa decided she hadn't gotten the thrill of the spotlight out of her system yet. She wanted "to be on TV, Mommy," and since I was still working the business at that time as assistant to a prominent writer-producer at Disney Studios in Burbank, I thought this a simple request to fulfill. But things had changed in six years — there were more kids than before asking to "be on TV, Mommy," and more starstruck mommies schlepping around town in pursuit of family fame and fortune.

Three years later, my daughter is still acting — and I'm still schlepping. By now I've met hundreds of other parents who have helped their sparkling offspring create family businesses, and Risa's worked with many talented people on national commercials and films. She even spent two weeks in Orlando this year shooting a short film which, the producers told me when she was hired, "will still be playing as part of the MGM-Disney Studios Tour when Risa brings her own grandchildren to Disney World." I remember well the day of the big shoot with director Garry Marshall, watching my tomboy-daughter — costumed in prissy satin dresses, big glasses, and hair ribbons — sing scales deliberately off-key like a trouper, take after screeching take. I'm sure everyone on the crew went home that night like me, unable to squelch the off-key tunes echoing in their ears. And since we can't see the film in local movie theaters, we're ready for a vacation, or better yet, another film project in Orlando so we can view *The Lottery*, a funny two-minute film starring Bette Midler as Risa's lottery-ticket-losing-singing teacher, in context.

We also spent a full month in Utah this past spring when Risa was chosen out of several hundred girls to star in *It Nearly Wasn't Christmas*, a charming family telefilm which airs nationally in December 1990, produced by Jimmy Osmund and Ventura Entertainment Group in association with LBS Communications. Risa plays spunky Jennifer Baxter who helps Santa Claus (veteran actor Charles Durning) regain his Christmas spirit after he decides Christmas has become too commercial and quits his job. This odd couple journeys across the country to bring her struggling songwriter father home for the holidays and encounters a variety of situations which test their own "goodwill to all men."

While Risa rose to the demands of the six-day shooting schedule at locations ranging from Osmund Studios to snowy mountain tops to an old-fashioned railroad train, I saw firsthand how much stamina and flexibility are demanded of child actors when cast in significant film or TV roles. I also learned through experience how their parents are often faced with unexpected situations and decisions on the set which can range from dealing with working long hours, resolving financial and contractual details, working out jealousies or lack of communication with production personnel and among actors, living out of a suitcase for weeks at a time, and keeping the high energy of a bright child actor from clashing with the older actors or the production crew. Parents must also keep the children well-fed and rested, help them learn their lines each night, work closely with the studio teachers to make sure the children's academic schedule is met, and keep the kids occupied during free hours through bowling, museums, zoos, movies, etc. In retrospect, it was both a wonderful and highly educational month, and we are eagerly waiting to see what impact, if any, this project has on Risa's continuing career.

Each of the showbiz parents I've spoken with has a unique "how I got my child into the business" tale, as well as war stories gathered along the road to stardom. The standard "getting started" saga begins with either a beautiful baby "everyone says should be in commercials," or an outgoing youngster who badgers Mom and Dad to be on TV until they give in and agree to "get him an agent."

I recently watched thousands of potential child stars parade before me as I sat behind a booth at the Fallbrook Mall Baby & Children's Expo in Canoga Park, California, one weekend. Every parent who stopped at our table representing Hollywood Screen Parents Association, a professional showbiz parents' network, had the standard eager-beaver questions: how do I get started? ... who's the best agent? ... is three months too young for my baby to do diaper commercials? As I scanned the strollers and the sticky little faces passing by, I realized how excruciating it is for casting directors and agents to choose one of these adorable tykes over another. Each one has showbiz potential and just needs access to professional opportunities. Fortunately, in major cities such as Los Angeles, New York, Orlando, and Chicago, opportunities for talented kids are on the rise.

In Hollywood especially, it's difficult to move from acting-as-hobby to paying career without a well-connected agent to introduce your child to casting directors. Only agents and managers can receive the "breakdowns" (capsulized casting notices circulated daily by Breakdown Services of West Hollywood), alerting them to current roles being cast so they can submit photos of clients meeting the particular age-coloring-personality profiles. Sometimes a special skill or ability is desired, such as a two-year old who could say "Picasso" for director Jonathan Kaplan's *Immediate Family* (Columbia Pictures). "We put the breakdown out for kids who could say 'Picasso' on cue, and while they all could say it in the waiting room with their mothers," reports associate Patrick Rush, "when they went in to casting directors Sally Dennison and

Julie Selzer, they'd clam up. I think they got the idea this was a doctor's office — they were fine in the lobby, but inside the casting room they were scared to death. Of the forty kids we saw, only three could say 'Picasso' on cue."

Rush recalls the phones ringing when a blurb about the search for this particular child was mentioned in the *Los Angeles Times'* Calendar section. "We had cast the role in Vancouver as that item came out, but every LA mother of a cute toddler called our office anyway. Usually, casting directors wait until they get to location to find children that young, as we did in Vancouver. When you hire somebody from the location area, it saves on hotel bills, per diem, air fare. And they may only work a few days anyway."

The eager parents who called Rush were typical, but there are loads more down-to-earth screen parents to be found in Hollywood and elsewhere. David Ruben, who cast children for Paramount's *Scrooged*, the Jessica Lange/Warner Brothers *Men Don't Leave*, and 20th Century Fox's *War of the Roses* with Michael Douglas and director Danny DeVito, among others, feels that the parents are as important to "cast" as the child. "When casting kids, you must be conscious that you're also casting the parents, especially when an actor is on a full-run of the film or series. Producers, directors, and casting people are very aware of the dynamic between the parent and the child since the parent's going to be on the set a great deal. Parents, in general, don't have a great reputation, although it's the bad apples that cause this. On the Jessica Lange film, we were extremely fortunate to find talented kids — Chris O'Donnell from Chicago and Charlie Corsmo from Minneapolis — with wonderful parents."

The parent's role

Rubin emphasizes that it's essential for parents to treat acting as just another fun activity their child enjoys in a well-rounded life, along with school, sports, friends, and family. "There's a well-known young actor named Sean Astin who's sometimes hard to schedule because his Little League schedule is first and foremost in his life. His agents are instructed not to let anything interfere with it, which is impressive. This is the kind of kid you want to cast if you're going for reality in a story." (Sean's parents are unique. His mother Patty Duke Astin, a former child star herself, and father John Astin, both know from their own experience that there are dangers in letting a child's life revolve around showbiz.)

What parents can do first to help prepare kids for showbiz is to instill a strong sense of self-worth in them. Then, when the child can read, find a good acting workshop emphasizing improvisation, scene study, and on-camera and audition skills to prepare him for that first interview with an agent or casting director. These classes also give kids confidence and presentation skills useful in life whether they make it in showbiz or not. Most local parks, YMCAs, and performing arts centers offer low-cost classes for beginners.

Finding an agent

Next step is the difficult agent search, which should involve a minimum of expense. Well-lit, casually dressed head and shoulders snapshots will introduce agents to your child's "type" better than fancy portrait photos. Send them along with a cover letter detailing special talents or athletic skills, school/community acting experience, and ongoing training. A good agent will respond if he feels your child fits in with his current clients, and will call to set up an interview for both you and your child. Parents should "shop" for agents just as you do for schools, as the personality of the agent will influence his efforts for your child, including your ongoing relationship with the agent. When you find one who's excited about your child and communicates well with you, give him a chance to represent your child. During the first 90 days, agents, depending on production cycles, try to send out new kids as much as possible to get feedback from casting directors. If the child gets some callbacks, or even jobs, the agent will know your kid is "marketable" and will continue to work hard for you.

In major cities, acting, dance, and gymnastics schools may be friendly with local agents since these training grounds are valuable resources to help find showbiz kids. Some schools even hold showcases where kids can strut their stuff for local pros, and are a good way for parents to preview the class before enrolling. Community theater is also an excellent arena for training and exposure; many Broadway shows like *Annie*, *The Music Man*, *The Sound of Music*, and *Annie Get Your Gun* have key roles for kids who can carry a basic tune and shine on stage.

Once you've found the right agent to work with and your child begins making audition rounds, you'll find your job as a screen parent just beginning. It's your job to keep up an audition wardrobe (shopping at Sears rather than Esprit), as well as log in auditions and bookings for tax and unemployment records. (Working child actors can qualify for unemployment, just like adults.) On the set, it's up to you to keep your child prepared and alert for work when he is not in school with the studio teacher. And most difficult, it's you — not your agent — who will dry those painful tears when your child loses out on a coveted role after a half dozen callbacks.

Screen parents can be their child's best partner or worst enemy. The stage mom who gets angry at her kid when he doesn't get the role is still alive in some families. But despite the hard work, most showbiz parents discover a new bond with their kids through quality time spent together en route to auditions and on the set, and through their new roles as home-based business people.

Showbiz isn't right for everyone, though. The adult-level pressures, specter of rejection, demand for kids to "sell themselves" from audition to audition, and constant juggling of school-work-playtime, not to mention other siblings and family responsibilities, can take a toll on everyone when least expected. I continually ask my daughter whether she still wants to act professionally, emphasizing she doesn't have to be in the spotlight to earn my love. And while she's not a household name yet, nor does her college trust fund overflow with dollars, she has a stronger sense of self worth than many of her "normal kids" friends merely because she's earned a lot of positive attention, and some significant bucks, doing something she truly enjoys. As a proud parent, I can't ask for anything more.

> *Barbara Elman Schiffman is a screenwriter/journalist, member of the Women in Film Board of Directors, and founder of the Hollywood Screen Parents Association, a national network for parents of showbiz kids.*

CallBack's editor-in-chief, Alan Simon, is also president of On Location Education, a private tutoring service for child performers. His company has been responsible for tutoring young actors featured in *The Cosby Show, Kate and Allie, The Mickey Mouse Club, Married To The Mob, Brighton Beach*

Memoirs, and *Mermaids,* among others. In the following piece
that originally appeared in *Back Stage*, he offers his insight
into providing quality education for youngsters working on the
sets of professional productions.

A PARENT'S GUIDE TO EDUCATION ON LOCATION

In the musical *Gypsy*, Mama Rose is presented as the arche-
typal stage mother. She brings her children from one audition
to the next, instructing them on how to stand, where to look,
and when to smile. She thinks nothing of packing up her
entourage and moving from town to town, always worrying
about how she's going to feed them "on a buck." She also worries
how she's going to raise money to pay the members of her
company. When Mama Rose approaches her father for $88.00,
she sings a litany of the items that she needs to have in order
to get the kids on the Orpheum Circuit: "... new orchestrations,
new routines and red velvet curtains ... a feathered hat for the
baby, photographs in front of the theater." History and math
books are not included.

With so many children in Rose's charge one has to wonder
how they went to school. Unless we're to assume that Rose
taught them herself — although with her responsibilities she
couldn't possibly have found the time — the kids probably had
to forgo an education. Yet, at the end of the show, we see Gypsy
Rose Lee: mature, elegant, and articulate. Since this is a
musical comedy, we can suspend disbelief and assume that the
details of how these performing children were educated took
care of themselves. Life, however, isn't as magical as the
theater; somehow these matters have to be addressed.

Fortunately times have changed. What used to be roman-
ticized is now seen for what it is: a tough way to survive. Being
a child actor is difficult because both work and education have
to have equal significance. Most successful child actors must
strive to achieve this balance.

How in the throes of show business can children get a solid
education so that they do not find themselves wanting when
this business no longer needs someone cute, adorable, and
perky? It is difficult, but education on location can be as viable
as traditional classroom education. It should be clear, however,

that the parent has the ultimate responsibility for the standard of education that his or her child receives.

Dual responsibilities of the child actor

As professionals in the business, children are both actors and students. They carry two full-time jobs, each of which offers rewards and drawbacks.

School is the center of every child's universe. Children are concerned with how they did on an exam, what their next semester's classes will be, how they rate this teacher or that, what their feelings are for the new girl or boy in class. Attending school is the normal existence and is filled with long-term rewards and day-to-day problems. For the young performer, these "normal" problems quickly fade when compared to life on the set, where the child actor encounters the experience of a lifetime. This, after all, is what every acting class that children have taken for years prepares them for, and it is an education in and of itself. Imagine working with well-known actors, directors, and writers who share with the child their wealth of experience in television, film, and Broadway. Children receive on-the-job training while quickly learning a sense of responsibility. They're not just learning the importance of showing up on time for work; they fit into the grander scheme of things, too. If, for example, the child is late, the reading may not start on time. If a prop is lost or misplaced, it is costing someone (perhaps the child?) money. Essentially, children learn that in show business there is an interconnection of people's responsibilities and everyone is a part of a total production.

In the long run, the child learns the importance of working for a living as he earns money that can be earmarked for college. In a very real sense, too, the set is a home away from home. The cast and crew become an extended family, providing a child with a supportive environment and, especially in long running productions, looking out for the welfare of the younger cast members.

Most times, however, the human factor can get lost. On the set, the project comes first and often there is no room for mistakes. This directly contradicts what we teach our children; that is, to learn by trial and error. One might say that show business is "trial by fire," especially when you consider the meaning of the loss of a percentage point to a network's ratings or the possibility of a show's million-dollar budget going down the drain in one evening.

Parents should also remember that there are limited hours in a day for work and school. Also your child needs time to be a child. With so much to juggle, your child faces the possibility of feeling enormous pressure. Parents not only need to help their children cope with these pressures, but they must remain flexible and, if necessary, be willing to change the school and/or the work environment.

Alternative education

The family must decide what kind of school environment is best suited to the child and might consider seeking professional advice to help them choose an appropriate program. This decision is based primarily on the kind of career the child is pursuing. Children who work on long-running television shows face different choices from children who do a movie for two or three months. The former are out of school for at least six months and very few schools support this. A child who acts in an occasional movie presents little threat to the established school system.

If there is an indication that this is not a whim and is, in fact, a lifelong pursuit, the parent must consider a new type of long-range education. There are four possible school options: public school, private school, professional children's school, and correspondence program. Each of these options has pluses and minuses, but they all offer top-notch, quality education, and are taught or supervised by credentialed teachers in accredited schools. What the parent should note, however, is how each institution views the performing child.

A *public* school education is traditional and liberal arts oriented, and offers a well-rounded and solid education. The same holds true for *private* schools. Both systems offer sequential studies in math, science, the humanities, and the arts. They nurture the child's body and mind by requiring programs in physical education, as well as a wide range of elective subjects. Both prepare the child for college, including guidance in SAT testing. A private school charges tuition, but it offers smaller classes and more individualized attention.

Both public and private schools tend to support students who pursue outside careers and are often willing to cooperate with a family, but such support is not a given. There are some schools and districts that have no policy on working children because from their point of view they are not in business to support a career; they are in business to provide an education. Administrators may be displeased by the child's absence because there is a question as to whether the child's education on the set can remotely approach the school's standards. A school may require a student to get special dispensation from the superintendent or the headmaster to be excused from classes.

There are other considerations in dealing with a public or private school. The first is that the classroom teacher views a child's prolonged absence as a burden more than a blessing. The teacher is being asked to assume ongoing concern for a child who isn't present. Another more subtle factor is that there may be underlying jealousy on the part of the teacher towards the child. To many outsiders the set is a glamorous place to be, complete with salaries that far surpass a teacher's. The teacher may not be conscious of or acknowledge these feelings, but parents should know that they might exist.

Child actors who work are not only an oddity in the educational hierarchy; they are also isolated from their peers. In their school settings, these children often have to deal with being the outsiders. They're often absent and have to adjust to the school environment and to their fellow students each time they return. More often than not, classmates, like teachers, are jealous.

A *professional children's school* is designed for youngsters whose work coincides with regular school hours. Actors are not the only ones who fall into this category. The students might include musicians, dancers, gymnasts, ice skaters, and diplomats' children. A professional school understands the dual responsibilities of the working child and provides a correspondence program that reflects the sequence of the actual classroom assignments. A work sheet, for example, will say, "Monday read pages 6 through 8, answer questions 1 through 10, begin studying for quiz on Friday." The school will also provide the quiz for Friday that they expect will be administered by a professional tutor who will make sure that all assignments are returned to the school for grading. The school keeps a running tab on all work, usually designing projects that take into account the child's location work, access to libraries, and time pressures.

When the child returns to school, he or she enters the classroom and regular teaching resumes. This is different from a *correspondence school* which does not provide a classroom environment, but allows children to proceed at their own pace and even to spend a year completing a semester's worth of courses. In addition, when children excel, they may move up a grade level during a school year.

Parents should keep in mind that if children do not complete correspondence courses during the length of their working contract, they will have to provide tutors independently of the production company. If the child is taking geometry or chemistry, studying without the aid of a tutor may not be sufficient. Many correspondence programs do not require a tutor to work with the child and rely on parental supervision instead. This does not make up for the unique interaction between child and teacher. A professional children's school, by offering teachers, classmates, and a building to return to, creates a more conventional school environment. This kind of school also specializes in working with performing children. What regular schools and teachers see as a problem, this school sees as the norm.

A professional children's school, however, has its drawbacks. The student population tends to be homogenous. Most professional children are involved in their performing careers, which are the focal points of their lives. This environment may not offer a child access to extracurricular activities, such as team sports or school clubs.

Each school situation is different and it may only be by trial and error that the family determines which one works best. No matter what educational system is chosen, the family should be honest about the child's lifestyle from the very beginning. Most parents don't realize the value of open communication and tend to view the school as an adversary rather than an ally. If you tell the headmaster, principal, or director that your child is an actor and will be out of school from time to time, and an adversarial position is assumed, then it is best to look elsewhere.

When you approach the school, request an orderly transfer of work from the school to the set. You are developing a game plan that runs either daily, weekly, or monthly, depending on the length of your child's commitment to a given project. You will want to know:

- Who is the contact person (guidance counselor, assistant principal) at the school who will address the student's needs?

- What is the school's policy on absences? This question is more difficult to deal with in a public school, which is state funded, than in a private institution. Some public schools will automatically fail children for unexcused absences no matter how well they do in class. Is taking a job, for even a week's time, an "excused" absence?

- How does the school want the assignments handled? Do they want the set tutor to call weekly for new assignments or would they prefer to provide a general outline of the work they want completed for the duration of the job?

- Will teachers grade the child during his or her absence or will they allow the tutors to supply report card grades?

- How flexible will the teachers be if a project is due in two weeks, and the child needs three?

- Who makes up the tests? Will teachers require a classroom exam to be proctored or will they accept the tutors' exams?

- What about labs? Dissections and chemical experiments are not easily adaptable to a set. How much should labs be stressed or can children be excused?

- Can a duplicate set of books be provided for the tutor and will there be a charge for a second set?

- What about gym classes? Formal physical training is not usually possible on location. Is there an alternative to the health education requirement, i.e., dance or aerobic classes, that can be done in the student's spare (!) time?

- What happens if the child misses Regents exams and/or standardized tests, both of which can only be administered on school premises?

Never make assumptions! You want and need answers to these questions and it's worth your while to visit the school and meet with its administrators to iron out these details. The parent and child should meet with the principal and/or contact person, the child's teacher(s), the set tutor(s), and the production company representative to ensure that everyone is absolutely clear on these matters.

Students who have proved themselves throughout their school careers are obviously more likely to get leeway than those who have cut class and performed poorly. This is especially true in public and private schools where flexibility may have direct correlation with the student's general attitude. It's akin to the actor who shows up promptly on the set, follows directions, learns lines, and establishes a solid reputation for being reliable. Working consistently with the school is as much a priority as getting the job. Just as savvy parents send postcards to agents thanking them for their time, follow-up letters to thank school personnel for their cooperation are duly in order.

Unions, rules, and regulations

Congratulations, you've got the job! They want your child and you have a contract in hand. It can be assumed that you probably have an agent working for you who has negotiated the best possible deal on your behalf. As part of the deal, be certain to get in writing a specific clause that guarantees a tutor on location. Unless the contract states this clearly, there is absolutely no guarantee that a tutor is forthcoming. Issues of education and child welfare are not second nature to production companies, and rules and regulations governing working with minors vary from union to union and state to state, thus making a very gray area all the more murky.

Take the term "minor." In New York State anyone younger than 18 is considered a minor. The Screen Actors Guild (SAG) defines a minor in accordance with individual state regulations, but only when the child works under the Basic Agreement or the Television Agreement. Children who work under the Commercials Contract are considered minors only up to and including 14 years of age.

Virtually every state in the union has a different definition for the age of a minor and has established its own policies. California, for example, has the clearest and firmest policies regarding working children. The laws in California have been in existence since 1928 and are published and available for a family whose child will be working there for any period of time. They are compiled in *The Blue Book*, a policy manual devised and regulated by the state department of labor and available through its office.

California's tutors are also social workers and responsible for the child's welfare on the set. They enforce the law to the letter and are empowered to stop production when they see that the children are working past their allotted times. One ironic note is that these very policies, because of their inherent rigidity, have forced many production companies to re-evaluate California location shooting when they work with children. Production companies are relocating to other states in order to avoid these policies, thus adding to what California perceives as its problem of "runaway production."

It's recommended that you contact each state's film commission or, in New York City, the Mayor's Office of Film, Theatre, and Broadcasting, to know what its specific policies are in the area of minors in entertainment. But don't be surprised if you find that there is not very much information available. State regulations governing minors have not been a major concern to states that are lobbying hard to attract production within their borders. Fortunately, some unions are establishing national policies governing the use of minors. And, you should note that if the union's regulations are tougher than the state's in which the child is working, then the union's regulations supersede those of the state's.

But no two unions have the same policies, which may increase your frustration and confusion. SAG has the clearest policies regarding working with children. In addition to standard union benefits for all members, its contract defines the term "minor," and addresses the areas of education, supervision, working hours, dressing rooms, play areas, medical care and safety, and child labor laws.

The SAG education rules provide the following for children working under the Basic and Television Agreements:

• When a child is guaranteed three or more work days, a tutor is hired. If the child is not guaranteed but ends up working more than three days, a tutor is provided for every school day thereafter.

• A tutor must have proper teaching credentials from at least one of the 50 states, but not necessarily from the state of employment.

• The producer, not the parent, must pay the teacher.

• A tutor can supervise only a certain number of students and grade levels on any given production.

• A tutor can teach on only one production at a time.

• Bilingual tutoring is available when needed and if feasible.

• Tutoring usually takes place on the set, but under certain circumstances, it can be conducted at the child's or the tutor's home.

• A schoolroom facility is provided that closely approximates the basic requirements for classrooms and includes heat, light, desks, and chairs. The facility cannot be a moving vehicle or any other vehicle that is not used solely as the classroom.

• The parent provides schoolwork materials, although major items, such as a blackboard, come from the production company.

• An *average* school day is of three hours' duration, with no period of less than 20 minutes acceptable as school time.

• The tutor provides written reports to be submitted to the child's home school.

To its credit, SAG sees revising these regulations as an ongoing process. These provisions are not airtight so a children's committee, comprised of adult members whose concern is with the welfare of SAG's minors, is always looking to improve conditions. Parental input is appreciated and an integral part of updating regulations.

Children working in commercials rarely, if ever, get tutored since very few commercials employ children for more than three days. Thus, the Commercials Contract, a separate set of regulations, has no provision for the education of minors.

Neither the American Federation of Television and Radio Artists (AFTRA) nor Actors Equity Association (AEA) has made the inroads into education that SAG has. Although children who work on prime time television and are covered under AFTRA are usually tutored, the union has not been able to provide for its members who work in daytime soaps and variety shows. Many of the prominent child soap stars are either called into work after their school day ends — and thus work well into the evening and return to school the next morning — or they work all day on the set and either skip school or provide their own tutoring.

Children who work under AEA and whose presence at rehearsal is integral to the show are almost always tutored. Children with less significant roles whose rehearsals can be scheduled after school usually will not be tutored. When a child tours with a show, the production company will normally provide for a tutor. However, the tutor may be a member of the cast who has a teaching degree but can only teach after his or her own rehearsal schedule is met. This does not establish the child's education as a priority.

Many times a touring production will hire the tutor to travel with the company while it is on the road. When the show opens in New York the tutor is released and the parent has to make provisions for education. This may be workable for those members of the company who live in New York, but for those who are not from the metropolitan area it can be difficult to arrange for alternative education. A show may not run for a long time but the tuition payments towards a private school are usually non-refundable regardless of the family's change of plans. A public school may require proof of residence in its district before allowing children to enroll.

There are too many ifs, ands, or buts in this business. When it comes to your children's education, you can save yourself many worries if you determine early that education cannot be sacrificed and that provisions should be stated clearly in a contract.

Working with production companies

A production company works under tremendous pressure. A film crew, for example, can begin its day around 6 AM and not finish until 9 PM or later, usually five days a week. Crews work in pouring rain, extreme heat, or frigid cold, and sometimes venture into unsavory areas of the city where every piece of equipment has to be guarded.

Working within budget constraints is another fact of life and adds to the self-imposed pressures of production. There's never enough money. Backers, it would seem, always panic just as everything is supposedly ready, and the last thing that anyone on the set wants to worry about is whether Johnny is passing algebra or Sally's cursive handwriting leaves something to be desired. When the education has a direct bearing on the overall quality of the finished project, everyone in production will show daily interest in the children's lessons. The likelihood of that situation, however, is small, and the parent should become familiar with how to take control and avoid an adversarial relationship with the production company.

A production crew attends to thousands of details. As you did with the school, you need to communicate to the production manager or producer your expectations for a coherent educational system.

Find out who the production company can assign to take the direct responsibility for your child's welfare. You'll want this person to handle all matters pertaining to the child's education, including overseeing the tutors. In film, the person assigned to this job is usually the second assistant director, the Director's Guild of America trainee, or a reliable production assistant. In television or theater, the role is filled by stage managers or their assistants.

Ask for a tutor, allow the production company to make a recommendation or, if you know someone who is qualified, suggest that person. In any event, make sure that you are not getting an elementary school teacher to teach your child physics or a physics teacher who has never worked with a child younger than 17. The choice of tutor is among the most important factors in determining the success of the system you have worked hard to establish.

Choosing the tutor

Experience shows that the most important factor in choosing the tutor is academic ability. A valid concern is whether the person is certified in an area of expertise. Certification means that the tutor has taken college courses in education, including a year of student teaching. The person should have a background in "methods," similar to the actor's training in "technique." This means that he or she knows how to construct a lesson and work with children, in addition to having been approved by a state board of education.

If the tutor is not certified, find out if he has comparable academic credits. If you have found someone who has taught a subject in college for many years or has worked in a private school, then he or she is probably qualified.

You'll want to know that the tutor has worked with children and is well-versed in the subject. If your child needs help in Spanish then you shouldn't settle for a person who is himself struggling with the language.

Consider whether one person can teach all of your child's subjects. This is especially important in the older grades, when children study an advanced math, science, and a language. Since few individuals are capable of teaching all of these subjects adequately, you probably will need two or more tutors to teach different subjects.

While teachers may have excellent qualifications, they may not be able to adapt to the craziness of the set. Some teachers are terrific in a traditional classroom with 30 students and are comfortable working in an established institution of learning. The tutor, however, works one-on-one and must have the sense of humor that is needed to work under makeshift and often frenetic circumstances.

Let's imagine that the child and the tutor are in the middle of a midterm. Someone knocks on the door and the call is for "Wardrobe! Now!" The child stops writing, hurries to wardrobe, gets dressed, and is then told to report back to school. Just as the tutor has begun readministering the midterm there is another knock at the door and this time the call is to "Report to the set! Now!" There's nothing that anyone can do but finish the exam when there's time. The tutor has to look for ways to win in a no-win situation. It can be done, but it requires tremendous flexibility and resiliency.

The tutor must know what to do in unexpected situations. There can be very little communication on the set and the crew might not know what will happen on any given day. For the tutor, this translates into suddenly discovering that he or she will have to work with a couple of "extras." Can the tutor get the children to concentrate on their studies when the crew is hammering the set together or the chorus is rehearsing the big tap dance number?

Parents should be wary of the tutor who is there to break into production, whether in front of or behind the camera. It is already difficult for children to keep up with their studies when the teacher *is* focused on the schoolwork. It is next to impossible when the teacher is busy making contacts and declaring that he or she really wants to be an actor or a production assistant. Knowledge of the set's hierarchy and particular jargon is important for anyone wishing to work with production, but a tutor is there specifically to teach.

Other responsibilities of the tutor

The tutor should be able to relieve the parent of much of the educational burden. Tutors who work daily with the child will become familiar with that child's work habits and should be involved from the beginning of the project. They should be included at the initial meeting with the school hierarchy to discuss subjects, requirements, testing, grading, etc. Most schools, in fact, will not meet with the tutor unless the parent has called first to consent that this person may work on their behalf.

It is up to the tutor to establish an ongoing format for lessons; homework should be assigned; goals should be established at the beginning. The tutor is trying to maintain a reasonable facsimile of a regular classroom situation in an untraditional setting. The tutor must be able to use time successfully wherever possible.

The tutor is not the child's guardian. SAG states that tutors are responsible for children during school hours, but the parents are responsible for the ultimate care of the child. Once the child is on the set, it is the parent, not the tutor, who is responsible for the child. When the child is released for lunch, it is the parent who makes sure that the child is fed a decent meal. When the child and tutor are dismissed for the day, the parent or the production company arranges for transportation. This is not to say that tutors allow children to be unattended, or that they would find it an imposition to see the child to a company car or a cab. This, however, should not be assumed.

It is up to the parents to establish boundaries between themselves and the tutors. The parent/tutor relationship should be friendly, but professional. Parents should expect exactly what they would from the regular teacher. The circumstances may be different, but the relationship should be the same.

Finally, it is imperative that the tutor and the child are compatible. Children will not learn as willingly from people they don't like. Since a tutor spends a significant amount of quality time with your child, you must try to exhibit objectivity when choosing one. A professional consultation may offer a solution.

Inherent problems

An inherent problem of location education bears reinforcing: the "importance factor." Unless the child's schooling has a direct bearing on the quality of the production, there will usually be no departure from the normal routines of a set in terms of educational matters. Ultimately, the parents will find that they are usually on their own.

A contributing problem is that when productions begin, the casting comes together quickly. The child is chosen on Thursday, by Thursday afternoon there is a realization that a tutor is needed, and by Friday the tutor is hired to start on the following Monday. This obviously does not leave much time to set the situation up properly. The parents who have anticipated their needs may find that they're in a better position to act quickly.

A second factor, and one that goes back to Mama Rose herself, is the perception of the "stage parent." By consensus these individuals are overly aggressive and pushy. They would do anything to secure the role for their child.

Every parent is branded "stage parent" by virtue of the fact that he or she is the parent of the child who has been cast. And while it is often an unfair epithet, parents have to realize that it may be worth the risk of being so labeled in order to voice a truly legitimate concern. They are not asking for limousine service; they are trying to establish a coherent educational situation.

The fact that there is too little time cannot be stressed enough, and working on the set is analogous to Murphy's Law: what can go wrong will go wrong. The child is on the set to act and to go to school. Somewhere along the line he or she has to find time to sleep. For this reason, SAG has established the

"12-hour turnaround" period which requires that your child have a minimum break of 12 hours between work days.

Lack of time affects children in long-running productions in yet another way. Depending on the extent of the success of the project, interviews, promotional tours, or backers' auditions may be required. Where does this extra time come from? It doesn't come from the normal rehearsal period, which means that school time may be shortened. The parent who realizes this in advance may be prepared to finance additional tutoring hours.

There is another inherent problem for a child working on location, and it's one with no obvious solution. This is the issue of peer contact. The child who works on a project for a week or two at a time is not away from friends long enough to miss them. The child who works on a project for several months at a stretch, however, is in a completely different ball game. If yours is the only child on the set, then who does he or she talk with?

The young boy goes out on the road with a national tour. He is the only minor in the cast. When the curtain goes down, and the other actors are socializing, what does that child do? He can't go out with adults since they might go to a local pub where minors are not allowed. There's no one around for him to discuss important matters with, such as toys or baseball cards or girls. If the child is being supervised by his parent, then there's the risk of the two of them being at each others' throats. Even if there is a chaperone who has been hired to act *in loco parentis*, this person will probably socialize with the adult actors. What the child may not realize is that the adult cast members will be the chaperone's friends, and not his; this may create jealousy.

Those children who are cast in productions that employ other minors are more fortunate. They may be able to establish friendships quickly. However, if the other minors in the cast are older or younger than the child, the off-stage life might mirror the on-stage family, complete with bickering and tattle-telling. Children who are close in age may compete and develop rivalries that are based on who is offered more promotional work, or who gets more fan mail, or who is doing better in school than the other.

Children as children

Parents can't create playmates for their children on the set. Probably the most that parents can do is to help their child be a child. Children can't always be expected to act like adults even when they have adult responsibilities. Parents should not lose sight of the fact that children are children first and actors second. They must have friends. They can work to learn responsibility and earn money, but above all, children must be soundly educated, so that the child will have choices.

Children are not immune to the tremendous pressures that come with the business. There are million-dollar budgets riding on their performances. While parents may see their children as children, the business views children as commodities.

If the family unit can set viable limits for the child, if it can recognize the child's capacity as a student and as an actor, if it can make choices and changes as they arise, and if it can switch priorities as the child's needs change, then it will be helping the child learn and grow. And how often do parents have this kind of opportunity to help the children they love?

One of the types of schools referred to above is a professional children's school. The New York-based Professional Children's School has been in existence for more than 76 years.

THE PROFESSIONAL CHILDREN'S SCHOOL
Randall Short

The first thing you see upon entering the Professional Children's School is a display case crammed with résumé photos of teenage performers and models, some beginners, some easily recognizable, whose names are household words. The second is a little more mundane: a knot of three lithe, leotard-clad girls discussing, not movies, dance, or the latest fashions, but the problems they're having with a particularly challenging English Lit term paper. "I think we're talking two more drafts," one of them says.

A teacher approaches the receptionist and asks if she's seen a particular student, an apprentice dancer at the prestigious neighboring School of American Ballet. "Yes," says the receptionist. "She passed the desk earlier this morning."

"Hmm," responds the teacher calmly. "She missed her first-period class. I'll have to see what happened."

Welcome to the Professional Children's School, on Manhattan's Upper West Side, where such curious mixtures of entertainment industry glamour and regular school routine are the norm. At other institutions, these scenes might be out of the ordinary; at PCS, they're long-established.

"When I wasn't working, there was schoolwork," wrote Milton Berle in his 1974 autobiography, of his 1916 vaudeville tour. "When you were on the road, you took assignments with you from the Professional Children's School. I had schoolwork to do every day, and papers and homework to mail in." Although the school doesn't educate many vaudevillians these days — dancers, actors, musicians, and models, in that order, make up most of its present student body — its aims have changed little in the 70-plus years separating the term papers of Mr. Berle from those of the kids we recently overheard in the hallway. Now as then, PCS is a provider of quality academic, college-preparatory instruction in grades four through twelve in a flexible context, for students who face the special demands and irregular schedules of an early career in the performing world.

To many, the history of the Professional Children's School is nearly inseparable from that of New York theater. In the second decade of this century, the daughter of the Episcopal Bishop of New York attended with a friend a performance of the musical *Daddy Longlegs*. Impressed by the unusually large supporting cast of children in the show, the women visited the youngsters backstage after it was over. They were shocked to learn that the young actors, singers, and dancers were entirely cut off from school as a result of their employment in the theater.

With some help from the Church of the Transfiguration — the famous "Little Church Around the Corner," known for its wholehearted acceptance of and ministry to New York's show folk at a time when others considered them less than socially acceptable — the pair began a series of classes for the youngsters at the Rehearsal Club on Broadway (which was the setting for the movie *Stage Door*). The classes quickly evolved into an ongoing educational center for young performers. The roster of its alumni reads like an honor roll of twentieth century American entertainment; Ruby Keeler, Ethel Merman, Donald O'Connor, Celeste Holm, Itzhak Perlman, and Leontyne Price are just a few of PCS' stellar graduates.

The PCS program

The school's academic program is what one would expect of such a private institution: a strong liberal arts curriculum with classes averaging 10 to 14 students. What distinguishes it from other schools is an uncommon mission; PCS faculty and staff, many of whom have performing backgrounds themselves, are proud of the school's unique sensitivity to the needs of the working child.

"As far as I know, we're the only school of our kind in the United States," says Mary Bozanic, PCS' Director of Admissions. According to Bozanic, PCS' claim to singularity is based on its combination of flexibility (a word heard frequently from those describing the school) with rigorous formal and informal tracking of each student's work. "We don't tear our hair out, for example, when a model tells us she's going to be on location for five days. What we do is make sure that she has her work when she leaves and that it's done when she returns. And if it's not, the teacher and student will make time for it to get done. The teachers all regard that flexibility as an essential, basic part of their jobs here." It's an attitude, she feels, vital to a working child's stable educational progress. It's also an attitude rare at traditional public and private schools that find themselves working with young performers who have suddenly been catapulted into the limelight.

"Many schools," says Bozanic, who came to PCS from a similar position at Michigan's Interlochen Arts Academy, "have neither the inclination nor the resources to deal with the special problems of performing children, and it can make for some very difficult situations. We have parents coming to us who are going crazy. They've tried to keep their kids' lives as normal as possible, but, even though the home school may be cooperating — which is not always the case — it's just not working. But they don't want to give up entirely and go to a correspondence-school program. That's where we come in." Indeed, the PCS "family" sometimes seems to serve parents, who find the school a convenient focus for exchanging information and discussing shared concerns, as much as it does their children.

What the students think

This all sounds like good catalogue copy, but what do the students themselves think? Seniors Lauren Echo and Jen Rudin waste no time in answering: the Professional Children's School has become indispensable to both their careers and their sanity. Lauren, who does commercials and jingle work, and Jen, who's appeared in several made-for-TV movies, came to PCS from schools that were either indifferent to or actively hostile toward their situations. PCS, they agree, is entirely accommodating and first rate academically.

Inevitably, there are tradeoffs to be made; extracurricular activities like class plays and dances are difficult to organize, given that much of the student body is already acting or dancing professionally. Jen and Lauren believe that such drawbacks are far outweighed by the school's benefits. "You have friends who know exactly what you're going through, and that helps a lot. You might be saying to yourself, 'Oh, I'm unemployed; I'm having trouble finding an agent.' At a regular school, no one would know what you're talking about. Here everyone's been through it, and they all understand."

The secret seems to be getting around: as a result of extensive word-of-mouth recommendations (both Lauren and Jen, like most of their classmates, were referred to PCS by friends) and frequent visits by prospective students, who are encouraged to drop in and observe, PCS presently boasts an enrollment of 180 students from seventeen states.

Headmaster Jeff Lawrence oversees the administrative end of PCS with the help of an unpaid Board of Directors that includes many prominent New York business and stage figures. They're particularly proud of their ability, with the help of a modest endowment and substantial fund-raising activities, to offer the school's unique services at a tuition charge one to two thousand dollars lower than that of comparable institutions; young performers, explains Lawrence, simply have too many other expenses — New York living costs, professional lessons — to consider. Over a third of PCS' students receive scholarships. Whatever profit the school realizes is immediately put back into the programs and facility.

The result seems to be satisfaction on both sides. Leaving his office to attend a Friday afternoon faculty meeting, Lawrence is met by a student in an otherwise-deserted hall, who has stayed to thank him for his help with an exceptionally thorny scheduling matter. They chat briefly; Lawrence's eyes are alight with interest. "That came up quickly, didn't it? Everything all at once? But you've got it worked out now?"

"Yes," the student says, thanking him again.

"Good! Great! Wonderful!" says Lawrence, patting her on the back.

Randall Short's work has appeared in The New York Times *and* Newsday.

The hardest thing about being an actor is telling people what you do when you're still an unknown entity.

"What do you do for a living?" you'll be asked at a party.

"I'm an actor," you'll respond proudly, at least for the first 175 times that the question is posed.

"Really," comes the inevitable follow-up, said with a sense of awe and, often, challenge. "What have I seen you in?"

And you learn to embellish. A reading at the Public Theater becomes "an appearance in an off-Broadway showcase in which Joe Papp was in the audience." The class that you take at a local acting school becomes "a great audition for a noted director" who told you that he'll put you in the very next project on which he'll be working. A string of mindless, pointless auditions, none of which you're right for, becomes an example in just how seriously you're "pursuing your craft."

You begin to wonder if you're only as good as your last job (which is how everyone in the business sees you anyway). But what *was* your last job? A waiter? A go-fer? A temp?

Don't despair. The reality is *you have to live.* Whether you decide to adopt New York — where rents are outrageous and late night cab rides are a necessity — or Los Angeles — where a car and car insurance are part of the lifestyle — the days in which actors starve are no longer deemed glamorous. It's too impractical to struggle, as well as too demeaning, and you must do something to survive and keep your ego intact.

EARNING A LIVING BETWEEN JOBS:
THE WAITING GAME
Bruce Kluger

I'd already taken their order and brought them their salads; their steaks were on the grill and I had a couple minutes of free time. So I decided to go over for a chat. Why not? They seemed like a nice couple.

Straightening my bow tie and approaching their table, I kicked into my usual routine: "I'm only waiting tables for now," I told them, though they hadn't asked. "Just until I get my big break. You see," I added, "I'm an actor."

It was a speech I'd been tossing off at least a dozen times a day, each day I'd been living in New York City. Sure, it was silly, self-serving chatter — but I liked engaging in it; it somehow kept the spirit going in me. And, at this particular moment, it was also helping me forget that I was waiting tables instead of starring on Broadway. "Yup, I'm going to make it big," I told Mr. and Mrs. Steaks-on-the-Grill. "And not only that, I'm also a writer," I said. "In fact, my first show is opening off-Broadway next year."

"So you write," Mr. Steak said. "That's funny. I write a little, too."

I smiled politely, but to tell the truth, I was being anything *but* polite. "Ah, yes," I was thinking smugly, "another middle-aged man with an unfinished play in his top desk drawer; another dreamer still pining away at the fantasy that he'll someday make it as a writer. Not like me," I continued to think, rather full of myself. "I'm gonna make it big. *I'm* here and now. *I'm* happening ... "

At that point Mrs. Steak playfully socked her husband on his arm and said to me, "Oh, don't listen to him. He doesn't *just* write. He's a little more famous than that. He's Charles Strouse."

Now, for those who don't know, Charles Strouse is "a legend." He wrote the music for *Annie, Bye Bye Birdie, Applause*, and a seemingly unending list of movies and Broadway musicals. *I* knew who Charles Strouse was, of course — I'd been following his work ever since I was old enough to hum a Broadway tune. Naturally, I was overwhelmed.

Forgetting about the steaks entirely, I began to babble to Charles Strouse — completely dropping my oh-so-cool actor/waiter/writer demeanor and taking on my truer-to-life persona: that of a gushing fan. I told him I adored everything he'd done; I cited obscure musical references in his work; I even made a lunch date with him — which he not only kept, but at which he gently told me all the things I had yet to learn about the ever-bumpy road to theatrical success.

And all because he and his wife sat at my station.

Which brings me to my point: when I moved to the City, I'd decided that, in order to be able to pay the rent each month, I'd have to get some kind of "survival job." (Auditioning doesn't pay the bills, you know.) And because I'd decided my life was going to be dedicated to the theater, I knew that job would *somehow* have to be theater-related.

Well, this waiting-tables job turned out to be just the kind of job I'd been looking for after all — thanks to Mr. Strouse — and it led me to a string of other theater-related survival jobs throughout my early years in the City. And today, as I bounce back and forth between my two passions — writing and acting — I can honestly credit many of those part-time and full-time stints of employment with having prepped and nurtured me for the many subsequent phases of my career.

Below are just a few jobs you can look for in a big city while climbing the show biz ladder; they're jobs which may not land you in the spotlight, but will definitely put you close by in the wings — close enough to see the action.

Waiting tables

Waiting tables is still *numero uno* on the Survival Job Top 40. Why? Over the years the notion of unemployed actors taking waiting and bartending jobs has become such a tradition that today the restaurant community has become indiscernibly entwined with the theater community. It's almost cliché; nonetheless, it's true.

Let's say you do *decide* you're up for a little table-bussing, a little highball-serving. Initially, you'll find it a drag. "I can't believe it," you'll think, "I'm surrounded by people just like me — *all of us* wanting the pot of gold at the end of the rainbow, none of us getting it. And not only *that*," you'll continue, "but I'm stuck here in this restaurant and I'm not learning a blasted thing about the business!"

Slowly, however, you'll find that you're very wrong, that this job actually offers a lot more than you imagined. In fact, you'll find that from your new friends — your fellow employees, that is — you'll garner a wealth of theater information, *valuable* information that's yours, free of charge. Someone might have met a casting director whom you've yet to meet; someone might have a résumé-writing tip you never thought of; someone might have an "in" at an upcoming audition — an audition you didn't realize *was* upcoming. Get the picture? Before long, you'll be wanting to get to work almost as passionately as you want to get to a rehearsal.

And if you *really* want to add a little theatrical punch to your survival restaurant job, find one that's in or close to the theater district. When I began looking for my first waiting-tables job, I chose a restaurant on 44th Street and Broadway. I'd picked that particular spot because I wanted to be near Broadway shows; I *loved* talking theater with the patrons — finding out which shows they were seeing, which shows they'd already seen. And isn't it funny that one of those patrons turned out to be the composer of a musical playing just up the street?

By the way, there's one other thing about restaurant jobs that can't be beat, a fringe benefit appealing to actor and non-actor alike: you get to eat for free.

Go-fering

I had just been laid off by the restaurant I'd been working at and, though it was raining, opted to make the rounds anyway. First stop, I decided, would be a casting office that was considering me for a recurring extra role in the movie *Fame*. Once I got there — and only to further aggravate my already disastrous day — I was told I would not be cast in the film. "Great," I said, "I lose two jobs in one day — one of which I never really had in the first place." At that moment, the casting director, Joy Todd, made an unexpected gesture, an offer which I can honestly say changed my professional life dramatically: she asked me if I would like to work for her.

I spent the next year on roller-skates crisscrossing the New York streets to deliver packages for Joy, dropping off pictures and résumés at film directors' offices, checking-in extras on the sets of Manhattan shoots, reading opposite actors at final callbacks — *the works*. And how did all of this pay off? In a million ways: I learned the film industry inside-out. I met agents. I learned how an actor should approach a casting office. I learned how an actor should *not* approach a casting office. And, as a real bonus, after I'd left Joy's employ, I *also* got my SAG card. How? I was cast in a Joy Todd film.

Admittedly, not all go-fering jobs come so easily. The fact remains, however, that if you find just the right go-fer job in just the right place, it can turn out to be an incredible apprenticeship. Look for a job that's close to the heartbeat of your theatrical passion, a job that will put you within an arm's reach of your dream. There are dozens of them in big cities, each offering its own exciting glimpse into the theater world. Consider working as a box office manager, a talent agency telephone receptionist, an usher, a film set production assistant, an off-Broadway production coffee-runner, a rehearsal pianist, a rehearsal hall desk clerk, or a script-revision typist for a small-house production; the list goes on.

The only "downside" of a go-fer-type job is the toll it takes in terms of frustration: you're *so* close to the action, but not quite there. You can't let that get you down, though. Remember, I put in a lot of mileage on my skates to land that first movie job. And it was that wait that made the ultimate reward so much sweeter.

One problem that most actors face on a day-to-day basis is money. There never seems to be enough. In 1981, when things weren't going so well for me in New York, I took a vacation in Las Vegas and, while there, won a significant amount of money. In the wake of the excitement, I began to fantasize about what I'd do with my new-found booty. Unlike most Vegas winners, however, I wasn't thinking about a car or a new stereo set-up or anything of that sort. Nope; I remember thinking, "Good — now I'll be able to pay rent *and* get new pictures and résumés, and I'll finally be able to afford postcards, and I can do a mass mailing ... " And that's just where the money went.

Theater supplies

But how do you make ends meet if you don't have a lucky Keno card in your possession? Well, another kind of survival job that can help the fledgling actor is one in theater supplies. It's not as hands-on as go-fering — and maybe not as exciting, either — but it certainly can help your budget when it comes to procuring your much-needed theater supplies and services with an employee discount. And there are many types of theater supply outlets to consider: photograph duplication companies; photocopying shops; drama book stores; costume and make-up outlets; sheet music stores; and theater ticket brokerages, to name just some of the possibilities. Any sort of business that has roots in show business can turn out to be an unexpected haven for an employee, especially for one who's an up-and-coming actor.

Saving money isn't the only saving grace of a theater supplies job; such a job also puts the out-of-work actor, once again, *hip-deep* into the theater community, which is really the biggest plus to consider. Your patrons will be theater people, your store schedules will be dictated by theatrical time-clocks and, before long, your theatrical knowledge will increase tremendously. And, who knows? The job might even be fun.

And the most important job of all ...

There are countless types of employment, in addition to the few mentioned, that allow a peek into the kaleidoscope of the show business world and ultimately give the actor an opportunity to learn and eat while working and "starving." And with the computer age on the rise, and the theater community taking advantage of that, who knows what kinds of survival jobs will be available in the coming years?

But the most important job of all is the one that takes place in your heart: keeping your passion alive. No matter if you're serving chops or typing script revisions, the richest actors are the ones who stick with their dreams and each and every day try to spin those dreams into reality. And *that's* the job that pays best.

> *Bruce Kluger has appeared in commercials, on TV's* Diff'rent Strokes, *and in the film* Playing For Keeps. *He is now an associate editor of a major consumer magazine.*

How do you find those jobs between jobs that Bruce talks about? Well, ...

NON-PERFORMING TEMPORARY JOBS
Devorah Kaitz

Herbert Viola may have been an investigator for the Blue Moon Detective Agency, but as every true *Moonlighting* fan knows, he got his start there as a temporary accountant. "Sure," you might be thinking, "anything can happen in TV. But what happens in *real* life to people who do temporary office work?"

Well, one of them went on to become Herbert Viola! The TV role of a temporary accountant was a real life role, not all that many years ago, for Herbert's alter-ego, actor Curtis Armstrong.

The scene is set in New York City in the summer of 1976. Curtis Armstrong, armed with two years of acting academy training, a year and a half with an Ann Arbor, Michigan theatrical company that's since become Detroit's Attic Theatre, and a trunkful of talent and determination, arrives to make his mark on the theatrical world.

"I didn't want to wait tables — it was just something I resisted," he recalls. "I'd heard about temporary employment services from other actors, so two days after I arrived in the City, I signed up with one. It turns out that temping was invaluable for a few reasons. First, it was practical; it helped me get to know the City. I'd just arrived and didn't know my way around, but working in different companies forced me to learn. And second, and more important, it freed me so I was able to work when I needed to, but when there were auditions or important meetings — not that there were that many back then — I could work around them. And it just in general gave me a feeling of security because I was *doing* something ... I had a purpose ... I wasn't in New York just lying around waiting for the phone to ring."

The temporary employment industry is one that offers performers on their way to "making it" a true alternative to, as the song says, "parking cars and pumping gas." Virtually every city and town in the country has at least one temporary employment service, and large cities can have a hundred or more. According to the National Association of Temporary Services, in 1987 more than 945,000 people were employed by temporary services *each week*, and they earned a total of $8.6 *billion* during the year.

For each of these employees, a representative of a temporary service offered some sort of interview and screening process, and based on the results, matched the applicant with an *assignment*, a job whose description was provided by a client company, detailing the kind of work the temporary employee would be asked to do once on the job. In most cases the work was performed on the client's premises. The temporary employee was paid for the work by the temporary service, which withheld taxes, in many states provided unemployment and disability insurance coverage, and in some cases offered optional health insurance plans, bonuses, and other forms of "perks." The temporary service then charged the client company enough to cover costs and make a profit for each hour the temporary employee worked.

Perhaps the most critical feature of temporary work for the performer is that it allows the option of working — or not working — around the schedule of the employee.

If you're a young performer of an age at which you're expected to be earning a wage, and performing isn't yet providing all the income you need, you'd be right to be concerned about making a commitment to a job whose hours would conflict with lessons, auditions, interviews, rehearsals, and performances. Similarly, if you're the "chauffeur/parent" of a performer too young to be working outside show business, but you want or need to work on a flexible basis, "temping" allows you the freedom to be available for your child on audition or work days and to work — and get paid for it! — on the days that the child is in less need of your presence.

Many services advertise in the classified sections of newspapers, and the yellow pages, usually under the heading *Employment Contractors: Temporary Help*, will likely list all the services doing business in the area.

Mr. Armstrong worked exclusively with one service from his arrival in New York until the spring of 1979, with some occasional breaks for plays. Then he went on major tours with *Adventures of Scapin* and the road company of Broadway's *Da*, which kept him out of the City for six months. Back on home turf, a call to his temp service got him more office work, and only weeks later, he signed for his first film, *Risky Business*. Curtis lived on his earnings from that movie during a year of unemployment, and with funds beginning to run low, doing temporary work again wasn't outside the realm of possibility.

But along came a role in *Revenge of the Nerds*, which led to roles in *Clan of the Cave Bear, Better Off Dead, Bad Medicine, Summer Vacation,* and *Nerds in Paradise: Revenge of the Nerds Part II*, and ultimately to his current success in *Moonlighting*. Curtis isn't likely to do temporary office work again, role requirements notwithstanding, but for many others dreaming of and working toward similar success, the relationship with a temporary service can be an important one.

You might choose to register with services that are members of the New York Association of Temporary Services, Inc., the local affiliated chapter of the National Association of Temporary Services. According to Shirley Laufer, NYATS' executive director, "Each member firm has pledged to conform to a code of ethics, which means that the individual will be treated with dignity and respect. Member services have access to the most current information that affects the industry, and that therefore can affect the temporary employees themselves. In 1987, these services — that's just New York City members — had 50,000 people a day on temporary assignments, and the payroll for the year was $500 million." For a free list of current members of the Association, write to NYATS, 136-50 71st Road, Flushing, NY 11367 or call (718) 793-6711.

What can you do, before you call or visit a temporary service, to assure yourself the best possible chance of finding work when you want it? Carla Kroch, former manager of New York's Priority Temporaries, Inc., says, "Sit down and make a list of all the work experience you've had and all the office equipment you've worked on, including brand names and models. If you don't remember the name of the phone system, or typewriter, or photocopier, or computer that you worked on, sometimes a phone call to the company you worked with can get you the answer. This list can be very valuable because we pair the experience with the requirements of each assignment. Include in your list not only experience from paid work, but also from volunteer and school-related work. If they weren't too long ago, list school achievements, such as awards, or offices held, and all your extracurricular activities. These tell a lot about a person; they can show leadership, organization, ability to get along in groups and to complete jobs.

"Many people returning to the job market," Ms. Kroch continues, "have been active in community or church-related work. This shows that they're outgoing, and involved. Running a household and managing the schedule of a child performer and keeping all the family members going require great organizational skills. People who can do this are frequently good at both initiating projects and at being team players, both very helpful skills for temporary workers. Be sure to include them on your list."

Résumé now in hand, you probably feel ready to visit a temporary service or two, but don't leave the house just yet. Since the temporary service will be your employer, it must abide by the same laws and regulations as every other employer in the country, and that now means that it's obligated, before it can employ you for even one day, to verify that you're legally entitled to work in the United States. So grab your birth certificate, passport, or your U.S. Citizenship Certificate, or your Certificate of Naturalization, or your alien registration card, because the interviewer will have to see one of these in order to consider you employable.

There are a few other things you should do, too, before you set off to conquer the world of commerce. One is to brush up on any rusty office skills you may have. Did you take a typing course in high school? Relearn that keyboard! Did you do word processing at home for a summer? Put those computer games away and practice doing Mail Merge! Were you a stenographer before you became a parent of a budding star? Dust off the pad and pencil before rushing off to rehearsal, and see how much of the class play you can get down accurately! Did you proofread the high school literary magazine? Take out your good dictionary and review those proofreaders' symbols!

It's suggested that you call various agencies for an appointment. Some services interview new applicants only during certain hours or on certain days, so a phone call to find out when you can come can prevent disappointment and wasted time.

When auditioning, you probably dress for the role being cast. When applying for work in the business world, it's just as important to dress for the role you'll be playing there. In New York, this generally means jacket and tie, a dress shirt, and slacks for men, and dress or skirt and blouse for women. Sneakers, jeans, and other casual attire aren't considered appropriate for many New York industries. It's always better to be a bit *over*dressed than *under*dressed.

Once at the service of your choice, you'll likely be given an application. Without exception, representatives of the temporary services say that it must be filled out completely; writing *Please see résumé* or *Will discuss*, or other such non-answers to the straightforward questions asked will only unnecessarily lengthen your visit and will potentially cause the counselor upon whom you're depending for work to see you as difficult to work with. Résumés can and do accidentally become separated from applications, and it's one of the mysteries of life that when that happens, it's the application that's retained and the résumé that's lost. This means that any skill or experience that you didn't indicate on your application essentially doesn't exist, and you could lose out not only on assignments, but on salary increases, too.

In some services, all applicants are tested for skill in spelling, grammar, arithmetic, and office procedure, but only those who indicate they *have* the skill will be tested in typing, stenography, word processing, data entry, bookkeeping, or proofreading. If asked to take tests, don't resist; each service knows what skills it gets requests for, and taking tests is more likely to expand than decrease the number of assignments for which you qualify. These tests will serve to prevent you from being assigned to those jobs you won't likely do well.

Next comes the interview. Let the counselor lead it. Answer questions succinctly and directly, even if you feel they're answered on the application or the résumé. When the critical question of your schedule arises, be as honest as you can about your audition schedule. Are you working only with a manager or an agent, or are you going on lots of open calls?

Assignments placed with temporary services can be for as little as a half day of work to replace someone who's gone home sick, as well-defined as the two-week period during which a regular employee will be on vacation, or as indeterminate a period as "three to five days," or "a few weeks," or "until we hire someone," or "until the work's caught up." The client company is paying by the hour from the time the temporary employee reports in, and management generally expects that one employee will be trained for — and will complete — each assignment. But with your schedule, unpredictable as it is, how will you ever get assignments if you're honest?

If you're straight with the temp service, they can frequently work things out for you. If you aren't, and you fail to complete an assignment without having made arrangements first, the service looks bad, and you look bad. If you're honest, your counselor will certainly try to help you work around your schedule.

Says Barbara Cohen, former director of Career Blazers Temporary Personnel, "In today's market there are never too many good candidates for temporary work. More important, there's plenty of work not only for skilled secretaries, typists, and word processors, but also for high school and college students, homemakers, and others who can do clerical and reception work, with or without experience."

"While there's always a demand for those who can type or do word processing, others can do clerical work or can work as product demonstrators or convention hosts and hostesses. With so many trade shows taking place in New York, there are lots of opportunities, especially for actors and actresses, to work at registration and information booths, or to handle telephone inquiries," assures Frank Santora, regional manager of TAC/Temps.

Many clerical assignments may require nothing more than stuffing envelopes or filing, but companies love the bright and enthusiastic person who works as though he or she *wants* to be there. Someone who learns quickly can earn as much as $7.00 an hour without even knowing how to type. There are so many assignments for these people, especially in the summer, because temporary employees are so frequently hired to replace regular employees on vacation.

It's suggested that you plan your week as much as possible. You can work one, two, as many as seven days in a week; full days are best for getting work, half-days are possible. One of the wonderful things about doing temporary work is that, depending on your skill level, you can work weekdays, nights, or weekends. Many performers work during the day and rehearse or perform at night; others use their days for auditioning, and work at night.

Stuart Geminder, of Continental Word Processing, points out that the temporary help industry operates 24 hours a day in New York. "You don't need to have the more technical skills, such as word processing, in order to work your choice of shift. Proofreaders, for instance, are needed around the clock, especially in law firms, and those who pass spelling, grammar, and syntax tests can earn anywhere from $11 to $15 an hour, depending on the shift they work. For those who *do* operate personal computers, especially if they're experienced in certain word processing programs, the chance of getting work at $15 to $22 an hour is great. People can be free during the day to work with their kids or to develop their own performing careers, and then work weekends or 'graveyard' shift and make a nice income."

Your counselor, who may have different job titles in different services, might well offer you an assignment on the spot. Before you accept it, be certain that you ask for a complete job description and that you feel qualified to fulfill the job, and that to the best of your knowledge nothing will prevent you from showing up at the assignment for the specified duration. What if the assignment is only for a few days and you were hoping to work for a few weeks in order to save money before your next round of auditions?

Many people find that doing temporary work allows them to add to their repertoire of skills. Curtis Armstrong took an assignment as a mailroom clerk in a publishing company; by the time he'd completed the assignment, he'd learned all the postal equipment, regulations, and rates, and "I earned more money after that, because I'd become skilled."

Now, armed with all this sage counsel, you're on your way to finding out firsthand how temporary work can offer exactly the opportunity you've been looking for. There's no other industry that can offer the young performer the flexibility of scheduling, the diversity of work, the opportunity to learn about so many industries — and the chance to play so many different "roles" — and get paid for it, too! Perhaps one day you'll tell the next generation of performers, as Curtis Armstrong, former temp, current star, tells you, "Doing temporary work was good on many levels; I did work which was frequently very interesting, and I got to know a lot of people. Temping, for me, was really an invaluable experience."

3
Training the Young Performer

I went to Intermediate School 70, not a very tough school, but it was easy to get on the wrong track. My mom was worried about me because I would get into fights. She heard about a children's repertory company called the [now defunct] First All Children's Theatre. It was pretty serious. It was every day after school from 4:00 to 7:00, and weekends for about five years. I did that in sixth and seventh grade, and it was fun. It kept me off the streets a bit, and it taught me a lot of discipline. Before that, I could never be anywhere on time, and I was obnoxious.

Josh Hamilton, featured in Women in Wallace

Having "technique" is knowing how to work with a script. It's knowing how to break scenes down into bits. It's knowing the actions and motivations behind the creation of a character.

It's learning to work with a director. It's learning the choreography and the song lyrics, while speaking like the character and developing a thick Italian accent.

It's knowing where to find music in your key. It's learning what your vocal range is and how to strengthen it. It's learning what songs work well for you at an audition.

It's the confidence you exude when you're auditioning. It can be seen by the method in which you attach your pages of sheet music together before presenting them to the accompanist.

It's the way in which you set your mind to following through on details, like writing letters to agents, or following up with them by regular phone calls, or attending x number of auditions per week, that helps make you a contender.

It's understanding how to do cold readings. It means knowing what clothes to wear to a commercial audition for Nintendo. It means knowing how to "sign in" at the audition. It's knowing the proper etiquette of working with a casting director.

It's learning how to use your energy to make each evening's performance seem like opening night's: well-rehearsed, clearly defined, and insightful.

How old should a young performer be before beginning to study formally? The answer is as different as the discipline. Dancers often begin training at very early ages. So do musicians. In acting, however, many professionals feel that children should not be pushed into classes too early. A youngster's natural talent, charm, poise, and honesty, it's believed, are technique enough.

Regardless of the differing viewpoints, children who like to act may at some point take acting classes. The following articles by Rita Litton and Bambi Everson suggest that if your child wishes to study, you should know what to seek from the experience.

ACTING CLASSES FOR CHILDREN? YES!
Rita Litton

In 1975 I established, and since then have developed and taught, a professional acting training program for young adults in New York City. I wouldn't be an acting instructor if I didn't believe and, in fact, *know*, that I have made a significant contribution to the growth and development of my students. Sometimes my effect on the students is immediate and professionally tangible, as many of them have won significant roles in film, television, and theater. Sometimes their growth is personal — a blossoming of poise, creativity, and confidence — they like themselves more!

I recently taught a young boy who had left school at 15 to "hang out." He enrolled at our school, worked hard, and showed real potential. One day he told me that he'd suddenly realized how much he had to know to be an actor. He had never been a "reader" and had little life experience to draw on outside his own small neighborhood. He was impressed with how much the other students seemed to know "about things." He decided to return to high school and get his diploma. I'm very proud of him.

Through the years I've heard professionals debate the value of acting training for children. Few bother to distinguish a child actor from a teenager and the different professional and emotional demands on each group. Certainly young actors need to retain their freshness and exuberance. I also strive to have my students *be* the character rather than *act*, or show it. But I believe most young actors past puberty (and I only work with those ages 13-20) have lost their natural sense of play and make-believe. They become mired in self-consciousness, peer pressure, "looking good," and "acting right."

It takes a lot of courage to be an individual. I believe the right instructor can help a young actor rediscover his uniqueness. Actors need some sense of stability in a very competitive business, especially at this sensitive age. They can benefit from a technique or foundation, of sorts, to help them when they're nervous, under pressure, or not getting the job — to help their confidence in auditions and in stretching to tackle more challenging roles.

Great directors, including Steven Spielberg (*E.T.*, *Empire of the Sun*) and England's John Boorman (*Hope and Glory*), admit that child actors can play only one role — themselves. Not many teenaged actors contemplating a career in acting would aspire to such a limited repertoire! In fact, when Spielberg was casting the young male role in the Oscar-nominated *Empire of the Sun*, he screened 4,000 boys, mostly amateurs, but ultimately chose the more experienced Christian Bale, after *six* auditions. To quote *Newsweek*, "... his Oscar-caliber performance — in which he grows from a snotty schoolboy to a savvy, hollow-eyed black marketer — was doubtlessly helped by his training."

I also think a distinction should be made between *acting classes* and *coaching sessions*. A certain status has been attached to working with a private acting coach. Besides being prohibitively expensive, this is not in my judgment an ideal way to learn to act. If the coach, often a former actor or actress, is working opposite you in a scene, he or she is *acting* with you, and is not able to truly watch and judge *your* performance. If he or she is not acting fully, but rather is sitting back to observe, then you are losing out on the wonderful give-and-take, the "spontaneous combustion" that actors give to each other — and without that feedback, you'll have trouble learning to develop your character's relationships. The possibility is that the actor will learn to act alone, in isolation, a "solo turn" — a selfish and potentially harmful presentational style. Actors in training need to work and perform *with other actors*, on stage if possible, and in the classroom. I've also found that working with video cameras, far from inhibiting a young performer, actually enables him to see immediately what does and does not work in a performance. The actor quickly learns that the more effortless performance is often the more *real* and affecting!

I would recommend private coaching only for specific auditions, monologue work, or very special needs, and then I would choose my coach *very* carefully! I have seen disastrous performances and auditions coached by anxious managers, teachers, and well-meaning parents. Usually these coaches are "result-oriented," meaning the parent or the coach can see how the scene should be played and therefore will demand a *result* from the young actor, often in the form of mimicked line readings. A sensitive acting instructor, on the other hand, knows that a coaching session for an audition requires great delicacy and must be approached in a manner so as to retain believability and adaptability.

A coach should also know when to leave well-enough alone. Case in point: A young student who had been studying with me for three years called me to be coached for an audition for *The Cosby Show*. His scene was brief and involved reactions and participation, but few lines. I heard him read the scene and thought he was terrific — good energy, and knowledge of the situation and relationships. I told him he was terrific — to keep his money, go home, put the script under his pillow, sleep on it, leave it alone, and he'd be great the next day. In other words, he needed only reassurance to go in and do his best! P.S.: He got the part, which has since become a recurring role.

It would have been detrimental to work his audition when he was so perfectly on the mark. I have seen other students appear for auditions totally unprepared or completely oblivious to what the scene was about. These otherwise talented actors occasionally need an "outside eye" to guide them to discoveries regarding the action, objective, or problems in certain situations. But I would never cram an actor auditioning for a role with line readings or give so many suggestions that he becomes more confused or anxious. My job in this situation is to encourage, to comfort, to enlighten, and to make the actor feel he can and will do his best!

I would say that when shopping around for an acting program or coach, you should start with professional recommendations and then ask for a personal interview. Find out the teacher's credentials and the amount of time spent teaching. Ask for specific affiliations, as many teachers will exaggerate "home teaching." Find out the teacher's own training background and professional accreditations. Auditing a class can be very helpful, but it is not necessarily a bad sign if a teacher refuses or has reservations. If the class enrollment is small, or the work involved intimate, an observer is an intrusion and a disruption to the concentration of those paying for the class. There may be times when obtaining a full description of the program, biographies of instructors, and course outlines, and weighing the reputation of the establishment will be sufficient to make a careful decision.

I recommend that if a student is unhappy in any way about his training program — *complain!* The old adage "you get what you pay for" is not necessarily true. Many parents and actors have come to me after spending *hundreds* or even *thousands* of dollars of instruction in other institutions, highly dissatisfied with what they received compared to what was promised or implied.

Be very cautious here! No acting school should — or can! — promise you work! And even graduate success ratios can be misleading and hard to document. I believe an actor should approach a school only for *solid acting training*, not for exposure, showcases, or the promise of discovery. The time for showcasing is when and *if* the benefits and results of training are clearly visible. While I have personally helped many students get started professionally, I believe young adult actors have to learn how to *do* the work before learning how to *get* the work. They have to fight for their own careers, do their own leg work — and learn "the business" of acting.

And if they spend half as much time developing their *craft* (their vocal, physical, and emotional instruments) as they do dreaming of success, they'll be ready and able to handle the opportunities ahead.

> *Rita Litton is the founder and director of the Weist-Barron School's Acting For Teens program, which includes workshops in commercials, film acting technique, theater, and speech. Ms. Litton has been a professional actress since 1970 and has appeared off-Broadway, in regional theater, in films, soap operas, and commercials.*

SCENE STUDY FOR THE YOUNG PERFORMER
Bambi Everson

On the surface, the leading character is just a very nervous girl trying to make a friend. What the audience doesn't know is that this girl has a terrible relationship with her mother. It's so bad that she's just stabbed her with a bread knife and left her lying on the kitchen table. A scene, from Leonard Melfi's *Birdbath*.

As an actress, I know that the young actor has to work on specifics: how to make a friend, how to keep a secret, and how to cover up. She has to think of her role in actors' terms, to work through the *process* instead of going for an end result. Instead of saying to a child, "I want you to be nervous here," I'd rather encourage her to look at her scene partner and observe the look on his face. I'll tell her to look into his eyes, keeping in mind where her mother is at all times, and remember that no one has ever listened to her before. Maybe this man can fix it all. If, as a teacher, I hadn't read this play thoroughly and worked through the scene in my mind, the child would never get past the words on the surface. Not only do I have to be well read, I have to be able to help that child find the core of the character.

I believe that it helps to understand the process of acting when you're working with children, and that it requires more than just having a vague idea of what you want to teach them. When I help children work through monologues or scenes, the actress in me can really appreciate the young actors' problems.

I give youngsters improvisational work before we actually get to scene study. We start with very simple situations. Two kids are talking. Child A is very upset because she thinks that her best friend, child B, doesn't like her any more since B is spending more time with C. A begins to tell B how she feels. Unbeknownst to A, B is actually planning a surprise party for her. B *has* to keep it a secret.

I question my actors, "Do you have a best friend? Have you ever felt jealous?" Now we fill in some of the blanks with specifics. What does the other person look like? Is she nice? Remember the time she really came through for you. Is she smarter than you? This helps give the actors a point of reference.

Child B, the one planning the surprise party, has to come up with huge lies to cover up her plans. She may say that her newfound friend is coming over to help her with her homework, or that she's left something at her house and she needs to come by to retrieve it. If done properly, it's honest. If we were then to turn the improv into a script, I would have to keep reminding the actresses to go back to when the words they spoke and the ideas they had were fresh. I'd encourage them to go back to the persons they were at the moment they first played the improvisation and try it again. If the actors stay honest, they're building a foundation to create a role several times a week.

Kids love improvisation; it gives them the freedom not to be tied down to the page. They feel comfortable with each other and comfortable with the group. If they say something funny and get a big laugh, there's the relief of knowing that they can think on their feet. I'll suggest a line with which to begin the improvisation: something like "How could you do this to me?" From that, they'll start to create a character. When the other person responds to their opening, a scene develops. Initially, we'll create a six-line play. From that, they'll eventually grow into studying established scenes. The work necessary for scene study is no different than the work necessary to develop an improvisation. You have to question: what makes you say the first line? The second line? The third line? It's done on a step-by-step basis.

As an example, let's look at the play *Saint Joan*, which I've done with 12-year-olds. I say to the child, "Think of what it's like to be grounded for life. Your Benetton clothes are taken away. You can't listen to your music. You can't have your Michael J. Fox poster in your room. You can't smell pizza." I'd go through a series of deprivations that would mean something to a 12-year-old until she said, "Oh, I get it." I'd start her very slowly. I'd suggest that she think these thoughts and say Joan's words at the same time. The result is often very effective.

Photos courtesy of French Woods
Festival of Performing Arts

Everybody has gone through something that he or she can relate to. Without getting personal with children, a teacher should be able to help them find something that they can use that sparks some kind of response. If there's something internally happening, then children aren't self-conscious about what they're saying and they can use Shaw's, or Shakespeare's, or Tennessee Williams' words.

I try hard to stay away from notions that will hurt a young actor. Some teachers — some schools, in fact — like to take a psychological approach to acting. They play mind games with children which can often lead to them doing brilliant work. But when it comes to recreating the experience, youngsters find themselves unable to relive the situation.

I'd rather the actor have his or her own little secret. If they're supposed to be protective towards a baby, and they don't have a younger brother or sister at home, they can substitute an animal or a best friend. Some kids have a great need to express themselves, and I'm more than happy to listen to how they wish to play a certain part and to what they're feeling inside. But it's not the audience's, nor the teacher's, business what they use to create the on-stage reality. If it works, if it doesn't traumatize, if the actor can let go of it once the scene is played out, then I'm all for it.

In terms of choosing specific scenes, I would always stay away from those "original" monologues geared towards teenagers. They're usually about kids who are doing a lot of weeping. I personally avoid the material like, "My parents don't love me." I'd rather look for scenes that have obstacles: something that you have to get over, something that you need, something that gets in your way. Unless you have these elements, the scenes are flat out b-o-r-i-n-g.

What also seems to be happening these days is that playwrights are writing about precocious kids, which is not scene work that I like to assign. Often, the only characters available for children are the ones that used to play with silver spoons and are now putting them up their noses. The "I'm a drug addict" roles are not ones that I recommend. If given a choice, a 10-year-old will say, "Wow, it's about a drug addict. I want to play that part." I try to talk them out of those roles and into a list of *more suitable* scenes for young people.

Some of the Brat Pack movies have wonderful monologues. In Rob Reiner's film, *The Sure Thing*, there's a monologue in which a young man says that if he doesn't have the girl he's pining for help him with his English assignment, then he's going to be a bum for the rest of his life. He's going to end up selling french fries at McDonald's.

The Breakfast Club also has a couple of good monologues that require some character work, but they're people that a ten-year-old will recognize. The class jock, the class misfit, and the class intellect have all, at one point, made an appearance in a young person's life. The young actor can work through the character in his mind and ask himself, "How would this character walk across a room? How would this bully deal with the other people in his class?" If the actor has a point of reference, it's easy for him to crawl inside that character's head. I call that "getting possessed" by another character.

There's a wonderful monologue in the Tennessee Williams' play, *This Property Is Condemned*. The character, Willie, who is 13, has ideas of grandeur. She thinks she's really hot stuff. The actress has lots to work on. Willie's living in a condemned building. She has a strong need to impress people. She desperately needs a friend. She misses her sister who has died recently, and she must prove to everyone how well she can make it on her own.

I'd ask an actress who's preparing this role: Have you ever been *really* alone? Have you ever *really* needed a friend so badly that you'd talk to anybody? Then, when you see a real person standing there flying his kite, question what it is about this person that you like. Is he cute? What color eyes does he have? What's he wearing? Does he have a sympathetic smile? I'd instruct the actress to work through why she needs to tell him how wonderful she is. Most girls who pick this scene imagine that it's Kirk Cameron they're talking to. I'll ask, "Is he paying attention to you? If he's just turned his head, how are you going to get his attention back?" It's decisions like these that help you say the next line.

I still think that *The Children's Hour* works well. The Mary and Rosalie scenes are especially good because you're always going to find one child who loves to manipulate another child or who has always been in the position of being dominated by somebody. It's a timeless piece.

Anything from *You're A Good Man, Charlie Brown* is effective, especially the lunchtime monologue. For Charlie Brown, lunchtime is a horrible time of day. The actor has so much to work with, including the little redheaded girl, feelings of isolation, wanting to get up, and the fear of rejection. Lest we forget — peanut butter, "again! When you're really lonely the peanut butter sticks to the roof of your mouth."

The Member of the Wedding, Carson McCullers' play, requires a youngster to fantasize about what's going to happen after big brother gets married. Big brother suddenly has a place in the world, and the child thinks that her place is going to be very different from this point forward, and infinitely better, and the actor must work through these feelings.

In *A Tree Grows In Brooklyn*, there's a wonderful scene of the new girl in the neighborhood meeting the streetwise kid who's been there forever. The two start off bickering and eventually work out their differences.

To Kill A Mockingbird has a scene in which the older brother is taking his younger sister to school for the first time. He explains what's in store. She fears being alone, being left out, and not living up to her brother's standing. The actor playing the brother must must work on his feelings of protectiveness for his little sister, and on the confidence of teaching her something he knows so well.

Mrs. McThing is bizarre. It's a strange play about a witch who can turn children into eerie creatures. There's one scene between two children, in which the daughter of the witch manipulates a young friend into becoming her slave. She says, "My mother is a witch and she can turn you into anything, unless you do what I say."

The Bad Seed is great. The child playing the mother could use a doll, or a younger sister, or anything she feels she wants to protect to offset the shock of a daughter doing these truly dreadful acts. For the actress playing the child, I try to incorporate the child's active fantasies with a private improvisation. In our minds we are all capable of the most violent acts. I ask her to think about what she would *like* to do to that kid in school who's always pulling her hair. Young actors' imaginations are very active, and it's not hard to substitute hitting a kid over the head with a shoe, then dumping him in the river and stealing his medals.

I also encourage kids to write. It's wonderful for them to have something on paper because they can then give it to another child and really discuss and dissect it. Does this scene have obstacles? Do the characters have needs? Is it interesting to watch? Do you care about this person?

With the advent of VCRs, it's so easy to find pieces to work on. If you see something you like on television, tape it, transcribe it, and work on it. Sometimes TV sitcom scripts have really great obstacles and objectives, sometimes they just have funny lines. If it's just a scene that's set up to be funny, it's difficult to act well. There are some good sitcoms, though. *Family Ties* has some wonderful brother/sister scenes that are socially relevant. *The Cosby Show* also has some good two-person scenes where there are problems to overcome, negotiations to make, and feelings to consider. This is definitely preferable to people sitting around a table cracking jokes.

The good material is out there. The young performer just needs to know where to find it.

Here is a list of suggested scenes and monologues for the young performer:

For eight years and up

- *Summer and Smoke* by Tennessee Williams. Characters: Alma, John (Prologue).

- *The High School* from *The World of Sholom Aleichem* by Arnold Perl. Characters: Moishe, 13 (appears in many scenes).

- *The Secret Diary of Adrian Mole, Age 13 3/4* (the play) by Sue Townsend. Characters: Adrian, Nigel, Pandora (appear in many scenes).

- *Alice in Wonderland* by Eva Le Gallienne. Characters: Alice, the Red Queen, the White Queen.

- *The Dining Room* by A. R. Gurney. Characters: (from Act II) Sarah, Helen.

- *The Bad Seed* by Maxwell Anderson. Characters: Rhoda, Christine (the mother), Leroy.

For teenagers

- *Here We Are* by Dorothy Parker. Characters: He, She

- *Uncommon Women and Others* by Wendy Wasserstein. Characters: Muffet, Susie, Leilah, Samantha, Kate, Holly.

- *The Girl Who Loved the Beatles* by D.B. Gilles. Characters: Young Man, Young Woman.

- *Red Carnations* by Glenn Hughes. Characters: Boy and Girl.

- *Hello Out There* by William Saroyan. Characters: Emily, Photo Finish.

- *Five Finger Exercise* by Peter Shaffer. Characters: Clive, Pamela.

- *Accommodations* by Nick Hall. Characters: Pat, Lee (both girls).

- *The Day They Shot John Lennon* by James McLure. Characters: Sally, Mike, Kevin (both scenes and monologues).

- *Once A Catholic* by Mary O'Malley. Characters: (from Scene 5) Mary Gallagher, Mary Mooney.

Monologues for girls

- *Crimes of the Heart* by Beth Henley. Character: Babe.

- *Happy Birthday, Wanda June* by Kurt Vonnegut, Jr. Character: Wanda June, Age 8.

- *The Search for Signs of Intelligent Life in the Universe* by Jane Wagner. Character: Angus Angst, teenager.

- *Alice In Wonderland* by Eva Le Gallienne. Character: Alice, any age.

- *This Property Is Condemned* by Tennessee Williams. Character: Willie, 13.

- *The Member of the Wedding* by Carson McCullers. Character: Frankie, any age.

- *Runaways* by Liz Swados. Characters: Many and varied.

- *Talking With* by Jane Martin. A book of monologues for women.

Monologues for boys

- *Where Has Tommy Flowers Gone?* by Terrance McNally. Character: The Nephew, teenager.

- *Steambath* by Bruce Jay Friedman. Character: The Attendant, any age.

- *You're A Good Man, Charlie Brown* by John Gordon. Characters: Charlie Brown, Snoopy, any age.

- *The Dark At the Top of the Stairs* by William Inge. Character: Sammy, teenager.

- *A Separate Peace* (the novel) by John Knowles. Characters: (accident scene) Phineas, Gene, teenagers.

- *A Thousand Clowns* by Herb Gardner. Character: Nick, age 8.

- *Brighton Beach Memoirs* by Neil Simon. Character: Eugene, age 15.

- *Stand By Me* based on a story by Stephen King. Characters: Any of the four teenage boys.

- *House of Blue Leaves* by John Guare. Character: Robbie (Huckleberry Finn monologue), teenager.

> *Bambi Everson has been an actress for 10 years. She studied at the High School of Performing Arts in New York City, Webber Douglas Academy in London, and with renowned acting teacher, Michael Schulman. She presently teaches at the 92nd Street Y, the 14th Street Y, and the Usdan Center for the Performing Arts.*

Part of an actor's training is knowing the importance of the rehearsal period. Knowing how to work with others and learning what's expected after the part is in hand are signs of a professional. Ken Bush discusses how to be one.

AVOIDING THE ACTOR'S NIGHTMARE
Ken Bush

As a teacher and director of young actors, I have noticed a strange phenomenon when we moved from the classroom to the theater. The student who showed imagination and ingenuity in scene work suddenly loses focus and becomes overly dependent on the director in a production situation. Even performers with film and TV experience can get frustrated with the long hours needed to mount a play. Often, these rehearsals stretch out even further because the work we accomplished two nights ago is forgotten.

The culprit here usually isn't a lazy actor or (heaven forbid) bad directing on my part, but a lack of rehearsal technique. Young actors simply do not know what is expected of them. The following, then, is a brief summary of the actor's responsibilities that should help de-mystify the rehearsal process and keep it from seeming like a bad dream.

Who does what in rehearsals?

Let's start with job descriptions of a few important personnel.

The director is there to help you integrate your performance into the show. If, after trying several times by yourself, you are not sure why you are saying or doing something on stage, ask the director (a good director will see you are lost and give suggestions). Blocking or "cleaning up" the actor's movements is also the director's job. Don't expect the director to be your acting teacher. She/he is looking for you to make strong, informed choices about your character based on what you have read in the script.

All practical matters are covered by the stage manager (S.M.) and assistant stage manager (A.S.M.). Any problems with sets, props, costumes, lights, rehearsal schedules, personal injuries, and backed-up toilets should be directed to either the S.M. or A.S.M. In addition, they will cue you when you forget lines or blocking (sometimes this includes notes on missed lines or blocking given at the end of rehearsals). Once the play opens, the stage manager calls the technical cues from the light booth while the A.S.M. runs the show backstage.

What can I do before we start rehearsing?

Before going to the first rehearsal, read the entire script at least three times; once to get the story line (plot), then to determine what your character does (major actions), and finally to see what is said about your character by yourself and others. Don't waste time imagining how your character would say or do something; that is part of the rehearsal process.

Plan to show up early for every rehearsal. One of the things directors can't discover in auditions is a discipline problem, so they tend to judge tardiness very harshly. Of the three actors I have had to replace in shows, two were fired in the first two weeks for being repeatedly late. Also, bring your script, two sharp pencils with erasers (not pens), and a date book. You should be given a rehearsal schedule for each week (staple these inside the back cover of your script) but the date book is handy to note special times and days for costume fittings, lines due, photo calls, and first dress rehearsal. These dates should all be on the stage manager's master calendar which outlines the entire rehearsal period through opening night.

The first rehearsal

So now it's time to start rehearsing, usually with several read-throughs of the play around a table. The room is charged with expectation and the actors are champing at the bit to repeat that wonderful reading they gave in auditions. Why? You've already got the role. Now is the time to relax and begin to work with your fellow cast members. Go slowly and make as much eye contact with others as possible. The characters in the script are beginning to be embodied by the actors around the table, and it is important that you are involved in this transformation. The first tentative looks, gestures, and facial expressions are the start of a relationship, just like in real life.

Movement on stage

Generally, the first weeks of rehearsal are given over primarily to blocking. Here is where the novice stage actor gets lost.

To start, know what and where everything is on the set. The S.M. should have spiked (marked in tape) where all set pieces are located and arranged rehearsal furniture accordingly, but go ahead and ask questions: Does the window open?

Can I lean against the tree? How high is that platform? If you can't imagine how the set will look opening night, keep probing until you get a clear picture. Both the director and the S.M. will have answers since they have been working directly with the designers. You should be able to make a rough ground plan (a bird's eye diagram) of the set before you begin blocking.

As an actor, I have been subjected to both extremes of blocking style, i.e., "move two feet to your right, turn and say your line" or "just move around when you feel like it." Most directors fall somewhere in between. They will ask you what you are doing and suggest movement to enhance the action or they will take movement that you are already doing and focus it in a more dramatic way. In any case, the best advice is don't move until you know what is making you move. This will keep you from either wandering aimlessly or being manipulated like a puppet by the director.

Once you have tried a piece of blocking and it works, write it down in the margin of your script. Use a pencil since today's blocking may change in a few days when you and the director have made more discoveries about the scene. Be sure you know how to notate blocking. Any good book on stage management will tell you. I suggest Lawrence Stern's *Stage Management*, because he gives several methods and also shows how to notate blocking on thrust and arena stages. Directors tend to block faster than actors can write, so don't be afraid to stop the rehearsal in order to get your blocking written correctly. In a pinch, you can also check with the S.M. or A.S.M. during a break.

All this does no good if you don't find time to review. For some reason, young actors will spend hours memorizing lines and never give blocking a second glance. Instead, check the rehearsal schedule to see what scenes are being worked, look over the blocking notes in your script, then show up early and walk the blocking while reading or saying your lines. This should also help you remember why you were moving so the first hour of rehearsal won't be wasted re-discovering your actions.

What about all these lines?

At the start of the rehearsal period, you'll be given a due date for when your lines should be memorized (or when you're to be "off-book.") This normally happens at the halfway point in rehearsals, with lines for an act or scene due on a particular day. No one expects you to know every word, so don't get stressed out over memory lapses. Simply call "line" or ask for blocking and try not lose your composure.

I picked up some memorization techniques when I was acting that might be helpful here. First, try to memorize in a monotone. Clever line readings and character voices are OK for TV and radio commercials, but the complex circumstances of a play require honest listening and responding to other actors on stage. A memorized vocal pattern prevents this from happening. Second, give yourself about two hours to study your script. I've found that the part of my brain that records lines doesn't really kick in until I have been at it for 30 or 40 minutes. By the second hour, I'm memorizing faster and retaining longer. Third, whenever possible, corner your scene partner(s), sit down together, and run lines. You not only get the benefit of reviewing the script, but can also make some subtle discoveries about character relationships that you might have missed while moving about on stage.

Countdown to opening

The last week of rehearsals is called production week when the set, lights, costumes, recorded sound, special effects, live music, and any other technical aspects are brought together.

At least two weeks before this you need to be asking questions about your costume, make-up, and props, just as you did with the set. If you think something might throw your concentration, ask to work with it early on. Don't wait for dress rehearsals to find out you are wearing a long wig, floor length cape, and brandishing a 17-pound sword. However, try to make difficult props and costumes work before rejecting them. Long hours have been put into their design and construction; there may not be any alternative.

Technical rehearsals are meant to incorporate light and sound cues into the show. They are not for the actors. Tension can run high between directors, designers, the S.M., the A.S.M., and the running crews, so be patient and cooperative. From this point on, you are expected to muddle through if you forget your lines. The S.M. and A.S.M. are too busy to give you line cues.

If you are moving from a small rehearsal space, be aware that you must now fill an entire auditorium with your voice. Also, note where the dark and bright areas of light are on the stage and adjust your blocking slightly so you can be seen. Take some time before or after rehearsal and walk leisurely around the set to notice details or idiosyncrasies. Remember, you have spent many weeks relying mostly on your imagination to create a set. Now that one has been constructed by the designers and crews, you need to reconcile the differences between your respective visions.

How not to offend

Finally, a few rules of rehearsal etiquette that will help you get a good reputation.

- At the first rehearsal, let the S.M. know about any days when you will not be available. Should an emergency arise, have the S.M.'s phone number and call immediately so he or she can reschedule around your absence.

- If you must leave the rehearsal early for any reason, check with the S.M. or A.S.M. first. Let them know where you have to go and for how long. Also, never assume you are finished rehearsing until the S.M. has okayed it with the director.

- When the director gives acting notes at the end of a rehearsal, write yours down without arguing or asking questions. Discuss them later when you're not wasting other cast members' time.

- The S.M. and A.S.M. are there to trouble-shoot problems for the whole show, not just you. Treat them courteously or your requests will begin to get low priority attention.

- Never tell another actor how to act. Wait until you are asked and then choose your comments very carefully.

- All rehearsal props and costumes are your responsibility until you return them to the prop table or costume rack.

- There is no talking off-stage or in the auditorium during the rehearsals; that is why some genius invented the green room.

Exceptions to the rules

Not all shows rehearse this way. Community theaters, off-off Broadway, and many educational theaters simply don't have the money to hire all the technical staff to make things run smoothly. Often, there is only one director and stage manager (who may also have a bit part in the production) with the actors expected to help build sets, make costumes, hang lights, run the box office, and even wait tables (at dinner theaters). There is always plenty to learn in the theater so don't be afraid to gain experience under less than perfect conditions. Knowing the rules also means knowing when to bend them.

> *Ken Bush was an actor and director in New York for 12 years. He has taught and directed at Usdan Center for the Performing Arts in Huntington, Long Island; Duke Ellington School of the Arts and Catholic University in Washington, D.C.; and Adam Mickiewicz University in Posnan, Poland. Currently, he is an assistant professor in the Department of Theatre and Drama at Indiana University, Bloomington.*

✪

Young performers must be happy studying and must be comfortable with and have confidence in the person in whose care they're entrusted. Nowhere is the teacher/student relationship more symbiotic than in the world of dance, as the following article describes.

CHOOSING A DANCE TEACHER
Jacqueline Kolmes

For a young person interested in dance, finding a competent dance teacher is essential. Dance is a physical art form, and the physical well-being of an individual may be compromised by poor dance training. Dance is also an art form in which the student is asked to expose part of his inner being to his teacher and fellow students. This experience should be positive, not humiliating, especially for young students who are just starting out.

Many young students start out with a physique that is not considered to be "perfect" for dance; a good teacher will help to

Frank Hatchett teaching a dance class   Photo by Eduardo Patino

protect children from becoming self-conscious about their bodies, and will keep the focus of the class away from the issue of body shape and proportions. Granted, many talented professional dancers have received bad dance training at a young age, but they have often had to retrain on the way to professional success. Sometimes they harbor permanent injuries that could have been avoided.

How do you recognize a high quality teacher if you are not already involved with dance? There is no simple answer to this question. The first step might be to use available tools to educate yourself about dance. The public library has books with pictures of correct dance positions in them. Other dance books are available on a mail-order basis, as are video cassettes of outstanding performances. Television features performances of well-known dance companies. By using these tools, you can begin to get a sense of what dance looks like when it is well executed. When the time comes to select a dance studio, you will have to observe a class, paying particular attention to the teacher, and generally soak up the atmosphere of the studio.

Students will typically exhibit some very bad body positions. If you see that the teacher leaves these positions uncorrected, it may be best to look for another studio, or at least another teacher. And since the subject of picking a good teacher is a complicated one, *CallBack* discussed the problem with experts in the field. We selected three teachers who are known for their excellence as instructors, their impeccable technique, their knowledge of anatomy, and their ongoing devotion to the art of dance.

Peff Modelski

The first is Peff Modelski, who teaches teenagers and adults in New York. Ms. Modelski's résumé is formidable. Among her many teachers were Nenette Charisse, Margaret Craske, Hector Zaraspe, Vera Volkova, Stuart Hodes, Frank Wagoner, and May O'Donnell. She attended the Royal Academy of Dance in London, England, and has worked with some of the world's great companies. She taught ballet at the High School of Performing Arts for five years. Presently, Peff owns a company that produces ballet videos and she travels throughout the country restaging classical ballets for regional companies. Peff is proficient in ballet, modern dance, and jazz dance, although ballet is clearly her first love.

Peff brings some very special qualities into the classroom with her. One of these special gifts is her ability to describe even the most difficult aspects of dance technique. She gives her students words and images to work with that make difficult feats seem possible.

What does someone with these qualifications advise you to do about selecting a dance teacher? First, she emphasizes the importance of scrutinizing a teacher's credentials. Peff feels that the teacher's résumé ought to be available to you. "The teacher must be able to tell you where she was trained, and by whom." She adds that a good teacher will be able to specify whether her training is in Cecchetti, Russian, French, or Danish technique, or if her background represents a mixture of techniques. Modern and jazz teachers should be able to explain the influences in their backgrounds.

Ms. Modelski feels that, ideally, teachers should have a plan, or even a syllabus for their courses. Parents or young prospective students need to be permitted to watch a class; theoretically, a good teacher has nothing to hide. Peff also advises the observer to take a good look at the teacher; the posture of a dance teacher ought to indicate to you that the person has dance training. A teacher's clothes should be tidy, and appropriate to the kind of dance she is teaching.

Once you step inside the studio to watch class, Ms. Modelski suggests that you look very carefully at what is around you. Make sure the studio is equipped with barres, mirrors, and a good floor. Peff feels that ashtrays and food are out of place in the studio. She adds, "Music should never be played so loudly as to hurt young ears."

If teachers or assistants are in the studio between classes, their conversation should not be derogatory toward their students in any way. Ms. Modelski suggests that you " ... watch the teacher's facial expression while teaching; is the message conveyed a pleasant one?" Make sure that the teacher both praises and criticizes the students, but never humiliates or embarrasses them. Peff asks parents to consider whether they would like to expose themselves to this particular teacher; if the answer is that you feel uncomfortable with the teacher, you might expect your child to feel the same way.

A superb technician, Peff contends that it's very important to recognize the signs of bad technique. Students or parents have to learn to identify bad pliés, bad posture, sickled feet, and scarecrow-like arm positions. Teachers should teach the difference between straight knees and locked knees. If a studio offers classes in pointe work, make sure that you don't see children under the age of 11 wearing pointe shoes. In beginning ballet classes, children should work in third position, rather than in a tight fifth position. Ms. Modelski notes that in tap class, emphasis on making a loud, hard noise is a sign of bad technique. No matter what's being taught, the teacher must never move a child's limbs quickly; this can cause serious injury.

What does Peff consider to be the earmarks of good technique and good teaching skills? The best teachers, she feels, are knowledgeable about music *and* other academic studies, particularly in areas which overlap into dance. Porte de bras, which she defines as " ... the carriage of the arms, shoulders, and head," is a classroom essential. Also, rhythmic clapping and walking exercises for young dancers in pre-dance class should be stressed. In cold weather, good teachers in all disciplines lengthen warm-up time. Tap teachers are not exempt from giving their classes warm-ups either. A barre and exercises to stretch the long muscles should be included in their classroom work. Finally, Peff feels that a good studio will offer boys separate classes, into which gymnastics and a mild form of weight training are incorporated.

Natasha Baron

We brought our question next to Natasha Baron, a jazz teacher of teens and adults. As well as teaching in New York, Natasha has choreographed two MTV videos and has choreographed productions in Japan, Spain, and Mexico.

Natasha began to study dance at three, and even at that young age, began the study of jazz movement. Ms. Baron is from the small town of Edinboro, Pennsylvania. She considers herself lucky to have been taken under the wing of a teacher from Edinboro named Luana Bunting Moran who recognized her talent early on, and encouraged her to dance every day from the time she was seven. Before she moved to New York, Natasha attended Point Park College in Pittsburgh, earning a Bachelor of Fine Arts degree in dance. Although still in her 20s, she has a fine portfolio of performing and teaching credits.

Natasha is another teacher who brings something very special into the classroom with her. She has a gift for clarity, for simplifying movement without ignoring detail. She makes long dance sequences accessible even to beginning dancers. She is also a superb technician, setting a high standard for clean technique for her students. She encourages students to work as technically in jazz class as they would in ballet class.

Not too surprisingly, Natasha's views on what constitutes good teaching were generally in agreement with Peff Modelski's. Natasha reiterates the importance of jazz and modern teachers being capable of naming the influences on their styles. She stresses that teachers shouldn't say that their technique is based on television or video dance. Ms. Baron points out that a good jazz or modern teacher should be able to create choreography, rather than rehashing combinations picked up at last summer's convention.

Natasha reminds us that studios should be properly equipped with barres and mirrors, and adds that if at all possible, they should not be in a church basement or any other environment not well adapted for dance. Natasha emphasizes the importance of learning to dance in an emotionally healthy atmosphere. She advises us to watch out for overly possessive teachers who discourage students from taking class at other studios.

The issue of a studio's focus is an important one. Natasha suggests finding a studio that offers more performing opportunities than just a June recital. She also suggests finding out whether a studio you're considering has produced professional dancers.

She emphasizes that good studios divide classes by discipline, rather than squeezing three kinds of dance into a one-hour class. Class levels should be determined by students' abilities, not by their ages.

Natasha offers some thoughts on tap dance. She notes that tap teachers should be able to identify the steps they're teaching, and should be endowed with a strong sense of rhythm. Young children should never be taught to tap in heels.

What would Natasha add to Peff's comments about the earmarks of good studios? She feels that a good ballet program should be at the center of a school's curriculum. "Go to a school with a great ballet program, and take jazz or modern somewhere else if you have to." She adds that young students like jazz a lot because it's fun, but that serious technique should be taught in jazz class as well. In Natasha's opinion a good studio should offer young people the opportunity to take class more than once a week, and preferably three times a week as they become more advanced.

As someone who grew up in a small town, Ms. Baron has a suggestion for dancers from isolated places. If possible, attend a dance camp in the summer. This way, you'll be exposed to many teachers, " ... and you'll get feedback from different kinds of teachers constantly."

Lynn Simonson

Lynn Simonson is a renowned figure in the world of jazz dance. Ms. Simonson is a founding co-director of Dance Space, in New York, where she also teaches. She has been the director of the Jazz Project at Jacob's Pillow. Her portfolio of credits is enormous; she travels the world constantly choreographing and guest teaching.

Lynn hails from Seattle, Washington, where she was originally trained in classical ballet. She came to New York at age 18 to dance, and continued her studies of classical ballet at American Ballet Theatre. She also studied Horton technique, and pursued jazz studies with Jaime Rogers, Luigi, and Claude Thompson.

Ms. Simonson joins our other experts in bringing very special elements into her classroom. She believes strongly in the integrity of jazz dance and its relationship to jazz music. Her studio is one of the very few in which real jazz music is used for class. She also emphasizes the importance of feeling movement, rather than relying on the mirror to know whether you're working correctly. Lynn saves a few moments of class time for improvisation, giving her students the opportunity to discover their own ways of moving.

Lynn had some excellent suggestions for finding a competent teacher. If students or parents know a performer they admire, they can ask where the person was trained. Lynn thinks that a good reputation can be a guideline, but that your personal instincts should be trusted as well.

She emphasizes the importance of finding a responsive teacher, one who is not oblivious to students. She notes that a teacher should not only be able to explain movement in class, but must also be able to re-explain it when necessary. She suggests asking a teacher about her background knowledge of anatomy; she should not draw a blank in response to such a question.

The importance of finding a studio where kids have their own classes is stressed by Ms. Simonson. If teens are allowed into adult classes, they should have the maturity to behave appropriately.

Lynn Simonson feels strongly that jazz is not really a discipline for children; it's best to start with ballet, or from about age 12, modern dance. She feels that suggestive movements are out of place in children's jazz classes. If you're enrolling your child in jazz class, make sure that the teacher isn't letting students work in a swaybacked position, which can damage the young spine. Watch out for teachers who do lots of head rolls in an uncontrolled fashion. This can eventually lead to arthritic spurs in the neck. And when modern or jazz students work in a flat back position, they should not be leaning back into their heels with their backs slightly arched.

Among the items on Lynn's warning list for bad studios is overdone turnout. She reminds us that turnout should be natural, and that 180 degrees is a rarity. Forcing turnout causes feet and knees to roll in, causing injuries. Lynn advises prospective students and parents to look at the basic alignment practiced in the classroom. The body should make a vertical line from head to neck to ribs to ankles. Ms. Simonson warns us away from teachers who force students' bodies into positions that they can't hold naturally.

Lynn feels that tap dance is not quite as dangerous to young bodies as are some other dance forms. However, good tap classes begin with a thorough circulatory warm-up.

A dance teacher who is concerned with the students' welfare makes sure that there is enough space between students to prevent them from falling over each other. If students in the back of class are unable to see, a good teacher will encourage them to trade places with people in the front periodically. New students who are beginners or who are unaccustomed to a teacher's style should not be left alone to fend for themselves. Some principles of the teacher's technique should be explained to them, and they should be placed in a spot where they can follow more experienced dancers until they get the hang of things.

Dance class should not be chaotic or overcrowded, nor should it be an opportunity for a few people to show off their prowess while other students struggle to find enough space in which to dance.

One thing we can learn from observing our three expert teachers is clear. Good teachers can come from east or west, from urban or rural environments. All of our experts have positive attitudes toward their students' ability to learn. And all three are dedicated to making dance possible for their students, rather than keeping all the secrets they've acquired to themselves.

When you select a teacher, look for someone who gives this ultimate gift of sharing knowledge. And keep the word longevity in mind. Think of all the years of dancing still ahead for a young person. Look for a teacher who'll nurture students physically or psychologically. A good teacher is the beginning of a lifelong love affair with the art of dance.

The following is applicable to all disciplines. It's the age-old question of whether or not there's a reason for a young performer to attend college. And while it's a question that each family will have to answer on its own — an answer that will more than likely depend on the status of the child's career at the time of entry — there's good reason to believe that a career and a college education are not mutually exclusive.

College provides opportunities to explore more than just performing disciplines. A liberal arts curriculum could open the student to the world of design, theater management, film study, writing, directing, and thousands of other heretofore unexplored opportunities.

DANCE AND COLLEGE: MAKING A CHOICE
Jacqueline Kolmes

Dance and higher education aren't considered to be the most natural of partnerships. The belief in our society is that the two are mutually exclusive. After all, isn't school time wasted dancing time? Aren't the college years, from 17 to 22, a critical period in the making of a dancer's career?

With the exception of modern dancers, whose talents are often nurtured in a college environment, it's assumed that the best, most successful dancers didn't attend college. The careers of many famous dancers are testimony to the belief that higher education is irrelevant to dance. As a matter of fact, for those gifted and lucky individuals who have a professional, well-paid job waiting after high school, a college education would be difficult to obtain. There aren't enough hours in the day for rehearsal, class, daily performances, *and* college; a certain amount of self-education is about all that can be realistically expected. There are young dancers whose single-mindedness of purpose doesn't allow them to consider college as an alternative to a life immersed completely in dance; there are others whose academic background may not make them college material.

But there are lots of other young dancers who are thinking it over: How about going to college and majoring in dance? How about majoring in something else and continuing to study dance as well? How about going back to school part-time in order to maintain a lot of dancing time? Is it possible to devote time to education and still function as a professional dancer? Can you possibly have it all?

Jeffery Ferguson

Jeffery Ferguson looks as though he has devoted his life to dance. Not only a talented dancer, but an inventive choreographer, actor, singer, and teacher, he has performed with the Alvin Ailey Repertory Ensemble, with Agnes de Mille, and the Joffrey Ballet Company, in theatrical productions from Shakespeare to *Showboat*, and worked extensively in industrial shows and commercials.

Jeffery is proficient at multiple dance techniques, and looks equally wonderful doing lyrical work and fast moving jazz combinations. He has the unusual quality of seeming to be motivated in his dancing by joy and a pure love of the art form; he communicates this pleasure in movement to his audiences and students.

Surprisingly, he never set foot in a dance classroom until college. He comes from a family background in which books were the major form of entertainment; access to television and movies was limited. Jeff attributes his vivid imagination to the fact that his upbringing made him self-reliant in terms of entertainment. He was an excellent student, served as student council president, and participated in football, track, and basketball.

Jeffery has always been purposeful. He had no doubts about going to college, and "wanted to attend a school that was intellectually excellent and close to major cities." Princeton University fit the bill perfectly; he didn't apply to any other schools. Told that he had the makings of a good lawyer, Jeffery says, "I went to college assuming that I would go to law school and I majored in psychology."

Among Princeton's requirements was a certain amount of physical education, so Jeff thought he'd try modern dance. The instructor spotted his talent immediately, and insisted that he come to the Princeton Ballet Society to pursue dance. From then on, Jeff studied jazz, ballet, and modern dance. Princeton had no dance major at the time, and only the beginnings of a creative arts department, so Jeff continued to take academic courses. During exam periods, he went to dance class only a few times a month; otherwise, he attended several times a week. Because dance time was limited, he brought the maximum amount of concentration to the classroom. He concentrated on his academics when it was time to study; his schoolwork was never threatened by his time in the dance classroom.

Jeff began performing at Princeton with the Ballet Society, the University Dancers and, between semesters, with the June Taylor Dancers. He performed leading roles while in college with the P.J. and B. Players and Princeton's Triangle Club. By the time Jeff left Princeton, he had *Fiddler on the Roof, Jacques Brel is Alive and Well and Living in Paris, Sweet Charity, Oklahoma*, and *Mother Courage* under his belt.

Any thoughts of going on to law school ended when he saw the Alvin Ailey Dance Company perform for the first time. From then on he knew that this was exactly the kind of dance that he wanted to do, and that he would eventually postpone further education in favor of a dance career. "When I saw Ailey, I told myself that I'd be in that company in four years. Four years later, Alvin Ailey gave me a scholarship, and there I was."

Although the time came when Jeff lost interest in pursuing an academic career, he has no regrets about taking time for school. He was able to shift his energy completely to dance when it became appropriate to do so. He sees college as a positive experience which opened up new horizons and helped to make him the kind of individual he is today. And indeed, in conversation with Jeffery, he reveals himself to be a well-rounded individual with an inquisitive nature and a wide knowledge of fields unrelated to show business.

What are Jeffery's thoughts for young dancers considering college? He believes that education is very important; the mind needs exercise as well as the body. He's inspired by individuals who are multi-talented, and for whom the performing arts are not the only area of interest.

Asked who shouldn't bother with college, Jeff says that the lucky few who have a solid professional gig waiting for them are best prepared to skip school, at least for a while. He feels that college can wait for those who are completely uncertain about what they want to do.

Who, in his estimation, should attend school? Just about anyone who has the desire to do so. Some dancers, he feels, will enjoy school just for the joy of learning and growing; others, who are security conscious, will want to have a backup for dance should they need to earn a living some other way. He adds that, for those who are in the doldrums after a few years of auditioning without substantial results, "College can be a wonderful opportunity to refocus."

Jeffery stresses the importance of self-education as well, suggesting reading, attending performances, and going to museums. His favorite teachers stressed these things, and he feels that a love of education needs to be passed from one generation of dancers to the next. Jeff notes that show business will make you streetwise, but those who don't read and educate themselves will become limited. He believes that, "Training the mind can help in the long run with picking up choreography, with learning new styles of dance. One form of discipline leads to success with another."

Natasha Baron

To look at Natasha Baron, with whom we consulted in our search for the excellent dance teachers, one would assume that she'd never have had time for college. Not so! Natasha graduated from Point Park College, a prestigious school in the dance field.

Before college, Natasha was already an accomplished dancer who might have gone to New York immediately. But she was a young lady with a different plan; she decided to finish high school and college in less than the usual amount of time by taking more than the usual course load each semester. She completed both in under six years, and still arrived in New York quite young to pursue her career.

In order to find the right college, Natasha attended a general audition in Chicago where schools with dance departments were represented, and, on receiving several acceptances, decided to attend Barat College in Lake Forest, Illinois, since the school not only had a good dance department, but also offered her a scholarship. After a semester at Barat, she heard about the University of Wisconsin's Dance department and the opportunity it afforded to work with the Milwaukee Ballet. She contacted the university during Christmas break and was told to come enroll. She attended that university for three semesters. While at home nursing a broken foot, Natasha heard of Point Park College in Pittsburgh. The school was one of the top three for dance in the U.S., and had a large jazz dance department. Natasha applied to Point Park, and finished her college education there. She feels that each school she attended had numerous strong points. A great deal of personal attention was always offered. By changing schools, Natasha was able to fulfill her individual needs in terms of dance education.

She found that pursuing a dance major was hard work. Good grades were by no means automatic. She danced, choreographed, studied dance history, and took music courses designed for dancers. She did two hours a day of pointe work as well. She found the dance taught in universities to be pure, not flashy. "If a student relied on flashiness, this reliance would be subdued in favor of good technique." Natasha observed, upon arriving in New York, that nothing she experienced in terms of studio training was as intense as her university experiences.

And she has no regrets about taking time for school. The only problem she encountered upon arriving in New York was one of re-acclimating herself to the competition and the crowd scenes in the professional world. For a while it seemed overwhelming, but her present success is testimony to the fact that college doesn't mean giving up a career.

Natasha has a number of recommendations for young dancers. She stresses that there are virtually no stars in the dance world, with a few notable exceptions. Only the most extraordinary combination of talent and luck make stardom possible. Very few dancers are financially secure; they aren't as secure as their peers in the music, movie, or television industries. Even stars end up as humble teachers someday. Natasha reminds young people that, "The majority of jobs are on cruise ships, in nightclubs, in commercials and industrials; that's the reality no one tells you about when you head for New York." Unless you have a major dance job waiting for you, she suggests that you might give school a try. Why not develop other interests that can carry you through when show business and dance become rough going? Natasha feels that taking time for college is "far better than burning out at the age of 20."

Majoring in dance can be an opportunity to dance six hours a day, as it was for her. She feels that even budding ballerinas needn't worry; pointe work awaits you in college. She points out that American dancers aren't given the more complete education about their art that dancers trained in countries like Russia receive along with their dance training. They have to get their education outside the context of the dance studio. She suggests that college students experiment with a wide variety of courses, and study voice and theatrical skills as well as dance.

Natasha adds that college can be a time to gain lots of performing experience that looks good on the résumé. Once a dance department accepts you, they'll put you to work since they consider that you've already passed the test. Men can do an enormous number of shows in college, and are very likely to receive scholarships as well.

From observing her fellow students who worked professionally while in college, Natasha notes that many schools have a liberal attitude toward taking time off; you may well be able to leave for a while to work in a company and return to finish school. Attending school needn't be an absolute end to working as a dancer for several years.

Words of wisdom from Natasha for parents: it's only natural to think that your dancing offspring is very talented, and that you shouldn't encourage further schooling. But you need to be objective. The best way is to take your child to professional auditions and see how he or she holds up in the eyes of the decision makers. It's worth a few plane tickets to do this. If you do prefer that your children bypass college, try to get them instruction in theatrical skills at a young age; at least this will put them a step ahead of the competition.

Diana Zeydel

Diana Zeydel is probably not aware of the admiration she receives from her fellow dancers. But people always peer in when she takes class, admiring her technical prowess and seamless movement. One hears some whisperings about her, something about the Joffrey Ballet and something else about her being a lawyer.

Dance is a sideline for Diana, who is a trusts and estates lawyer. She loves her work in the field of law, and is only as involved with dance as she feels like being for her own enjoyment. Diana is a Yale Law School graduate who went to college when she decided that dance wasn't turning out to be a satisfying career.

When she was 16 years old, Diana came to New York to study dance; she was on scholarship at the Joffrey Ballet School. She was very much the serious young dancer. "I tended to be so focused I couldn't shut it off. I was involved 24 hours a day. It was confining." Well-suited for classical repertoire, Diana worked with the Chicago Ballet, and was accepted into the Joffrey's second company and the Pennsylvania Ballet. She had always been a good student who enjoyed school but had attended no college at all. She tried a few correspondence courses and read on her own.

A soloist with the Chicago Ballet barely in her 20s, Diana was making some unhappy observations about the dance world. She saw that dancers' weaknesses were harped on, and that scholarship students were seen as the sum of their weaknesses rather than their strengths. She noticed that negative reinforcement was used to force improvement, that "There was a lot of unnecessary feeling that you were fat and incapable." She also found performing quite taxing, and pre-performance periods fairly unpleasant.

Coming from an academic background, Diana started to miss the intellectual aspect of life; she was bored. She decided that school would be a more comfortable environment than the dance world, where financial and emotional insecurity were standard. Accepted by Yale, she entered school at 22, and went straight through, graduating from Yale Law School. Diana presumed that she would stop dancing altogether, since she had no stake in a dance career anymore.

Entering college without a definite idea of what she might want to study, Diana enjoyed experimenting with various subjects. She decided to major in philosophy, since the subject matter was satisfyingly broad. She found the discipline she'd developed as a dancer extended itself right into school; concentration on details seemed to be relatively easy.

In her sophomore year, Diana found herself involved with dance again, to her own surprise. Having abandoned a successful dance career, she found she didn't feel at odds with the art form. Dance class became an enjoyable experience, rather than a source of enormous pressure. She began to teach classes in the athletic department, and had blocks of time for dance and choreography.

She enjoyed teaching students from Yale's theater department; some of her ex-students are now working as professionals.

When Diana performed in college, she still realized dance wasn't the full-time career she desired. She wasn't searching for a direct replacement for the performing experience. Diana has no regrets about taking on a career in law; she loves what she is doing now and says that any performance she ever did was more trying than taking the bar exam!

Like Jeff and Natasha, Diana encourages dancers who are inclined to go to college. She acknowledges that professional dancers with American Ballet Theatre may not be able to find time for college, but that for others college is a possibility. She says, "Any way of doing things is possible if you put your mind to it. You really can have it all. The recognition that I had choices about what I wanted to do really made the difference for me."

Diana suggests that dancers examine their own career motives honestly. Are they really in the dance field for the artistry? She feels that those who go to college have proven to have a different feel for dance than those who concentrate solely on dance. Educated dancers tend to concentrate better and to learn and take corrections well. "You get a special kind of dancer from someone who does both school and dance, someone with a real ability to concentrate and a real dedication." Diana observes that, as she learned from the successes of her Yale classmates in New York theater, college training can be invaluable for a dancer's career.

Diana feels that older people needn't be frightened of the difficulties awaiting them in the academic world. She assures them that their discipline will make school much easier than it might otherwise have been.

As for the ongoing role of dance in her life, Diana doesn't know whether dance might someday be integrated into her career. She takes one day at a time, and lets the future unravel as it will. She finds that staying in shape physically is a help in maintaining mental balance and offsetting career stress. She dances frequently enough to be in shape to perform if she decides that she'd like to do so. For the present, she's content to practice law, to make a different kind of contribution to society than the one she would have made as a dancer, and to dance on her own terms, rather than lead a life controlled by dance.

If *you* decide to give school a try, you'll find many resources to help you find the right program. If you are focused on a dance education, *DanceMagazine*'s *College Guide* is a good resource, listing programs and enrollment details. There's the College Board's *Handbook and Index of Majors*, Cass and Birnbaum's *Comparative Guide to American Colleges*, and college admissions guides. There are books that tell you where to get scholarships, which schools are the best for the money, and how students feel about the universities they're in; and books guiding parents through the admissions process. Once you've singled out schools that interest you, you'll find that they're happy to send you all the information you need. Happy hunting! College will be one of the most exciting and enriching times in your life.

TRAINING THE YOUNG VOICE
Frank Schindelheim

As a vocal coach and director of three performing arts centers in New York and New Jersey, I'm often asked, "Does my child have the voice to be in show business?" To most of these parents, my answer is an unequivocal "Yes!" However, a youngster's voice must be trained. After all, we wouldn't expect a person to sit at a piano and play a musical selection without having undertaken a specific program of developmental instruction. Such a program would consist of technical studies in scales, finger studies, rhythm identifications, and the understanding and interpretation of dynamics.

Voice training should be approached in a comparable fashion. Because the child has been using the voice since infancy, we can expect faster results than we would from piano lessons, which would necessitate the acquaintance of keys and positions. In classical teaching for the adult voice, emphasis is placed on proper breathing, tongue placement for articulation, vibrato, projection, and range extension. Training for children, too, includes these musical techniques, but in dealing with the young, immature voice, the instructor must *always* be aware of the limitations of the undeveloped vocal cords. Instruction for a youngster should begin with a combination of tone and breathing exercises, with style and interpretation explained by the teacher. Simultaneously, the child should be encouraged to develop his or her own style. The teacher should then introduce new material in order to build the child's repertoire. At the same time, the child should be exposed to the various styles of different composers.

Although we often marvel at the six-year-old girl with the ability to perform a Barbra Streisand song, be aware that Streisand has an exceptional range and many of her songs have key changes which should not be attempted by a juvenile. It's true that in the child's training, the teacher should strive to expand the child's vocal range, but that should be a slow process in order to avoid straining the child's vocal cords. In essence, the teacher should stay within the parameters of *the child's range* and keep the repertoire youthful and simple until the vocal cords have developed after practice over time.

In teaching distinctive style or interpretation, the use of live demonstrations or recordings will enable the teacher to express a goal for the child to strive for, at the same time allowing the child to develop his or her *own* style and stage presence. Because children have a great ability to imitate, in a few weeks the child will likely begin to sound very much like the targeted style, but with his or her *own* inflections.

When a youngster is auditioned for a voice-over or a singing commercial, the casting director is usually listening for a simple voice, one that rings of innocence. If the casting director wanted or needed a mature voice, an adult would have been sought in the first place. *So keep it youthful and simple.* Remember, the type of voice usually heard in commercials is mellow and sweet; it's a voice that rings of innocence. After all, isn't that what childhood is really about?

Frank Schindelheim is the owner of Star*Time Dance and Performing Arts Centers in Brooklyn, New York and in New Jersey. He's been a vocal coach for nearly 20 years, during which time he's perfected his own methods of teaching and has turned out many professional children. Currently, Mr. Schindelheim is creating and producing a children's showcase for television.

COMBATING STAGE FRIGHT
Gerald Lee Ratliff

The role of the body in performance is just as important as the voice and proper breathing techniques.

The most obvious visual clue to nervousness and anxiety is your body, especially if it's shaking or twitching. In developing a relaxed, comfortable body posture, it's important to learn the basic principles of concentration and amplification, and to think of the parts of your body in isolation.

Your voice and breathing technique are influenced by your body responses. A relaxed, comfortable posture enhances your breathing technique and results in fluent, expressive speech. Study your posture before considering what the voice must do in performance. Make a checklist of gestures and facial expressions before considering what breathing techniques you will use. Think of your performance as a total involvement of the voice, breathing techniques, and body working together for a successful presentation.

Each of the exercises that follow presents steps of body control that ask you to practice muscular coordination, movement, and gestures with self-confidence, poise, and style. In approaching each exercise, imagine you are a dancer who is capable of fluid, graceful movement. Concentrate on the almost-musical quality of your body actions, and explore expressive and meaningful gestures that give a rhythmic quality to your performance. Remember that body movement — from the tip of your toes to the top of your head — should be an indication of your mood or attitude.

Poetry in motion

The role of the body in conveying character insight is of primary importance in creating a relaxed, natural visual portrait of self-confidence and poise. In this exercise, your goal is to voice the following poem from William Wordsworth's *It Is A Beauteous Evening* using only gestures and movement to suggest the poem's meaning. First, analyze the poem to determine the probable setting and mood, and then decide on an appropriate age for the character being described.

Next, perform the poem silently with subtle gestures and movements to convey the action described by the poet. Be sure your "performance" builds to a climax. Gestures and movements should be both fluid and flexible, and be executed with strength and vigor. Repeat this silent performance three times, refining your gestures and movements while you "suit the action to the word," as Hamlet suggested in his famous advice to performers. You may wish to videotape another performance for comparison with later efforts.

> *It is a beauteous evening, calm, and free,*
> *The holy time is quiet as a nun*
> *Breathless with adoration; the broad sun*
> *Is sinking down in its tranquillity;*
> *The gentleness of heaven broods o'er the sea:*
> *Listen! the mighty being is awake,*
> *And doth with his eternal motion make*
> *A sound like thunder — everlasting.*
> *Dear child! dear girl! that walkest with me here,*
> *If thou appear untouched by solemn thought,*
> *Thy nature is not therefore less divine:*
> *Thou liest in Abraham's bosom all the year,*
> *And worship'st at the temple's inner shrine,*
> *God being with thee when we know it not.*

Now, turn your physical attention to spelling out the following characterizations using only gestures and body movements: A young lover mourning the loss of his sweetheart; A young woman saddened by loneliness; A grandmother recalling her youth; A father grieving quietly for a lost daughter; A young girl singing a song of joy.

End the exercise by incorporating the gestures and movements developed earlier as you perform the Wordsworth passage again. Are your gestures and movements compatible to interpret the poem accurately? What adjustments will you have to make to sustain the characterization developed?

Puppet on a string

To cultivate the total physical concentration needed for good relaxation technique in performance, it's necessary to develop muscular coordination that is fluid and flexible. A basic requirement of physical concentration is the ability to appear natural and relaxed, with your posture suggesting that the bones of your body are in proper alignment. Although at ease and comfortable, your posture should suggest alertness and anticipation of action to follow.

Begin by holding your body erect, chest high, chin up, back flat, and arms and legs straight. Place one foot slightly in front of the other, with the weight centered on the ball of the forward foot. This position creates a pleasing and alert visual portrait and also facilitates later movement necessary to convey changing moods and attitudes.

Spread your legs slightly so that you have a solid sense of balance. Let your upper body sag so your head and arms slowly dangle toward the floor like a puppet on a string. Swing your arms forward and backward in a slow rhythm, and repeat the sounds *ah* and *oh* in an intonation that parallels the movement of your body swaying to and fro.

Slowly raise your body while continuing to swing your arms forward and backward in a slow rhythm. When you are standing upright, begin to rotate your head in a slow circle left to right and then right to left. Repeat the *ah* and *oh* sounds in short bursts, then slightly longer bursts, and then in the longest burst possible on only one breath. You should now have experienced a marked release of physical and vocal tension. If you do not feel physically and vocally relaxed, repeat this part of the exercise more slowly.

When you are confident that your muscles and vocal cords are relaxed, proceed to complete the exercise. Open your mouth as wide as possible in a yawn. Prolong the yawn as long as possible, adding as many *ah*s and *oh*s as a single breath permits. Repeat three times, each time slowly inhaling as you sustain as many *ah*s as possible on a single breath. Then begin to take deep breaths from the diaphragm as you repeat as many *oh*s as possible on a single breath.

You may conclude the exercise by slowing repeating the following excerpt from the popular song "Running On Empty" in short, breathy phrases.

> Running on.
> Running on empty.
> Running on.
> Running blind.
> Running on.
> Running on empty.
> Running on.
> Running into the sun.

Noodle soup

In developing movement awareness in performance, think of your body as an expressive instrument that conveys a portrait of self-confidence and relaxation. Graceful, fluid movements help to suggest poise and to communicate thoughts. Before attempting any movement exercises, you should be aware of your own sense of movement. Do you walk gracefully? Are your shoulders erect? Do you think you were born with three left feet? Can you follow the tempo of music? Once you have a sense of your own movement potential, you should be able to concentrate on weaknesses.

Begin by bending from your waist, trying to touch your toes. Relax your arms in front of your feet once you have touched your toes. Begin slowly to swing your head and your relaxed arms in a pendulum-like motion, as if you were a limp noodle in a pot of boiling water. Now begin to relax your legs and your chest cavity as you continue slowly to swing all parts of your body from side to side, finally collapsing in a soggy heap in the middle of the floor.

Next, lie flat on your back and slightly elevate your knees while keeping your feet flat on the floor. Be sure your pelvis is tilted toward your knees and your arms are flat on the floor at your sides. Inhale deeply for a count of 35, then exhale slowly for a count of 35. When all tension has been expelled from your chest cavity, purr like a playful kitten and sustain the sound produced for a count of 35, being sure that your throat is open and that you are breathing deeply.

Keeping your pelvis tilted toward your knees, continue to inhale deeply for 35 and then slowly exhale for a count of 35 as you growl like a dog, hum like a bird, snort like a horse, buzz like a bee, whimper like a puppy, hiss like a snake, hoot like an owl, bray like a mule, squeak like a mouse, and crow like a rooster. Next, stand up and let your body respond to the following movement suggestions. In this part of the exercise you may wish to play 10 minutes of popular or classical music to create spontaneous movement patterns that help to free your body from tension. If you choose to use music, allow one minute for each movement suggested below.

Move like a witch doctor exorcising evil spirits from a tribesman. Move like a juggler performing on a street corner. Move like a medieval king in mortal combat with his arch rival.

Move like a policeman directing rush-hour traffic. Move like a villain stealing slyly toward a beautiful heroine. Move like a burglar entering an empty house late at night.

Body count

Graceful and fluid coordination of all parts of the body is necessary for expressive movement in performance. A basic approach in cultivating such movement is to hold your body erect with chest high, chin up, back flat, and arms and legs straight. When you have developed this primary stance for good posture, it should be possible for you to suggest alert, energetic, and natural movement in performance.

Once you've achieved a "posture portrait" that is comfortable, you should concentrate on developing all parts of your body to express changing ideas or emotions. One way to enhance your posture portrait and suggest coordination is to "count" with the body. Start by standing in a natural, erect position in a large, open space. Begin to count in the air from 1 to 10, using only the fingers of your right hand. Repeat the count using both the fingers and the wrist of the right hand. Repeat the count using both the fingers and the wrist of the right hand and the right shoulder. Next, repeat the exercise using the left hand, wrist, and shoulder.

Now begin to count from 1 to 10 with the left leg. Stand on your right foot with the left leg elevated slightly, and make your counting as specific as possible. Repeat the count using the left ankle and toes. Conclude by counting from 1 to 10 with the right leg, the right ankle, and toes. Then count from 1 to 10 using the entire body. Count with your head, chest, waist, and arms. Involve as many separate parts of your body as possible in the count and strive for graceful and fluid posture. Conclude by using your body to spell out the ideas and emotions suggested in the following excerpt from Shakespeare's *Romeo and Juliet*.

Make your gestures precise, and try to capture the mood of the passage. Any movement that you incorporate should be fluid, and your body should be relaxed. You may wish to accompany yourself in the silent expression of the passage by playing a tape or record of the film music used by Franco Zeffirelli in his production of *Romeo and Juliet*.

O, then I see Queen Mab hath been with you.
She is the fairies' midwife, and she comes
In shape no bigger than an agate stone
On the forefinger of an alderman,
Drawn with a team of little atomi
Over men's noses as they lie asleep;
Her wagon spokes made of long spinners' legs.

The cover of the wings of grasshoppers,
Her traces of the smallest spider web,
Her collars of the moonshine's watery beams,
Her whip of cricket's bone, the lash of film,
Her wagoner a small grey-coated gnat
Not half so big as a round little worm
Pricked from the lazy finger of a maid;
Her chariot is an empty hazel nut,
Made by the joiner squirrel or old grub,
Time out o' mind the fairies' coachmakers.

Ten-finger exercise

Effective gestures should originate within you, convey specific meanings, and be executed with strength and precision. There should be no confusion about the location, the physical description, or the general properties of the person, thing, or object in question. As a prelude to communicating silently with gestures that suggest a calm and relaxed performer, the following exercise is designed to help develop precise hand gestures to convey mood or attitude and to spell out specific shapes and forms of objects.

Begin by rotating each finger of your hands, first clockwise, then counterclockwise. Now move each finger up and down and then from side to side. Keeping the fingers straight, move the outer fingers away from the inner fingers and slowly return them together. Holding your hands out, with palms up, slowly repeat the following sequence.

Starting with the little finger of your right hand, close the hand by rolling in each finger one at a time. Now open your hand in reverse order, starting with the index finger. Repeat with the left hand.

Now repeat the exercise at least five times in each of the following tempos: First, very slowly so that your hands are free of tension. Second, very quickly so that you are able to control the speed of your gestures. Third, at moderate speed so that your hands are free of tension and yet you are in control of the gesture. Fourth, very slowly so that you refine and clarify the role of the fingers and the hands in executing gestures. Fifth, very quickly so that your gestures appear specific and yet spontaneous and natural.

When your use of fingers and hands is both relaxed and controlled, execute the following hand gestures with as much precision and detail as possible: Open an umbrella. Pour a cup of tea. Peel a potato. Pinch a penny. Wash a window. Dial a phone. Eat a doughnut. Crack an egg. Open a window. Swat a fly.

To evaluate the precision with which you have executed these specific gestures, conclude the exercise by gathering all of the objects needed to perform the tasks described. Place them in a large box, and then draw each one out at random. Note the size, weight, and texture of each object and use it to perform the task described. Now discard the objects and repeat the tasks using only your fingers and hands to describe the action needed.

Is the imaginary gesture as precise as in your use of the actual object? Is the imaginary gesture as specific as to the size, weight, and texture of the object? When the answer to those questions is "Yes," repeat the exercise, remembering to perform each task with silent precision.

May I have this dance?

The performer should always be free of tension in order to use movement effectively, but that movement should always appear motivated and spontaneous. Aimless wandering and nervous pacing are both distracting and irritating and may result in audience fatigue and performer collapse. Movement used wisely should be direct, energetic, and emphatic. If used sparingly, movement may also help to reinforce major ideas expressed in the script.

The most common uses of movement in performance are *toward* the audience to reinforce a fact or to share a confidence; *to the side* to direct focus on an element or aspect of the speech or the dialogue; and *away from* the audience to suggest that distance is needed to contemplate or rethink the implications of what has been said. Although there are no hard and fast rules regarding the amount of movement in performance, a good rule of thumb is that movement should be used in moderation, and then only when it is essential to communicate ideas that cannot be expressed as well with facial expressions or gestures.

A good exercise to encourage variety of movement — and to relax the performer physically — is the use of music and dance in rehearsal. Tape record a classical sonata, a popular song, a folk ballad, and a jazz tune. Listen to each separately until you have a sense of its tempo and rhythm. Move slowly to the lyric tones of the sonata; move quickly to the accelerated pace of the pop song; relax and sway to the repetitive notes of the folk ballad; and then sense the strident and yet free movement suggested by the jazz tune.

Repeat the exercise without the music, and adapt the movements that you improvised to an imaginary performance situation. Movements requiring a forceful step forward may now be thought of as disco steps; movements of deliberate intent may be expressed in sonata steps; movements to redirect audience attention may be inspired by folk steps; and movements of emotional intensity or intimacy may be motivated by recalling jazz steps.

Now expand the exercise in dance movement by executing the following passage from Alfred Lord Tennyson's *The Princess,* moving to the beat first of a classical sonata, then of a disco tune, a folk ballad, and a jazz tune.

> *Tears, idle tears, I know not what they mean,*
> *Tears from the depth of some divine despair*
> *Rise in the heart, and gather to the eyes,*
> *In looking on the happy autumn-fields,*
> *And thinking of the days that are no more.*
>
> *Fresh as the first beam glittering on a sail,*
> *That brings our friends up from the underworld,*
> *Sad as the last which reddens over one*
> *That sinks with all we love below the verge;*
> *So sad, so fresh, the days that are no more.*

Gerald Lee Ratliff is Professor and Chair of the Department of Speech and Theatre at Montclair State College, Director of the nationally-known touring Reader's Theatre ensemble The Wordmasters, an active national participant in children's theater and youth drama.

Bands and singing groups often need demo tapes to present them at their best to people who hire for cruises, club dates, and music videos. The following describes some of the important elements of putting together a useful tape to introduce yourself and your musical ability.

MAKING A DEMO TAPE
Scott Knipe

You think your band is pretty good. It's developing a loyal and enthusiastic local following. The reaction to your original tunes has been positive. School dances and local club owners are clamoring for your services. How do you step into the big time and land a recording contract?

It might be time for your band to consider making a demo tape to submit to the powers of the music world. There was a time years ago when a rough tape made on a home recorder in your garage or basement would suffice, but this is no longer the case. With today's sophisticated recording techniques, those in charge of selecting new artists and materials want to hear the most refined product possible. There are many choices and considerations to make when you decide to make a demo tape, both financial and artistic. The manner in which you handle these choices will play a large part in getting your band past the front door.

Your repertoire

The choice of repertoire is crucial to any successful demo tape. Most people will only listen to two or three songs at most. The length of each song should be from two and a half to four minutes, which is typical of the length of hit tunes played on the radio. The tape should feature one style or image. Tapes exhibiting many styles show a lack of direction.

While a variety of factors contribute to the success of a hit tune, most have several features in common. Almost all hit tunes have a hook, which is a catchy phrase, title, or line. Sometimes the title and the hook will be the same. The hook is easily remembered by the listener and helps to give your song an identity.

Listeners prefer lyrics which relate to them. Melodies should be both easy to remember and easy to sing. While a melody that jumps all over the place may seem interesting to you, the listener likes to hear something he or she can hum. Consider these factors when choosing the songs for your demo tape. Remember that you must give your best shot in a brief eight to 15 minutes of tape time.

The quality of your vocals is a crucial factor. The listener focuses on the voice first. Constantly strive to improve your vocals. Make sure they are in tune and of a good basic quality. Make recordings at rehearsals for yourself and others to critique. Do the instrumental parts have clean, logical chord progressions? Is the bass line clean and in tune? Does your song contain an instrumental solo or performance that will dazzle the listener? These are all important for showing you in your best light.

Choosing a producer and a studio

You've rehearsed and chosen your material for the demo tape. What is the next step? For many groups a producer should be hired to oversee the process at this point. A producer can listen to your songs and offer suggestions for improvement and expansion. Some recording studios can recommend producers and many even have a producer on staff. Do you need to bring in an arranger? Will additional instruments enhance your tunes? What is the right choice of studio and recording engineer? The expertise of the producer will aid in these decisions. Good producers do not come inexpensively. For most, you can count on spending between $1500 and $2000. In selecting a producer, look for someone who shares your artistic goals and is a master in the art of recording. It is possible that a member of your band may be so talented; this is one way to cut down on costs.

Next is the selection of a recording studio. The first and most important consideration: Is your band comfortable in a particular studio? The sound ambiance or acoustics of the studio is a vital factor. Live or "wet" studios are best for acoustic instruments, while dead or "dry" rooms show electronic instruments to their best advantage. Studios come equipped with 4, 8, 12, 16, 24, or 48 track recording equipment. How many tracks do you need?

Think of each track as a separate tape recorder capable of recording one line or instrument. For the best possible sound each line needs its own track. Considering that the drums alone can use up to four or more tracks, you can see how tracks can be used up very quickly. It is possible to combine lines on a single track, but there is a loss of quality each time this is done. If your band makes use of MIDI technology make sure the studio has a tape recorder with a MIDI track. What instruments does the studio have on hand? Most are equipped with a piano, while others may have drums, synthesizers, amplifiers, and various percussion equipment. Check to see if the use of these instruments is included in the studio rental or if there is an additional fee. It is also important to see if free setup time is provided.

Studio time can be very expensive. Shop around. Your local home-town recording studio may prove more costly than one in a competitive market such as New York or Los Angeles. Today, prices seem to vary between $15 and $75 per hour, with the average being about $45 per hour. Estimate needing about 10 to 15 hours of studio time for each song. The average three-song demo will cost between $1350 and $2225 in studio time alone. Add to this the cost of tape and duplication, which generally runs between $200 and $300. While you can purchase tapes on your own, it is usually worth it in goodwill to purchase from the studio directly. A cassette tape rather than a pressed record is the generally accepted format for a demo today.

The selection of a recording engineer is vital to the success of your demo. The right engineer is able to interpret the wishes of you and your producer in the recording and mixing process. Engineers average about $18 per hour, so count on an additional $750 to $1000 dollars for your production costs. If you need additional session players for certain effects you can count on spending about $150 more.

As you can see, the financial demands of producing a good demo tape are considerable. Average total costs range between $2250 to $6750. For the lower figure you must serve as your own producer and have friends serve as extra players.

The studio is not the place to rehearse and experiment. Be totally prepared before going in. If you have never played wearing headphones before, practice before going to the studio. Make sure you have lead sheets available for reference and that instruments are in good repair. Have extra strings, fuses, and drum heads available for emergencies that may occur. Work as if you are making an actual recording. The most professional sound possible is crucial and many demos may be independently produced if the record companies fail to show interest.

Where to send the demo tape

When your demo is complete it is vital that it is heard by people with clout or power in the music business. Most important is the artist and repertoire person of the various record companies. The 'A and R man' is responsible for recommending new artists and materials for each record company. If he likes what he hears, his superiors will get to hear it at a future meeting. With most record companies, decisions to sign an artist are committee decisions rather than the taste of one individual. Others with influence in the music business that should receive your tape include top managers, record producers, music attorneys, publishers, and agents. Recommendations of these people carry much weight and can make all the difference in having your tape heard. Lists of people accepting submissions appear in the annual guides of *Billboard*, *Record World*, and *Cashbox*. Try to limit your submissions to those that deal in your style of music.

Make sure your tape is labeled properly when you send it out. Information on the label should include composer, song titles, playing time, and the name and address of the contact person or person in charge. With the demo, you should also send a press kit including photos, biographies, press clippings, lead sheets, and a cover letter. Additional costs to the band for these materials will average about $350 for such things as photographer, duplication, folders, envelopes, and postage. If you can afford it, a logo for your band makes a favorable impression. Always send a self-addressed stamped envelope (SASE) if you expect to have your material returned. Be persistent. A follow-up phone call to the people you send your demo may help, but don't be too pushy. The result may be that they are totally turned off and will not listen to your demo.

Your original material should be copyrighted to protect you from unauthorized use or pirating. The safest way to do this is to register your copyright with the Copyright Office of the Library of Congress. To order forms by phone call (202) 287-9100 any time. If you have other questions, call (202) 287-8700 between 8:30 AM and 5:00 PM Eastern time. Form PA is used to register published and unpublished works of the performing arts.

There was a day when record companies concerned themselves with developing and promoting new artists. This is not the case today. Record companies are primarily concerned with the distribution end of the business. They want to hear a finished product. If you have the financial backing it is sometimes wise to independently produce and record. Promotion and distribution among your local and regional following will give your band something that may make the major labels sit up and take notice. Try to get your local radio station to play your material and get the album into local record stores. The major labels like to see a proven track record. A local or regional following can be quite valuable.

Making a demo tape is a major step for any band. Make sure that you are ready to put in the time, effort, and finances to produce the most professional product possible. You may even have to engage in some fund raising in order to bankroll your project. Make sure that the tape is heard by those in the best position to help you. Don't be discouraged by rejection and keep plugging away. With the right approach and some luck you just might be on your way to a major record contract.

How do you take your talents and package them so that it shows your range of ability to business professionals capable of hiring you? One way is by developing your own one person show.

Such a production might include well-known songs and monologues or original characters and material that you've created. It may feature a back-up band or a single piano. It could present you as a talented musician, dancer, or actor, or as a "triple threat performer," one capable of doing it all.

HOW TO PUT TOGETHER YOUR OWN ONE PERSON SHOW
Barbara Sarbin

If you're like me, agents and casting directors are always telling you they don't know what to do with you. They recognize your abilities, but they can't figure out what category to put you in, or how to market you. You're not exactly ethnic, but you're definitely not all-American. Not weird-looking, but not gorgeous either. Not a stand-up comic, but not soap opera material. They tell you you're interesting, you're funny, you're different — and they always give the job to somebody else. So what do you do? Get totally frustrated? Wish someone would tell you you're lousy so you could just get out of the business? Become an agent yourself?

You could always write, produce, and perform in your own show. If you're passionate about acting, and you want to perform with integrity, even if it's for no money, you may have the nerve to put together a one-person show. And that's exactly what it takes: a lot of nerve. People often say to me, "I don't know how you could do it, get up there in front of all those people by yourself." I tell them I didn't have any choice.

When I graduated with a BA in theater several years ago, I knew exactly what I wanted to do. My lifelong dream was to be a member of a touring theater company. For the next three years I did tour with the Adaptors Movement Theatre in the U.S., Canada, and Mexico. But strangely enough, after your dreams come true, the question becomes: what's next? I looked at the performers whom I most admired: Lily Tomlin, Whoopi Goldberg, and Gilda Radner. What they all had in common was experience in improvisation. I joined the in-house improv company at Who's On First and spent the next three years learning how to improvise with an audience, as well as with company members. During that time, I also developed my own material. I had performed solo in college as a mime and monologist, and I had characters and ideas that I was ready to develop further.

The following outline is how I create, develop, and present a solo show, and some of the process may be applicable to you. Keep in mind: there is no one way to do anything in this business, but you can take hints from other performers' experiences as you create your own path.

Getting started

My favorite way to work is with a tape recorder. After several weeks of recording different characters talking about themselves, I transpose and edit what I have into monologues. Everyone has their own method for generating ideas, but the main goal is to get something written down and/or memorized. You can torture several friends into listening to you and offering their opinions. You can even crash a class, or audit one legally, where you will be given the perfect workshop situation to test out your new material. If the responses are favorable enough, it should give you enough confidence to take the material onto a stage.

The demo tape

First, though, you need a demo video. There's a great way to do this if you have no money. The Stanley Greene Audio/Video Center in New York costs about $15 for a yearly membership, and they'll do videos of you for free, which make for good, first-time demo tapes. You do have to be a member of AFTRA, though. If you're not a union member, find someone with a video camera and befriend him, or approach a film school student who needs experience. This first tape just needs to exist as a record of your material that presents you looking halfway decent, like your picture and résumé. In the same way, it needs to be concise, no more than 10 minutes long.

Then respond to one of the many ads that run in the trades seeking solo performers. I was invited to do my earliest material, *Just Another JAP,* at Good Times, just on the basis of my demo. Once you have a gig set up, make a lot of colorful fliers and mail them to everyone you know. You'd be surprised how many people will come to see you in a solo performance piece. First of all, they know they'll get to see you, and if nothing else, they'll admire the fact that you got up there and did it.

Performing at a club is great for a beginner, because you only have to make a minimal investment. In return, you make half of the cover (meaning you're guaranteed some kind of profit if you have enough of an audience).

Moving up

When I needed a more substantial demo tape of my new material, I approached a local public access station in Westchester, where I live. (By the way, don't ever let anyone tell you that you can't live outside Manhattan and still make a living. It's clean, safe, usually less expensive than the city, and after a day of rejection, trees look really friendly.) They were more than happy to film a live version of a solo performance that they could air for free as often as they liked on local cable. No one made any money and no one lost any, but I got a broadcast-quality version of my show which I then edited down to another ten-minute promotional tape.

When you get to the point of editing your demo professionally, you're starting to talk money. Unless you have a friend in film school who wants to edit your video for free, you'll have to hire someone, and pay for rental of an editing room. You can cut these costs down if you watch yourself on tape a million times and figure out exactly which sections are the most flattering, timing each piece before going to edit. Even so, there are always unexpected extras. The master tape you have to edit on is an extra. If you need titles, that costs extra. Labels for the video cassettes cost extra. At the least, editing and duplicating can cost anywhere from $100–$300, depending on how fancy you get, and how many copies you make.

You'll need lots of copies. Start out by making 10 of each, but you'll probably need as many as 20. Each time you send a tape out, you need to include a stamped, self-addressed envelope, in order to get the tape back (that's close to $7.00 for mailing bags and postage, *per tape*). But considering how much you spent to make copies, it's best to get them back. I primarily used mine for agents (who still got excited about me, and did nothing). But better yet, I sent them out to colleges and was hired to perform my show at various schools for $400 plus transportation. A hundred of that went to pay my technical person, and the rest was mine to reinvest, or pay rent with.

Where to get more money

Once you establish yourself a bit, you can begin applying for grants from the New York State Council of the Arts or the National Endowment for the Arts. You can go to the Foundation Center or the Center for Arts information to find out more about grants. This is less fun. Most organizations don't want to recognize you financially for a few years, and even worse, they have very little money to give out. It's still worth looking into, though, because if you stick with solo performing long enough, you'll eventually be given some support money.

Classes for solo performers

After two years, I felt that my performance needed more depth. I noticed that two female solo performers I knew, Stephanie Silverman and Jane Gennaro, had developed their material under the tutelage of Wynn Handman, artistic director of the American Place Theatre. There are other teachers who work with solo performers, and you just have to seek them out. I joined Wynn's professional acting class, and he began to work with me on my writing. At his suggestion, I took one of my characters all the way back to her childhood and then worked forward with her, in a series of monologues. Although this was intended as an exercise, and is excellent for working on any character, this ultimately became the material for my new show, *Adolescent Wilderness.*

Real theaters

This time around, I felt the material and my abilities as an actress were strong enough to warrant a bigger investment. I went looking for off-Broadway theaters that rented space inexpensively on dark nights so that I could perform for an audience under more respectable conditions. I was tired of hearing the clink of silverware during my more dramatic moments. I also had dreams of wooing agents, casting directors, and reviewers, and I knew most of them wouldn't venture outside Times Square. I approached an independent producer, Jeri Slater, who had produced a revival of Jane Gennaro's show, *The Boob Story,* at the John Houseman Theatre. She gave me a list of places to contact, and the range of prices for rental ran from $150 a night to $900 a week. I ultimately chose The Producers Club, because I liked the fact that it had a bar/cafe attached to the theater where the audience could relax before and after the show. The director there had been looking for something that could fill the theater's empty nights, and he offered to co-produce the event with me. By this point I had developed a mailing list of 500, and I was pretty sure that I could fill his theater for two weeks of performances.

Where to get an audience

My show was, in fact, filled with audience members. You can ensure an audience by listing your show with Audience Extras, Theater Development Fund, and all the newspapers in the city. To cut costs, use every friend you have as an usher, house manager, dimmer board operator, and press agent. If you run the production as an Equity Showcase, you can't charge more than $8.00 a ticket, which makes it impossible to make a profit. With postage, photocopying of fliers and programs, phone calls, transportation, press kits, photos, ticket services, and rental of the theater, you'll be extremely lucky to break even. I had to keep telling myself this was an investment.

In the end

I'm back where I started now, making a video of *Adolescent Wilderness* and planning a tour of colleges to recoup the money. Still, I haven't given up. Rather, I've formed my own company, Third Vector Productions, an expression which means that instead of struggling against your opposition, deflect it and come at it from an oblique angle. I like to think of it as the Tai Chi of acting.

This approach to performing is not for everyone, but you'll know if it's right for you. If you're not a great writer, get one to write a show for you. This can mean anything from using your friend's work, to hiring an expensive professional. You can also adapt something from a novel, or from the life of a historical character.

Most important, go see other solo performers and check out where they perform and what kinds of material they get away with. Let people's work inspire you, as Spalding Gray's did for me. If it hadn't been for seeing his work, *Swimming to Cambodia,* at Lincoln Center, I never would have thought it possible to do mine. See Jim Calder, Jeffrey Essman, Frank Maya, David Cale, or Scott Carter. Go to La Mama, Dixon Place, The Duplex, BACA, or The West Bank Cafe. Rent videos of Gilda, Lily, and Whoopi. As I've said, there is no one way to do this, and other solo performers can offer other routes.

Barbara Sarbin has been writing and performing her own material since 1983. Her one-woman shows Alone Together *and* Adolescent Wilderness *have been seen in comedy clubs, on cable TV, and at colleges throughout the New York area.*

4
Legal-Ease

I think I'm more realistic about the fact that it is a business. However, I also see that no matter how commercial it all gets, there are still people out there who are willing to make a personal sacrifice to work on projects that don't necessarily make money. If you can make money doing television, for example, you can devote some time to not earning as big a paycheck for a couple of months. Much of the work available to an actor may be considered 'garbage work,' but you do the garbage because it allows you to do what you really want to do. Who could ask for anything more?

Christopher Collet, *featured in* The Manhattan Project

Today's young performers and their families can't simply hide behind the label of "artiste" without also acquiring some business savvy. They have to know, for example, how to read a contract before signing, how to keep accurate records for tax purposes, and how to meet and influence people. If they don't learn to be somewhat self-sufficient in the business world, what happened to Dick Moore could happen to them.

AN INTERVIEW WITH DICK MOORE

Dickie Moore began his professional acting career in 1926 when he wasn't quite one year old. If you're a true film buff you know that he was *Oliver Twist;* he was one of the *Our Gang* kids; he was Gary Cooper's younger brother in *Sergeant York*; he was the child dying of rabies while Paul Muni looked for a cure in *The Life of Emile Zola*; he gave Shirley Temple her first screen kiss in *Miss Annie Rooney*; and he played the son of Barbara

Dick Moore   Photo by Mikki Meyer

Stanwyck, Marlene Dietrich, and other renowned actresses. He is married to Jane Powell and he has hobnobbed with the likes of Mickey Rooney, Judy Garland, Jackie Coogan, Jackie Cooper, Donald O'Connor, Roddy McDowall, and other great child actors of the 20s, 30s, and 40s.

The days of the powerful studios are gone and so is little Dickie Moore. In his place is Dick Moore, public relations executive, publisher, and author. He now owns Dick Moore Associates, and in 1984, his book *Twinkle, Twinkle, Little Star (But Don't Have Sex or Use The Car)*, was published by Harper and Row. The book provides a realistic look at an era long gone, when child stars could carry a movie on the strength of their personalities; when a film that starred Shirley Temple was *a Shirley Temple Film* and all that that represented to a public ravaged by the Depression and hungering for escapist entertainment.

Alan Simon: You mention in your book that you see the child actors of your generation as a throwback to the Dickensian age, when children were mini-adults. Why do you feel that way?

Dick Moore: Because I don't think that there has ever been an era — certainly it doesn't exist now — when children were cast as stereotypes of themselves. I mean you go back to *Oliver Twist, David Copperfield*, or any of the Dickensian stories and, frankly, children were perceived as mini-adults. Oliver Twist was an adult in every sense of the word except that he didn't have the capacity to govern his own life. He was easily victimized and he was small enough to squeeze through windows and open doors from the inside so that Fagin and his gang could enter. He was very amenable, he was very anxious to please. He was tractable. Aside from that he was an adult. He was expected to behave and to perform and to provide the same way that an adult does. That was the case in the 1930s and on into the 1940s as far as — not just the reality of the child actor in his relationship to his family — the child actor was perceived by the whole society. I don't think that condition existed before the 30s and 40s because child actors weren't in vogue, except for Lillian Gish, and that was different because she wasn't an infant star. It certainly hasn't existed since, not since World War II, which kind of blew our illusions and a large number of our fantasies away. From the 50s on there was something more real, more immediate, more urgent to focus on than the fantasy that Dickie Moore could fix a broken marriage or that Shirley Temple could solve the country's problems.

AS: Is it true that if your tutoring hours were put in during the morning, then no one minded how long you worked at the other end of the day?

DM: Well, that was true before I came on the scene. By the time I got there, there were child labor laws that limited one's ability to be on the set for longer than eight hours, with some exceptions. But prior to me, when Diana Cary (Baby Peggy) worked, or when Jackie Coogan did the bulk of his work, there were no limits. Lillian Gish was working at fourteen and there were absolutely no limits. But had there not been child labor laws there would never have been limits. I never knew a parent to say to an assistant director, "The child is tired. He can't do any more today so we had best quit." I never knew a director to say it, since he was always fighting for daylight and against budgets. I never knew anybody but a teacher to say, "Enough!" It didn't come from the parents; it didn't come from the children. The children were too anxious to please and they really didn't know any better. Shirley Temple thought everybody worked. If you were a child who didn't work and Shirley met you, she wouldn't understand what was wrong with you.

AS: Franklin Delano Roosevelt said, "As long as our country has Shirley Temple, we will be all right." If each child actor stood for something different in the American psyche, what did Dickie Moore stand for?

DM: Innocence and purity and goodness. I was not a rebellious child. I was able to reconcile dissenting adults (not consenting adults), like Marlene Dietrich and Herbert Marshall. I made it all okay.

Dick Moore's career began in 1926, and he appeared in approximately one hundred films, though he wasn't quite certain of the exact number. It was difficult to keep a record prior to the institution of Social Security and the creation of the Screen Actors Guild in the early 30s.

AS: When did your career end?

DM: The last feature motion picture that I did was either *Member of the Wedding* or *Eight Iron Men*, both for Stanley Kramer, and one right after the other, so I'm not sure which was which. That was 1952 or 1953. I continued acting, but those were my last feature films. I was on television, stage, and radio until 1957, when I finally found a way to permanently escape.

Despite having done so many classics, Moore still described himself as having neither singing nor dancing abilities nor being able to perform without a script. How did he survive for so long, if that was the case?

He admitted that it was no longer the case, but it was a trap that he had to dig himself out of. According to Moore, "When you are conditioned to reading other people's lines and performing in other people's scripts and behaving according to others' specifications, and you do that while living in an atmosphere or a climate that does not encourage you to express yourself, you don't make waves. You have to be very strong or have to get a lot of help to escape from that kind of pattern, which becomes lifelong. By that, I mean the anxiety to please. All of us grew up in this way, anxious to please the adults in our lives. When you depart from that script, you risk disapproval."

AS: Do you still equate good acting with being able to cry on cue?

DM: Natalie Wood talked me out of that. But I must say that a good actor has to have technical facility as well as emotional intensity. A good actor has to do whatever he's supposed to do.

People who say to those of us who were child actors, "Don't you just love acting more than anything else in the world?" are surprised to learn that most of us don't really feel that way. I certainly didn't. I couldn't wait to quit. I just didn't know what else to do. But I feel very strongly that to be a good and effective actor, you have to really want to do it so much that you are willing to forgo many of the things other people in other professions take for granted. You must be willing to risk the kind of rejection, denial, pain, and privation that goes with the territory.

I don't think that is a choice that can be made by anyone but a mature adult. So when a child has grown up as a performer, and reaches the point when that choice has to be made, often he doesn't know that there's anything else to do.

AS: So who did you do it for? Did you do it for parents, did you do it for the studio, did you do it for some combination of both?

DM: It was some combination of both.

AS: Have parents changed as far as you can tell?

DM: Not so far as I can tell. I think that the entertainment industry is not so sharply focused on children anymore, but I don't think parents have changed. We used to work on a now-defunct project called *The Milliken Breakfast Show* which was an immense annual theatrical fashion event in New York. *The Milliken Breakfast Show* was the foremost industrial show in America. It engaged stars like Ginger Rogers, Don Ameche — everybody — and they had 13 or 14 children in each show, 30 or 40 performers in the chorus, plus a score of principals. They spent an astonishing amount of money to display their fabrics in garments within a theatrical framework.

I stayed away from the children's auditions. As promotion director I didn't have to go, which is a good thing because I couldn't stand them. On one floor were the auditions, on another the children and their parents waited to audition. I remember one little girl, about five years old, who simply wasn't right. Now actors and parents never know why they're not right; they always believe that if they do something 'right' they'll get the part. Most of the time it has to do with other things entirely beyond the ability of an actor to change — the sizes of the dresses, or they want three dark girls because the colors for the fall collection happen to go best with a dark complexion. It could be anything! ... Who knows? It's totally beyond your control.

But performers tend not to understand that. So this little kid was sent back to her mommy in the upstairs waiting area. They were very kind to her, very gentle, but she was rejected. The child went back to her mother, not terribly disheartened, and said, "Okay, Mommy, they said I wasn't right." So the mother opened her purse, took out another dress, ripped the first dress off the child, put her in the second dress, changed her hair-do on the spot, and pushed her back in line to go down the treadmill and be rejected again, which, of course, she was. I happen to think that people like that should be put away.

So when you asked me if I see any great change in parents, no, I don't see any great change. I just think that sensitive people who are not in the families are a little more aware of the psychic damage this sort of thing can do. That mother wasn't thinking about her child, she just had some neurotic need that she was acting out by forcing her child to perform for her sake, not at all for the kid's.

I have a litmus test. People say, "That's not fair, that's not fair!" I'm not interested in being fair. My test, to help a parent know if he or she is doing something for the child, is to see if the parent is willing to take every cent that the child earns and put it in trust for the child and not touch *any* of that money. They can't delude themselves by thinking that they have to buy a bigger car because agents will be more impressed, or get a bigger apartment so that the kid will have a place to rehearse, or any other line that is pure justification, complete self-delusion, rationalization of a basically unhealthy situation. If the parent is willing to do this, then I think that that parent may have the child's best interests at heart. Otherwise, if they touch the money, they are not performing in good faith.

Because when this isn't understood, the delusion begins. I'm sure Jackie Coogan's stepfather, who stole $10 million from him, talked himself into the fact that this was in Jack's best interests.

AS: In your book you've said, about your own era, that parents often discouraged their children from forming solid friendships because friends might tell each other about a part that was coming up and then the wrong child, in the parent's view, would get the part. So the competition, apparently, was there more among the parents than it was among the children?

DM: Sure, but we learned to compete also. Children pick things up very quickly.

AS: Did you have many friends outside the business?

DM: Yes, all kids in the neighborhood. We played football and baseball and kick-the-can. I would get bruised and battered and tear my clothes up occasionally. My parents were really good that way. I was encouraged to have outside relationships, much more than many of my peers. I was not so lonely.

AS: So you wouldn't say that "isolated" was a way of describing ...

DM: Oh, I would. I definitely would because I didn't talk to anybody about things that mattered. But still I wasn't so isolated as many others, as Jane Powell was or as Roddy McDowall, for example. And when you are young and you experience those feelings of isolation and loneliness, it tends to affect your feelings later on and encourage you to make bad choices in terms of friends, husbands, wives, lovers, colleagues, even agents. You tend to settle for anything just so you won't feel lonely. It takes a long time to get over that. It's a very difficult problem.

Yes, I think that isolation is a great danger. You see these kids know about close-ups, know about long shots, they know how to find the key light, they always know their lines. But so what? They don't know anything that's going on in the third grade. They don't know anything that matters to anybody else.

AS: Why did so many of you find the studio to be a home away from home?

DM: It became a kind of family. That was not true for me because usually I was not under contract. But to those that were under contract, it was home. You studied there, you were taken care of, you got your play, you got your lessons, you got approval. That is to say, whatever approval you got, you got there. It became very important — it was populated by authority figures.

In his book, Moore seemed to indicate that it was easier to relate to some of the adults than it was to relate to most of the children.

AS: But who were the adults that you most respected?

DM: Always the director. There happened to be some nice directors who I really liked. Whether this was true or not, this was certainly the person I related to the most and was most anxious to please. In my case, this was especially true because this was the person that my parents were also most anxious to please. So I learned by example. Children learn good lessons as well as bad lessons, but bad lessons more quickly than good ones.

AS: You speak about confusing reality with make-believe and I wonder if you could talk about that, specifically as it has affected you in later years.

DM: I think it comes mostly in not being able to sort out one's feelings. That is, knowing how you feel about something and maybe being conditioned to think that you must feel another way about it. You'll have doubts and you'll say, "I shouldn't be feeling that way." For example, everyone tells you that someone is very nice and there's no reason that you shouldn't like that person. As you mature, you give comfort to yourself by learning to respect your feelings. One has a tendency, especially having had an early career as a performer, to want to channel feelings in the most convenient direction, and feelings don't work that way.

AS: How did the studios and parents try to prevent the children from growing up?

DM: I don't think it was any conscious effort to keep us from growing up. They might shave the hair on your legs, they might see if they could keep you wearing short pants. They might shave the fuzz from your upper lip when you were fourteen, and other garbage like that. They dressed us young. When Jane Powell was a mother, she was still playing little girls smitten by someone at the high school dance. She used to go to Louis B. Mayer, the head of MGM, and say, "Mr. Mayer, I want to play grown parts. I'm a mother." He'd say to her, "You will, my dear, you will." But then, as Jane said, "I could have quit."

AS: You did all these films and a year and a half of the *Our Gang* comedies. One might get the impression that you are set for life, financially speaking. Is this the case?

DM: Oh, no, that is not the case at all. Not at all. That's probably why I made the remark I did earlier about the money. There was no money put aside for me. I don't know anyone, with the exceptions of Shirley Temple, Jane Withers, and Jackie Cooper, that had any money saved for them.

AS: Were you paid any residuals?

DM: According to the contract that the Screen Actors Guild has with the motion picture producers, they are not required to pay residuals for any feature film that was made before 1960. Of course my film work, and most of everybody else's from that era, was done before 1960.

AS: Is there resentment?

DM: Absolutely. I must make the point that most of us had great ignorance when it came to money. We were not encouraged to take an interest. Some of us still don't know much about it. It seemed to be the antithesis of everything that we were taught to be interested in. Even as adults making decent salaries, many of us don't understand money.

AS: Would you put your child in this business?

DM: No, and I think my son is quite angry with me because I didn't do anything at all to help him or encourage him. He hasn't said so, but I think he would've liked me to try to do more. I couldn't have done anything even if I'd wanted to. I don't know anyone in casting. I have no contacts in that area anymore. Even if I did, I wouldn't have helped him, which may not be right. There are others who have benefited from having their parents in the business, but I simply didn't have that kind of clout.

AS: Would you do it all over again?

DM: Sure. I wouldn't want to be anybody else doing anything else in any other place. If in order to be here now I had to relive my past, then that's what I would do.

To avoid some of the pitfalls that happened to Dick Moore and the other child actors of his era, the family must know what to look for in a contract. Neil Burstein, an entertainment lawyer, offers some insight.

CONTRACTS AND THE CHILD PERFORMER
Neil A. Burstein, Esquire

In contract law, an agreement between two parties is generally binding, and each party is required to honor the terms of the contract. An exception occurs where one of the parties to the contract is a minor. To protect the best interests and welfare of children, the law deems minors incapable of possessing the necessary judgment to be legally bound by their agreements. As a result, a contract with a minor can be voided by the child. A noteworthy example is the case of Lee v. Silver. A child vocalist and her mother signed a contract engaging a business manager for three years. Shortly thereafter, the child repudiated the agreement, and the manager sued to enforce the contract. The court ruled that the child had the absolute right to repudiate the agreement on the grounds of infancy. The business manager's claim against the mother for inducing her daughter to repudiate the contract was also dismissed.

A minor may repudiate contract obligations at any time during infancy or within a reasonable time after reaching the age of majority. The adult party to the agreement cannot avoid the obligations of the contract should the minor seek to enforce it. The age of majority is determined by state law. In New York and California, a person is an "infant" or "minor" until age 18. The legal right of minors to disaffirm their agreements caused problems for employees in the entertainment industry.

Mounting most entertainment productions requires enormous investments, whether for movies, television, or stage production. In the past, the legal and financial risks inherent in employing minors without the assurances of binding contracts were especially troublesome to employers in the entertainment business. Entertainment companies were reluctant to hire minors, since there was no legal assurance that the contracted services would actually be provided by the child. For example, if a production company hired a minor to perform in a television series, the child performer could, upon receiving a better offer, repudiate the contract and leave the series midseason without any legal penalty.

Court approval of contracts

Recognizing the special problems of the entertainment industry, states with significant entertainment business established procedures for court approval of personal service agreements with minors. The purpose of such legislation was to provide assurances to parties contracting with minors by eliminating the minor's common law right to annul contracts. Thus, a contract approved by the court is binding on the child and cannot be disaffirmed on the grounds of infancy or on the ground that the parent lacked authority to make the contract. However, certain minimum requirements must be established before a contract will be approved by the court.

A court will not approve a contract employing a child in the entertainment business unless the terms are reasonable and in the child's best interests. To ensure that the terms are reasonable, most states (including New York and California) require that a copy of the contract be attached to the court papers seeking judicial approval. There is also a requirement that a portion of the child's earnings be held in trust for the child. This provision is commonly called the "Coogan Law," after Jackie Coogan, the child star of silent pictures. Despite making vast sums of money as a child, Coogan found his money depleted upon reaching adulthood. To prevent such occurrences, "Coogan Laws" were enacted. Each state with a "Coogan Law" sets guidelines whereby a judge can set aside a portion of a minor's contract earnings, to be held in trust until the child reaches adulthood. To implement the law, a court petition must be filed seeking judicial approval of the contract. The court petition may be filed by the employer, parent, guardian or relative acting on the child's behalf. It is usually the employer who seeks court approval, since he gets the benefits of a binding contract. Only a small percentage of contracts are submitted for court approval due to the time required for court appearances and the expense involved.

New York and California law

Both New York and California have procedures for court approval of contracts with minors. In New York, the Arts and Cultural Affairs Law provides that judicial approval may be obtained for contracts with minors rendering services as "performing artists," such as actors, dancers, musicians, or vocalists. Court approval is also available for management and agency agreements with minors. The Civil Code of California provides for judicial approval of contracts with minors employed to render "artistic or creative services." Under both statutes, court approval is frequently contingent on setting aside a percentage of the minor's earnings under the contract, to be held in trust until the child reaches majority. The amount held in trust is determined by the court, but no more than one-half of the minor's net earnings may be set aside. In determining the percentage set aside, the court considers the financial circumstances of the parent, other family members, and the needs of the child.

There are several significant differences in the New York and California laws. Under the New York statute, no contract will be approved if the term of the agreement, including any extensions, exceed three years. A contract which includes a two-year option to extend beyond the three-year contract period would not qualify for court approval. However, certain contract terms not relating to the duration of the child's services may extend beyond three years. For example, the court may grant a movie producer the perpetual right to use the child's likeness in advertising the movie.

California law allows court approval of contracts for up to seven years. Producers frequently file petitions for court approval under California law because of the longer contract period. In New York, court approval of the contract may be revoked or modified at any time if the well-being of the child is impaired. There is no similar provision for revocation of court approval in California.

Parental liability

Today, most entertainment industry contracts require the parent or guardian to sign as a guarantor of the child's performance. Parents who sign in this capacity are potentially liable for damages in the event of nonperformance by the child. To protect parents and guardians, New York enacted legislation providing that a parent or guardian is not liable as a guarantor of a minor's contract unless the agreement received judicial approval, and the parent signed the contract either as a party or guarantor. This means that unless a contract received court approval, a parent is not liable as a guarantor even if the parent signed in that capacity. In California, there is no statutory provision covering parental liability, so parents who sign as guarantors do so at their own risk.

Exceptions to the right to disaffirm

Parents and guardians are urged to consult an attorney before signing contracts or permitting their children to do so. Parents should know that not every contract is subject to the common law right of disaffirmance by the child. A court approved contract is not subject to disaffirmance on the ground of infancy or on the ground that the parent lacked authority to make the contract. Certain contracts providing necessities to children (e.g., food or clothing) are not subject to repudiation. A contract is also enforceable if ratification occurs after the minor reaches majority. There are other situations in which a contract cannot be revoked. In Shields v. Gross, the court ruled that the parent's consent was binding on the child. In this case, internationally known model and actress, Brooke Shields, sued to prevent a photographer from using nude photographs taken of her when she was 10 years old. Brooke Shields' mother had signed an unrestricted consent form granting the photographer permission to use the photographs for "any purpose whatsoever." Shields argued that she had a common law right to disaffirm the consent given by her parent years ago. However, the court ruled that Shields was bound by the terms of the unrestricted consent given by her mother. The court refused to bar the photographer from using the nude photographs in legitimate publications.

A photographic release was also upheld under California law. In Faloona v. Hustler Magazine, a mother had signed an unrestricted release for the use of nude photographs of her children, intended for use in a textbook on human sexuality. The release gave the photographer the right to use the photographs "in any manner." Following publication of the book, an adult magazine purchased the right to publish a 5,000 word excerpt with accompanying photos from the book. The mother sued on behalf of her children after the magazine published the nude photographs of her children. In addition to monetary damages, the lawsuit sought to void the photographic release, arguing that minors had the right to repudiate contracts. The court disagreed, holding that photographic releases were not subject to disaffirmance under California law.

Before signing a contract

The child's parent or guardian should carefully evaluate and analyze any contract before signing. The financial and educational needs of the child should be considered, as well as whether the contract provides for the proper development of the child's talents. In all contractual matters, parents should consult an attorney with experience in entertainment law.

> *Neil Burstein is an entertainment lawyer with offices in New York City. He is a section member of the Talent Agencies and Talent Management Committee of the New York State Bar Association, and author of numerous articles on entertainment law.*

TAXES AND FINANCES FOR
THE YOUNG PERFORMER
Alan Straus and Michael Chapin

You can probably balance a checkbook as well as the next person, and you feel that this represents the extent of your ability to understand financial matters. Like most people, you've probably made two basic assumptions:

First, you've assumed that you're incapable of understanding taxes and finances. Second, you've assumed that the subject is boring. Like most people you know, you've always relied on someone else — your father or brother-in-law or Uncle Sidney — to offer to explain tax and financial matters that pertained to you. It was so much easier than learning to ask the right questions yourself. These subjects were, after all, not only unfathomable and uninteresting, but *intimidating*, too.

You'd be surprised, though, at just how much information you can absorb. By approaching family financial matters with a sense of organization, the subject actually becomes *interesting* and *manageable*. And that's the point of this chapter. While there's much to share with you, perhaps the most important lesson is this: whether you're the parent or guardian or the young performer, you have a responsibility to understand *something*, if not more, about taxes, finances, and paychecks. To play dumb and to rely completely on someone else to take the responsibility for *your* money can result in disaster. You'll make a lot more wrong decisions out of ignorance than out of knowing what to ask.

Before we ask the questions, though, here's a glossary of some of the terms that should be added to your vocabulary.

- **IRS:** The dreaded Internal Revenue Service. This is the United States government bureau that's responsible for collecting our taxes at the end of the year. Income tax day, when all personal taxes are due, is April 15 of the year after the tax-year. Thus, on April 15, 1991, you pay tax for 1990.

- **Social Security Number:** A nine-digit number that the IRS uses to keep track of you, your earnings, and your taxes. Every working performer, even the youngest child, is required to have a Social Security number. (You're not being singled out! Every worker in *every* industry needs one!)

- **W-2 Form:** This is the form on which your employer reports to the government all the wages paid to you and the amounts withheld for payment to the government on your behalf. During January, your employer must send you a W-2 stating your total wages and the amounts withheld in various tax categories for the entire previous year. You attach a copy to each tax return you file.

- **1099 Form:** The form that replaces a W-2 if you're not an employee but instead are self-employed and don't have taxes withheld from your earnings. If you earn less than $600 from any one payor in a calendar year, that payor need not send you a 1099 form, but you're still responsible for reporting that income to the IRS.

- **Deduction:** An expense that can legitimately be deducted from the amount of income on which you pay taxes at the end of the year. We'll discuss *legitimate* business deductions in our question and answer section following this glossary.

- **Disbursements Ledger:** A working young performer should be thought of as a business, and a ledger allows the business manager to keep track of all expenses and all legitimate deductions in an orderly way. With a properly designed ledger, a family can keep track of the amounts being spent in given areas over the course of the year.

- **Per Diem:** A Latin expression meaning "by the day." A per diem is a daily allowance to be used for living expenses while traveling in connection with a performance. A performer who goes on the road gets paid a per diem for housing, meals, laundry, and other expenses.

- **Dependent:** A person for whom someone else supplies all or a major amount of necessary financial support. Children are usually the dependents of their parents.

- **Tax Form:** The form on which a taxpayer reports to the government information about income and expenses during the tax year. The Bottom Line shows whether the worker owes the government, the government owes the worker, or the score is even. There are separate forms for reporting to federal, state, and local tax agencies.

• **Accountant:** A person who specializes in handling the financial reporting of an individual, a corporation, or an institution. An accountant will use the client's disbursements ledger, receipts, W-2s, 1099s, and any other relevant documentation and information that will help him or her to prepare tax returns in accordance with the law and to assume every legitimate advantage for the client.

Questions to ask, things to know

Q. What kind of accountant should a family hire to provide the best advice for its situation?

A. The easiest analogy to draw is to the medical profession. You wouldn't go to a dermatologist if you needed open heart surgery. Accountants have various areas and degrees of specialization as well. Parents should look for an accountant who specializes in working with professional performers — of any age and any performance area — since all performers have parallel financial needs.

When an accountant or a tax consultant works with clients who make their livings in a particular field, he or she becomes familiar with the important issues of that area. A performer looking for an accountant shouldn't have to explain what a *headshot* is or what an *under 5* job is. An accountant should be familiar with the terminology and intricacies of the entertainment business as well as with all the tax laws associated with it.

Q. What are the questions to ask before selecting such a specialist?

A. You select a doctor or a dentist based on references of people you respect. That's a good first step, too, for selecting an accountant. But personal recommendation, while a good introduction, is only the beginning.

Parents should inquire about the specialist's credentials. Some financial specialists will have a law degree as well as one in accounting. Some are tax preparers, specialists who are not certified public accountants, but are knowledgeable about particular areas.

Ask who else in the business this person works for. How does he or she charge—by the hour? by the job? by other specified terms? How available is this person? If something comes up, can you call and ask questions ... for no fee? Or is everything "on the clock"?

There are no right or wrong answers to these questions, but it's always better to know the answers up front in order to avoid unpleasant surprises down the line.

Q. When should a child have a Social Security number?

A. The new tax law requires that every child over the age of two have a Social Security number. However, if your child works in a diaper commercial at the age of three months, he or she must have a Social Security number at that time. Therefore, it's a good idea to get a Social Security number before the child works, probably as soon as a birth certificate becomes available. As a matter of fact, you can't open a bank account in your child's name unless the child has a Social Security number.

Q. How does the new tax law affect the role of the young performer as a member of the family?

A. If a young performer is making money, his or her income is taxable. A child who works is, in the eyes of the law, at least for taxation purposes, an adult, and is taxed as one. This was true even before the new tax law came into effect.

The "new" tax law came into being as the 1986 Tax Reform Act, and was Congress' attempt to make taxation more equitable. The specific tenet of the 1986 Tax Reform Act that's relevant here is the "Kiddie Tax."

Before the "Kiddie Tax," parents could make all sorts of investments in their child's name. The interest that these investments earned would then be taxed at the child's rate, which was usually lower than the rate at which the parent was taxed.

Congress then got smart. It declared that any interest earned by a child fourteen and under must be taxed at either the parent's or the child's rate, *whichever is higher*. Children *over* fourteen are treated basically as adults, so interest earned on investments — also known as *passive income* — is taxed at their rate.

The point, whether your child is a performer or not, is that the interest earned on a family's investments really can't be hidden anymore. If your child is making money, you may want to consider several types of investment that may not be subject to taxation. There are several available; a good investments advisor can make you aware of them.

Q. Does it make sense for the young performer's accountant or tax preparer to know the family's entire financial situation?

A. Yes! Since the institution of the "Kiddie Tax," a child's tax returns can't be properly prepared unless the information from the parents' and siblings' returns is known. There are certain schedules, or forms, in which the whole family's income is considered together and charged as a unit, as if the sum had been earned by one person. A different person could prepare each family member's return, but the results probably wouldn't be accurate.

Q. What is a legitimate business deduction?

A. In the entertainment industry, a business deduction is anything that's ordinary and necessary for production of income but not lavish or extravagant.

All of the following are — or can be — business deductions: résumés, lessons, transportation expenses incurred while looking for work, unreimbursed per diem expenses incurred on the road, sheet music, telephone calls, postage, stationery, headshots, photography fees, union dues, trade publications, clothing, and legal and accounting services. Now, let's qualify some of these categories.

Let's take lessons. As long as the lessons are in a field in which the child has *already* worked professionally — that means for pay — and their purpose is to improve skills, they're probably deductible. This means that voice, acting, dance, movement, and cello lessons might be legitimate. If your son or daughter is taking Driver's Education, that's probably not deductible. If, however, the child is required to learn to speak Latin to fulfill the requirements of a role, then you can probably deduct the cost of Latin lessons.

Clothing is a category that you have to be very careful about. Any article of clothing suitable for "real life" wear is not deductible. For example, if your child is scheduled to go on an audition and is required to wear a blue suit and black shoes, the cost of that clothing is not likely to be deductible since, although not a common outfit in some circles nowadays, it's nevertheless one that could be worn in everyday life.

Suppose, however, that your child has a role that calls for him — or her — to dress as an Elvis Presley look-alike, with a gold lamé jacket and sequined pants. You'd not likely let your child go to school in that outfit. Therefore, the cost of this costume is probably deductible.

Costume is the key word to keep in mind to help you determine what clothing is likely to be deductible. Cyndi Lauper and Madonna can probably deduct their on-stage garb because even though they probably wear the same clothing to go grocery shopping, the overwhelming majority of us would consider their outfits *costumes*, not "real life" clothing.

Let's talk about musical instruments. Your child is a professional violinist and you pay $50,000 for an Amati that's going to last for the next 20 years. Sure, it's a deductible expense. The government, however, will not allow you to deduct the full cost of the instrument in one fell swoop; more than likely, you'll deduct little bits of it over time, probably for the life of the instrument. What you're doing is *depreciating* the cost of the instrument over time, or deducting its cost little by little.

Q. *What's the best way to keep the records needed for a tax advisor?*

A. It should be a given that a family sets up a separate bank account exclusively for the child's earnings. All earnings go into that account and all disbursements come out of that account. It's of paramount importance that the child's activities be kept separate from the rest of the family's finances.

The best way for a family to keep records is in a disbursements ledger, a book whose pages are divided into 10 or 20 columns. Each column is given a heading, such as Transportation or Headshots and Reproductions or Lodging. Each time you spend money in one of these areas, you note the day and amount. Then you keep a running total of all of your expenses, by the category and by the month.

A simpler method of keeping records is to use a checkbook's line-by-line transaction space and clearly identify the purpose for which each check was written. However, it would not be as easy to keep a running total using this method.

In addition to keeping accurate financial records, the family should keep a log, or a diary, of all of the performer's appointments. The book should detail auditions, rounds, jobs, rehearsals, and business meetings, so that if the IRS ever questions you, you can match each claimed financial transaction with evidence of what you did on the day the transaction took place.

Save receipts! But no matter how you keep your records, the one thing you shouldn't do — ever — is give your accountant a shoebox full of receipts and ask him or her to sort them out.

If you do, you'll find that your accounting bill will be astronomical. It's the family's responsibility to keep their books in order; it's the accountant's responsibility to find you as many legitimate deductions as possible.

Q. Are expenses incurred in seeking work tax deductible?

A. The IRS takes the position that unless you're making money at whatever it is that you're doing you're not engaged in that activity for profit. Therefore, expenses associated with it are not tax deductible. The activity is considered to be a hobby.

Stamp collecting, for example, is a hobby that many people engage in, partly because they assume that the value of their stamps will increase as time goes on. However, if the collector invests in a magnifying glass or a stamp album, the assumption of the increase in value of the stamps is not enough to justify these expenses as tax deductions.

Similarly, you can't deduct the costs of auditions and lessons on the assumption that one day your child will get *paid* for working in the performing arts. However, once your child has his or her first paying job, then all of the expenses we've discussed here which are incurred looking for *more* work can become deductible.

Q. How should parents invest their child's money?

A. Unless the parent knows what he or she is doing, it's best to turn to a professional, an exceptional accountant or an investments advisor. This person would prepare a portfolio of suggested investments and make valid recommendations based on what is considered to be in the best interest of the child.

Q. How important is it to clearly define a parent/child business relationship?

A. Very! Too often tragic mistakes get made when parents don't understand that a) it's the child's money, not theirs and not the family's and b) they must clearly define the role they're performing on behalf of their working child.

When your child turns 18, he can request an accounting of his money and how it has been spent. If the parents have been spending that money irresponsibly, the child can say, in effect, "I want that money back." Needless to say, this can result in some ugly situations.

The ugliest of all occurred back in the 1930s when then child superstar Jackie Coogan found himself on the short end of $10 million he had earned. It seems that Coogan's mother and stepfather had spent all of his money on themselves and very little, if any, was left for Jackie when the time came for him to claim it.

After that episode, the *Coogan Laws* were passed, laws which require that a family put away a certain percentage of the child's earned income so that something remains for his future.

The parent should also be aware that if he or she becomes the child's manager, and is paid a percentage of the child's income for performing this role, those fees become taxable income for the parent. If the parent takes the commission in the form of, for instance, a car instead of cash, then the money used to buy the car is considered taxable income. On top of that, the parent must keep a log that breaks down the use of the car into business and pleasure trips.

You can see that it's of utmost importance to define the parent's business relationship to the child. When your child works in the performing arts, you're not only his or her parent; you're also his or her most important business associate.

Every child's and every family's situation are unique. *CallBack* does not attempt through this chapter to give specific financial or legal advice. Parents are reminded to carefully check credentials of professionals who seek to offer such advice.

Mr. Alan J. Straus is a lawyer and certified public accountant and a partner in the New York City accounting firm of Perelson, Johnson, and Rones; Mr. Michael Chapin is a tax consultant for performing artists.

✪

Unions are organizations designed to protect all performers, and noted author and screen mother Barbara Elman Schiffman offers some insight into the workings of the unions, most notably AFTRA, SAG, and Equity. While her article is written from the Los Angeles perspective, her information is applicable for the readership at large.

UNIONS
Barbara Elman Schiffman

There are many concerns screen parents have regarding actors' unions and their children. Does the child have to be a member of a union to work, how does one become part of such a union, how much does it cost, and which one should he join are all relevant and legitimate questions which must be answered.

Children who work regularly in films and TV are usually members of the Screen Actors Guild (SAG). Some are also members of the American Federation of Television and Radio Artists (AFTRA). Both of these unions govern actors who work on TV (including commercials) while SAG also covers feature films and AFTRA includes radio, voice-overs, and sound recordings. But your child does not have to join an actor's union to be cast in films and commercials, and is in fact eligible for some non-union acting roles which union members cannot accept. Most of these roles are in independent productions (i.e., not made by major studios or TV networks) or locally produced educational and industrial films.

These projects provide paying work for many talented kids as well as credits which are helpful later in securing an agent or a union job. Educational film producers like Walt Disney Educational in Burbank (separate from Disney Studios and The Disney Channel) generally use experienced SAG or AFTRA actors for their high quality films seen at libraries and schools worldwide, but they frequently hire non-union newcomers (especially Hispanic, Asian, or Black youngsters since a balanced racial mix is desired in school-oriented productions) who are eligible for union membership. AIMS Media in Van Nuys, California is another well-known industrial and educational production company which produces films for business or educational markets including some based on popular children's books. AIMS casts mostly non-union actors including children who have starred in award-winning educational films like *The Tenth Good Thing About Barney* based on Judith Viorst's book and *The Red Wagon* about a child's reaction to his parents' divorce. These producers find young actors through local agents and managers, acting schools, groups like Hollywood Screen Parents Association, and by word of mouth.

While your child doesn't have to be a SAG or AFTRA member to be hired for his first on-camera job, he does need a valid California Work Permit (unless he has graduated from high school or passed GED or Proficiency tests prior to age 18). You don't need an agent, manager, or paying job to apply for Work Permits, which require evidence of a C average based on recent report cards (during non-school months) or teachers' signatures on the application. These Work Permits are renewable by mail and are valid for six months. Applications are available at local California Labor Standards Enforcement offices. If your child is cast in a role and has no work permit or it isn't current, it must be received or renewed before he reports to work. Otherwise the studio teacher on the production, who is responsible for compliance with California Labor Laws as a welfare worker and must sign the back of the permit when you arrive on the set, will not let your child work. The CLSE Van Nuys office will process applications within a few days under normal circumstances while the Hollywood office will do so while you wait, for next-day work.

As for union work, there are actually six unions your child might join depending on what type of work he does. They include Actors' Equity Association (known as Equity) which governs work on stage; AFTRA which oversees live and taped TV, radio, phonograph records, and non-broadcast recorded material (which may include educational and industrial films); American Guild of Musical Artists (AGMA) which covers singers, dancers, and other performers in operas, musical productions, and concerts; American Guild of Variety Artists (AGVA) which includes ice shows, nightclubs, theme parks, cabarets, and variety shows; SAG, whose members include actors working in films, TV shows (film and taped) and commercials, stuntmen, on-camera singers/dancers, extras and voice-over artists; and Screen Extra Guild (SEG) which governs background players for film and TV. (Note that print work and modeling are not included; these jobs, not regulated by unions, are governed by California Child Labor Laws which address working hours and conditions but not payment fees.)

Each union has a different set of eligibility requirements, membership fees, and annual dues. They also regulate and protect the employment of child actors in different ways. In addition, California State Child Labor Laws, being the most structured in the U.S., supersede any union rules that are less stringent. Payment of actors, penalties for late payment and overtime, working hours for children, and other regulations are determined and enforced by the unions, however. It is essential for parents of child actors to become familiar with both the California laws and the pertinent union rules as many decisions requiring the parents' involvement as well as the studio teacher and producer are made on the set, and some rules meant to protect the child may be inadvertently violated if the studio teacher is not attentive or is overseeing other children (only one teacher is required for up to 10 children).

In addition to protecting minimum payment rates and working conditions for actors, most of these unions provide useful benefits such as medical and dental insurance, credit union accounts, pension plans, educational seminars, publications, and casting information for members whether your child is currently working or not. SAG and AFTRA have an excellent joint medical plan at no cost to members for which your child must earn $5,000 in a 12-month period to be eligible for coverage the following year (as of 1990) and then $5,000 each subsequent quarter to retain insurance in additional years, for example. (Parents and siblings of SAG/AFTRA members are automatically covered at no extra charge.)

SAG and AFTRA also have Young Performers Committees which oversee and negotiate union rules affecting young actors and were involved in updating the California Child Labor Laws affecting young actors, in 1986. SAG publishes a list of franchised agents (who agree to abide by SAG rules and payment schedules for their actors, and do not submit union actors for non-union work) three times a year, available at the SAG office, free to union members and $1.00 to non-members. Current initiation fees paid when your child joins a union are: SAG: $838.50 initiation (including $796 fee plus first semiannual basic dues of $42.50), minimum yearly dues of $85.00; AFTRA: $800.00 initiation fee, minimum annual dues of $85.00 (there is a discount on annual dues if you were a member of another union before joining AFTRA, however); SEG: $670.00 initiation fee, annual dues $120.00; Equity: $500.00 initiation fee, $52.00 minimum yearly dues. (AGVA and other performers unions are not listed here as most LA child actors are SAG, AFTRA, or Equity members.)

Eligibility requirements are: Potential SAG members must (a) show proof of employment or prospective employment with two weeks in a principal or speaking role in a SAG film, TV program, or commercial, or (b) be a paid-up member of Equity or AFTRA for at least one year and have worked in at least one union project. Actors are eligible to join AFTRA by merely applying and paying the initiation fee; no commitment of work is needed to join. Extra players may join SEG if they are registered with a union signatory casting agency. Stage performers must join Equity when hired for an Equity production, but can join if they're a paid-up member of another actor's union.

Your child may work in one SAG or AFTRA production without being a union member under the Taft-Hartley Act — a federal law governing union work in all industries. This allows a non-union actor to be hired by a union production company for a union role, which is then reported to the appropriate union. The actor may also work on other projects governed by the same union within the next 30 days without having to join the union (although he is now eligible to do so). For example, if your child gets a SAG role in a commercial shooting February 1, he may work in other SAG commercials, TV projects, or films for the next 30 days without having to join SAG and pay the union initiation fee, which is a large outlay of your cash if he only works one day and never again. If his first job continues beyond 30 days (i.e., on a film or TV series) or he gets another union job after those 30 days are up (even if it is a year later), he is then required to join the union before work on that job begins. SAG requires full membership fees paid up front, while AFTRA often works out payment plans or deducts union fees from your child's AFTRA paychecks (after taxes) until fully paid.

For more information on unions or work permits, contact:

AFTRA
6922 Hollywood Blvd., 8th floor
Hollywood, CA 90028
(213) 461-8111

California Labor Standards Enforcement
6150 Van Nuys Blvd.
Van Nuys, CA 91401
(213) 464-8268

Equity
6430 Sunset Blvd.
Los Angeles, CA 90028
(213) 462-2334

SAG
7065 Hollywood Blvd.
Hollywood, CA 90028
(213) 465-4600

SEG
3629 Cahuenga Blvd. West
Los Angeles, CA 90068
(213) 851-4301

Editor's note: The AFTRA-SAG Young Performers Handbook is now available at your local AFTRA or SAG office. Presentation of your paid-up membership will enable you to get a copy. *The Handbook*, designed to promote an understanding of the rules and regulations governing the employment of minors nationally, goes into detail on topics such as benefits, parental dos and don'ts, education, marketing tools, labor laws, and often-asked questions. In addition, the manual offers appendices: one lists the major contract points; the other, the states' varying child labor laws.

★

There are rules and regulations that you need to know when you want to put on a show in your school or camp or community organization. You can't simply mount a production without having it licensed. Neil Graeme explains.

TAKING LIBERTIES WITH DRAMATIC LICENSE
Neil Graeme

We've all seen those movies: Mickey Rooney, Judy Garland, a cast of thousands; and at some point someone almost always says, "I know, let's put on a show!"

"We can use the barn."

"We can do it!"

Mickey and Judy made it sound so easy. The real world is usually not quite so obliging; however, their idea is not as far-fetched as it sounds.

Across the nation, groups of actors, directors, producers, and technicians band together in places ranging from a local high school or church hall to the most prestigious summer stock and dinner theaters to do just that: put on a show.

In the movies, of course, the kids write, compose, and build the whole thing themselves in about 10 minutes, creating sets and costumes that would make Radio City Music Hall green with envy, all on a budget of $12.65, using only crepe paper and cardboard. And the orchestra! Back on earth, the Smalltown Community Players will more usually opt for one of the "tried and true" Broadway hits of yesteryear accompanied, if they're lucky, by piano, bass, and drums.

Meredith Wilson's *The Music Man* has trumpeted those 76 trombones from River City, Iowa, around the world and back again. *Guys & Dolls* of all ages audition furiously in communities from *Shenandoah* to *Oklahoma*, be they *Damn Yankees* or *The Pirates of Penzance* because they want to ride the *Show Boat* down the *Big River* to *Fame* and ...*Superstar*dom. Of course we all know that while "There's No Business Like Show Business," it can be somewhat of a *Carousel* and, although many who audition *Can-Can*, there are many who simply can't can't!

So what happens now? Our merrie bande of strolling players has picked their show from the dozens of suggestions made; a show, let's hope, that suits their casting needs and the physical limitations of their performance space. Someone will fit the costumes; someone will handle the lights; someone will sell the tickets. But there is still the question of a script and the music.

The first step is to find out if the show selected is available. Shows still running on Broadway are usually not available for presentation by other groups, except as First Class presentations authorized by the Broadway producers. Such shows are few and far between. But when a show closes on Broadway, very often its life is just beginning, because it then becomes available for "secondary licensing" — for presentation in dinner theaters, by community groups, high schools, and the general public.

The creators of the show (author, lyricist, composer, et al.) select a licensing agent to control productions of their work around the world and to collect royalties on their behalf each time it is performed. Licensing agents issue the "Authorized Performance Material," i.e., scripts and scores, necessary to present the show. Usually the material is rented and is the *only* material authorized by the show's creators for public presentation. Each show is administered by only one agency and there is fierce competition among them when a show becomes "available" — especially if it is a big hit. Many factors determine in whose hands the show will end up and sometimes, though rarely, a show might move from agency to agency if circumstances change. Some shows, for any number of reasons, are simply not available.

Who are these agencies? Although there are various companies, there are principally four who handle major musicals: Music Theater International, The Rodgers and Hammerstein Music Library, TAMS-Witmark Music Library, and Samuel French. Some of these companies are easier to deal with than others, and for some people that is an important consideration in selecting their show. The name of the licensing agent is usually located on the copyright page of a published play. If the play is not published, however, call the aforementioned organizations located in New York City to ascertain the licensing agent.

Many shows are published and if you can find them you might be able to buy a script and vocal selections, sometimes even a vocal score, which includes most of the music. But beware. Purchasing a script in a store does not give you the right to perform the show. First, the published material is often incomplete. Second, unless you have a valid performing license, and have paid the required royalty, your production would be illegal.

All shows are protected by the federal copyright laws and in order to perform them, you must have a license and pay a royalty. Let's face it, if you made a commercial or TV movie, you would be very upset if it was aired all over the country and you didn't get your residuals. Royalties are like residuals, and the creators of shows also get upset if they find out someone is presenting their work and not paying for it. It doesn't matter if you are a community theater, a dinner theater, a high school or church, or a major regional stock theater. Royalties will vary considerably according to the nature of your production, the size of your theater, and the anticipated income of the presentation, among other factors.

And what about the shows themselves? Which ones do well and which ones just lie there? Without naming names, it's obvious that shows that were major successes on Broadway tend to have the greatest appeal in "syndication." Touring companies and big repertory companies know they will do better with a blockbuster hit than with a little known "failure." However, there are exceptions.

Some shows are too controversial for general audiences outside of New York City, even if they were hits there, such as *Sweeney Todd* and *La Cage Aux Folles*. Some shows are more appealing to Middle-America than to Broadway audiences, such as *Singing in the Rain* and *Roza*. Some are technically too difficult, such as *On the 20th Century*, to be done by small, low-budget companies, although many try. One of the biggest criterion is cast breakdown. A cast of all men (*1776*) is useless to a company with a large contingent of women in its ranks. A cast of four would be a bad choice for a group with thirty-five members. Some companies prefer shows with small casts (*Pump Boys and Dinettes* and *They're Playing Our Song*), few sets, and simple costumes, because those are relatively inexpensive to produce. Most schools, churches, and community groups, on the other hand, want big casts, such as *Fiddler on the Roof*, *West Side Story*, or *The King and I*, a chorus with lots of singing and dancing and, preferably, children's roles so they can include as many people as possible in the production. Some companies enjoy the more "sophisticated" and "demanding" shows like *Follies* or *Nine*, or the more unusual, less frequently performed shows, like *Lost in the Stars* and *Hair*. The biggest companies, needless to say, are not bound by the same economic or social restraints and will go for whatever is the most popular with the ticket-buying public at the time.

Do you still want to put on a show? Now you have your license and you're ready to go.

> *Neil Graeme has worked in the entertainment industry for the last 16 years in many capacities including designer, technical director, and business manager.*

5
Behind the Scenes

Versatility. Diversity of interests. We also think that being nice to people has a lot to do with it; maintaining a good attitude, a good work attitude, especially. Another part is being able to get along with your co-workers, and your manager, and your record company, and the radio people. You should always let them know that you appreciate everything that they do. Everyone you meet has something to do with your success. We don't have to take all the glory. Above all, like yourself.

The Jets, a hot top 40 group, on being asked what they think makes for longevity in the business.

The behind-the-scenes world of show business offers countless opportunities to young people seeking alternatives to careers in front of the camera. There are, for example, jobs in theater as stage managers, company managers, and general managers; in film as production assistants, assistant directors, and production office coordinators; and in TV as copy editors, camera operators, and line producers. This chapter details several of the aforementioned careers and describes how certain job holders approach their work.

CAREERS IN PRODUCTION AND DESIGN
Elsa Posey

You've tried singing, acting, and dancing but don't like being in front of an audience. You think you could be a lighting, scenic, costume, or sound designer, or work on production, planning, building, and executing the designs, or in the managerial jobs, such as production manager or stage manager, whose concern is the smooth running of all the show's components: electrical, scenic, props, costumes, sound, and special effects.

Where do you begin to get the experience for these jobs? Where do you go for training? What do you need to know to get your first job?

To prepare for a career backstage in production or design you'll need both practical hands-on experience and an education in the humanities (literature, history, art, languages), earning you a degree in theater followed by graduate study specializing in lighting, scenic, or costume design, or theater technology. You should experience many aspects of theater to determine your skills and interests before you decide on one aspect for your career backstage in production or design.

How do you get started? You probably already have!

Technicians often begin while in high school, assisting teachers with audio-visual equipment or operating a computer. They are scientifically oriented and might become engineers, mechanics, machinists, or computer operators.

Designers often begin in high school drawing things that express new ideas or new ways of doing things. Designers are artistically oriented people, who might become inventors, fashion designers, advertising, or graphic artists.

The difference is: you want to work in theater. Finding what you like to do relates to what you can do best, so try different jobs before you determine precisely what job you want in the theater. Volunteer to help the crew for school drama productions. Locate the nearest community theater and offer to help backstage. Look for a job in a summer theater or a theme park. Talk to people who work in the theater. Go to the theater whenever you can. Read about the theater. Be in a theatrical production in whatever capacity you can, even as a volunteer. You probably won't get paid while learning.

It takes persistence as well as knowledge, skills, and talent to succeed. Be prepared to work for nothing at the beginning. Do your job as well as you can no matter how small it may be; every contact you make can lead to a job.

Jerry Bloom, former electrician at the New York Shakespeare Festival, says, "It helps to be independently wealthy while you look for the first paying job! If you're not, try to find something else you do well that will support you while you are learning skills and gaining experience."

He warns that you may not be able to earn or learn enough to progress to another job pushing a scaffold around the stage and that you should have job skills in carpentry or painting. He notes that designers are not likely to wait on tables while they look for a lucky break but will take a job in theater doing carpentry, stitching, or electrical work.

Don Coleman was a junior in college when his interest in lighting became more important to him than other theater jobs. He had acted, stage managed, and done a little of everything, but designing held special interest for him. Now an assistant professor in the theater department at the University of Maryland, College Park, Don worked as a theatrical lighting designer. He advises, "If you want to be a designer, the best thing to do is to learn as much as you can about culture first."

Don recently attended an IATSE (International Alliance of Theatrical Stage Employees) conference in Anaheim, CA, where set designer Ming Cho Lee stated his belief that a strong liberal and fine arts background is preferable to specializing too early. Don agrees. "Shallowness and lack of depth in design can be the result of specializing too soon and becoming too narrow minded."

Mary Beth McCabe, President of Carp Productions, Inc., began acting in high school and community theater productions, and took summer jobs in theaters at theme parks while attending college. She moved to New York where she assisted a stage manager and got involved in stitching costumes. She got her first tour as a wardrobe assistant with a dance company through Technical Assistance Program, and has traveled as a wardrobe supervisor to six countries in two years including Brazil, Australia, Hong Kong, and Japan.

Ms. McCabe advises beginners, "Ask questions; don't assume you know it all."

She recalled a painful experience when she and a friend from college were doing electrical work at a theme park. Her 18-year-old friend was in charge of changing lamps on special effects equipment. She knew the instrument was turned off but no one had told her it was necessary to unplug the unit. The resulting residual discharge of electricity was enough to severely burn the pads of all 10 fingers. The tragedy was that her friend's college studies, talent, and ambitions were to be a concert pianist.

Ms. McCabe says, "Common sense is not enough. You need training. You need experience."

Lori Dawson, Technical Director and Designer at Dance Theatre Workshop, graduated from the University of Ohio at Akron where she studied lighting design. In high school, she was in the drama and glee clubs, but found she liked working behind the scenes.

Consequently, she worked in summer and community theater to learn more about technical production before she attended college.

"Freelance or union, you'll need all the experience you can get. Bombard the market. Send résumés and follow up with personal contacts. Put aside your pride and beg to work for nothing. If it's with the right person, at the right theater, you can get credit or learn something." Ms. Dawson adds, "You don't get paid for the first jobs; you take them to make contacts that lead to breaks later."

At Interlochen Arts Academy, in Interlochen, MI, there's a new light lab, and soon a sound lab will be ready. They seek students interested in theater craft and offer a program of individual studies geared to talented students from ninth grade to post-high school graduates who want an opportunity to work with professionals.

If you can't visit Interlochen, they interview by phone or in writing to determine individual goals. They request prospective students to submit a portfolio of design and art work, even if limited in scope.

Stephen Rinder, chair of the Division of Design and Production at Interlochen, asks his first-year students what knowledge they will need to know to be a designer in the arts.

This year's class listed over 62 professions such as historian, artist, electrician, plumber, and architect with specific knowledge in subjects such as math, engineering, history, and drawing.

You can gain valuable experience working in college productions while studying the humanities in almost every college in the country. Visit the college you are considering. Check the theater facilities available and ask what opportunities students have to work on technical production, to design, and to stage manage. For someone considering a career as a technical director or lighting designer courses in applied physics and electrical engineering, as well as applied art and art history, are helpful. Graduate work requires more specific training in theatrical techniques such as production organization, scenic construction, property making, and costume painting as well as practice in rendering, drafting, optics, physics, and engineering.

As you work you will do many jobs. You may find a job in an electronics or sound rental shop where you will assist the shop electricians by putting together the equipment needed for a production. As a designer, your first job may be assisting in a workshop produced with the intention of developing new talent — playwrights, actors, and directors as well as designers. Everyone agrees to work on the project for very little money in hope that their work will be seen. As you work you gain experience as well as learning from professionals, and others will get to know you and your work.

Finding that first job is a major undertaking. Put together a résumé, and, if you are a designer, a portfolio of your past work and previous experience to take to interviews. Check theatrical newspapers for job listings and send your resume to regional theaters, summer theaters, and theme parks.

Theater Communications Group (T.C.G.), 355 Lexington Ave., New York, NY 10017, (212) 697-5230, promotes communication between non-profit arts institutions. Its publication, *ArtSearch*, advertises job openings and internships at art institutions around the country.

Technical Assistance Program (T.A.P.) at Performing Arts Resources, Inc., 270 Lafayette Street, Suite 809, New York, NY 10012, (212) 966-8658, offers help for those starting in the business as well as those changing job levels. After a personal interview to determine your skills and experience level, they will recommend you to member organizations and theaters that call T.A.P.

Selected bibliography

Dupont, Betty, and Schlaich, Joan, eds. *Dance: The Art of Production*. Dance Horizons/Princeton Book Company, 1988.

Foke, Ann, and Harden, Richard. *Opportunities in Theatrical Design and Production*. Illinois: VGM Career Horizons, 1984.

Greenburg, Jan. *Theatre Careers: A Comprehensive Guide to Non-Acting Careers in the Theatre*. New York: Holt, Rinehart, and Winston, 1983.

Gruver, Bert. *The Stage Manager's Handbook.* Rev. ed. Hamilton, Frank. New York: Drama Book Specialists, 1972.

Williamson, Walter. *Behind The Scenes: The Unseen People Who Make Theatre Work.* New York: Walker and Company, 1987.

> *Elsa Posey is an Advisory Board Member of Performing Arts Resources, is Chair of the Studio Services Committee of the national dance association AAHPERD, and teaches ballet and children's dance at Posey School of Dance in Northport and Cold Spring Harbor, New York.*

INTERNSHIPS — PRO AND CON
John Attanas

To young people who wish to get involved in the backstage or administrative areas of show business, there can be many obstacles. Whereas there are few jobs available for prospective performers, no matter what their level of experience, there are a great many more positions waiting for the experienced stage manager, technician, or administrator. However, most young people coming straight from school do not have the experience necessary to obtain such a job. As a result, many find that the best way to get the experience needed to break into the field is by doing an internship.

What is an internship? According to Steve Kaplan, Artistic Director of New York's Manhattan Punch Line Theatre, an internship is a staff position with an organization where the rewards are not monetary, but rather in the *experience* you get from the work you do. While some organizations do pay their interns (usually large profit-making institutions such as banks or brokerage houses), in the arts, especially in the non-profit arts community, an intern will be lucky if he or she gets carfare or lunch money. Although many performing arts organizations provide perks to their interns, such as placing their names in the program, or giving them free tickets to whatever show is being performed, generally little or no money changes hands.

In some situations, especially where college credit is involved, it is the intern who *pays* for the privilege of being on the staff.

On the surface it seems a rather unfair exchange. An intern is expected to work, sometimes for many more hours than paid staff members, and in return receives nothing back from the organization other than experience and a "good night" at the end of the day. However, although fewer young people were interning with arts organizations in the late 1980s than in the early 1980s, according to Kenneth Schlesinger, former Artistic Associate at New York's Roundabout Theatre Company, doing an internship is still the best way to gain on-the-job experience, and to make contacts with people who may be able to give you paying work in the future.

How should a person go about looking for an internship? The first thing an individual must do is decide what area he or she wishes to work in, and for what type of organization. Once that is established the person should then start sending out letters of inquiry to see whether the organizations in question employ interns. In most cases, the reply will be a positive one, for nearly all arts organizations — whether they be theater companies, dance companies, TV stations, or art galleries — employ interns on a fairly regular basis. The main reason for this is to defray the cost of hiring permanent employees.

If the individual is enrolled in college at the time, he may wish to work through his department or the school's placement office. If the prospective intern is not in school, or if the school he is attending cannot be of assistance, an organization such as A.R.T./New York — which, according to its former Director of Membership Services, Catherine MacNeil, has a 100% record of placing interns with theaters throughout New York City — can be helpful in finding a position for the person. For people who wish to intern with organizations outside of New York, the publication *ArtSearch*, published by Theater Communications Group, which lists both internships and paying jobs, might also be of some help. Most arts professionals, however, agree that when pursuing an internship the most important thing involved is not simply getting a position, but rather getting the position you want.

"The most important thing in an internship is having a fulfilling experience," says Kathi Levitan, a former marketing director of Playwrights Horizons, who, during her tenure, employed numerous interns. "If you don't feel you will get that at one theater, try another."

Catherine MacNeil agrees, stating that she always encourages prospective interns to interview with a number of theaters, even if they are offered a position with the first organization they approach. However, if an individual is offered a position that he or she feels is right, the general recommendation is to take it and work as hard as you can.

"What you put into this is what you get out," says Paul Israel of Executive Internships, a department of City As School that places seniors from New York City's public high schools in internships of all kinds. "If a student is enthusiastic and goes into an internship with an open mind, the odds are he will have a very good experience."

What can a prospective intern expect from an internship? Mostly hard and not very glamorous work.

A typical situation is that of Robert Alfieri. When he was a senior at John Adams High School in Ozone Park, New York, Robert wanted to get a head start on college. A budding screenwriter, he thought that doing an internship with an arts organization would be a great learning experience. He contacted City As School's Executive Internship Program and worked as an intern at the Riverwest Theater. Robert worked four days a week from 10:30 AM to 5:30 PM and found that the internship more than fulfilled his expectations. While an intern, Robert reported, "It's great. It's very challenging, and I'm enjoying it a lot."

A slightly less typical situation is that of Elizabeth Karger. Now an actress living in New York, Elizabeth served as a summer apprentice at the Dorset Theater Festival, in 1986, one year after her graduation from Wesleyan University. A normal work day for her started at 9:30 AM, and did not end until 11 PM. In addition, she and her fellow apprentices were only allowed one day off every two weeks.

"Looking back, I see it as a wonderful experience," says Karger, whose duties included building sets, and working in the costume shop and as a dresser. "However, at the time I went through a whole spectrum of emotions. There were times when I said to myself, 'I can't believe I am working these hours.' But on the whole it was really fun."

While most internships are not as taxing as Elizabeth Karger's, any worthwhile internship will be both time consuming and physically draining. Ideally, an internship should be looked upon as a job; and a good intern must be as committed to it as he or she would be if a large salary were involved.

Some internships do in fact lead to jobs. Such was the case with Christina Rosati, a graduate of New York University, who was hired as an associate producer at the Manhattan Punch Line Theatre after serving as an intern during the Punch Line's One-Acts Festival.

"An internship is a balance between the employer, who has a desire to use you, and the intern, who has a desire to get new experiences, " says Christina, who is no longer with Punch Line. "If they aren't willing to give you anything else to do but lick envelopes, then the internship will not be successful. But if they are, then it can work out wonderfully for both parties."

Clearly, internships are not for everyone. Although most arts professionals say that the best time to do an internship is from late high school through early college, some young people are not ready to take on major responsibilities, and therefore should put off doing an internship until they are a little older.

"I look for someone who is outgoing and has a sense of humor," says Kenneth Schlesinger. "The best interns are fearless, easygoing, and are not thrown by what they are asked to do." Schlesinger also stresses, however, that since most interns are not paid for their service, they should be able to "draw the line," and not be forced to work excessive hours, or allow their supervisors to make unreasonable demands on them.

"Don't let your expectations get too high," says Christina Rosati, "or you might be disappointed. But don't get cynical about it, because that defeats the purpose of the internship."

Nevertheless, if you want to break into the non-performing areas of the arts, a good way to start is by doing an internship. Although the work will certainly be hard, and not always interesting, under the right circumstances the experience can be a rewarding one. The knowledge you take from it, both practical and personal, will probably be invaluable.

★

DIRECTING THE CHILD PERFORMER
Bill Persky

I've been a part of situation comedies, either as director, producer, or writer, for over 25 years. I first experienced working with children early in my career, on *The Dick Van Dyke Show*, which starred Dick Van Dyke and Mary Tyler Moore.

The average viewer probably doesn't realize it, but in the early days of television, children were used as filler in weekly episodes. They were rounding out the family which, typically, would have a mother, a father, a dog, a cat, and a kid. Very few of the stories were oriented toward the child. *Leave It To Beaver*, of course, was an exception, because that was a show about a kid. On *The Dick Van Dyke Show*, however, we would do two or so stories a year that featured the little boy who was played by Larry Matthews. Most of the other shows were about the adults, with a child needed perhaps as a catalyst for the action, but not necessarily to appear on screen more than once a week.

Today this has changed dramatically. Children are more of an emphasis in shows, primarily for two reasons. One, the audience is largely composed of kids who identify with the children they're watching. The other reason is that society has changed and children and their problems are considered more important than they were before.

Networks always update their demographics to learn who watches television at any given hour of any given day. In demographic studies over the years, they've come to learn one very important truth: children control the household television sets. Around the time of *The Dick Van Dyke Show*, television was such a new toy that it was the adults who controlled the family's viewing habits. But in television, everything reflects the sociological realities of the country and the breakdown of who the audience is. Television is about getting audience.

When divorce became a factor in American society, another reality was added to the framework of television. Now there were shows about split families. In many cases, those shows had more relevance in terms of the children who were being affected, both on and off the screen, than it did for the adults. This factor increased the number of young viewers who in turn dominated the television sets.

Kate and Allie was one show in which the issues of divorce and non-traditional families clearly reflected the time in which it was produced. As it turns out, all three of our young stars — Ari Meyers, Allison Smith, and Frederick Koehler — were from single parent homes. *Kate and Allie*, in a real sense, became their central organized family structure. It was a real family that they fit into, that had two mothers (Susan St. James and Jane Curtin), a father (me), and a steady, ongoing crew that provided a semblance, if you will, of a nuclear family.

I love to work with children. I think I work with them as though I were their father, which comes naturally, having raised three lovely daughters who spent most of their time living with me after my divorce from their mother. What I learned in raising my own children is what I apply in working with the children I direct. I never condescend to them. I am also very protective of them. When one of my own daughters wanted to be an actress, I wouldn't let her until she was old enough to do it on her own. God knows we need child actors! Still, I don't think it's a great atmosphere for kids, and I wouldn't have my child do it until she was ready for it. It's too rarefied an atmosphere for a child.

Furthermore, I think on the set children are exposed to "colorful" language that, even with reasonable self-censorship, still slips out in those moments of pique. Eventually, you find yourself treating the kids as "one of the guys." This can be very detrimental for some kids. On the other hand, Freddy Koehler literally benefited from being one of the guys because he learned how to play baseball and have other male-oriented experiences that hadn't been available to him growing up in a predominantly female household.

Additionally, I think a lot of shows are conducted in an atmosphere that simply isn't happy. I don't think this is true of the shows I am involved with, because I determined long ago that I wanted my set to be a place I would enjoy going to. On some shows, however, animosity abounds. Most shows are steeped in politics and that adds to the tension and stress of the cast and crew. That also has to have an effect on the kids.

Citing *Kate and Allie* again, I should point out that working in New York was a blessing for the children, because we were out of the mainstream of show business. In Los Angeles, television and show business are a way of life and that aforementioned rarefied atmosphere is constant. But in New York, where it would have been easy for our production to take advantage of the children because child labor laws are much more lenient than they are in California, we never infringed on the children's rights. Since I've always been aware of the kids as a parent would be, I would never allow any real or perceived abuse of them as children or as actors. A large part of this attitude, which pervaded the *Kate and Allie* set, was made possible by the cooperation and understanding of the two stars, Ms. St. James and Ms. Curtin, themselves mothers.

I wish I could say that due to the success of our show and *The Cosby Show* more production is assured of coming east. It's not the case. These shows were done in New York only because the respective stars of these series wanted to work close to their families. Los Angeles-based studios are not looking to come here; it's more expensive for them, as well as more disruptive to their normal day-to-day operations. Therefore, without the presence of a strong force — star, producer, or creator — New York production will not have benefited in the long run from the success of two hit series, both of which portrayed children and families in a positive light.

I approach directing children as a playful experience. I'll often say to them, "Try this" or "Try that." I'll invent a situation for them like, "You know how you feel when you walk into a room and it's dark at night, right? Well, that's how you feel here." So my goal is to put them in touch with the feelings that they have with the hope that they'll connect. You're cluing them in to the character, but the young actor has to find the part of himself or herself that relates best to the character and put that on top of it.

I believe that children can either act or they can't. I'm not a big believer in acting schools and acting study. I admit that some brilliant actors have come out of the great acting schools and I am aware that training can increase knowledge and awareness. But, as Spencer Tracy once said, you either have it or you don't, and this is no less true of child performers than of adults.

Bill Persky was the director and producer of Kate and Allie *for five seasons. He has also been involved in creative capacities for such series as* The Dick Van Dyke Show, Spenser: For Hire, That Girl, *and* Working It Out.

Finding representation and, ultimately, work, is not simple. Being cast is often a matter of luck, timing, and any of a number of intangibles. Show business is a microcosm of life and, as in life, there are some ugly realities to contend with. Casting director Pat Golden talks about one of them.

CASTING THE MINORITY VOTE
Pat Golden

To determine which actor types are in, one has only to turn on the TV set and see who's doing the selling. It's unpredictable and there's no one formula that you can follow, but since *The Cosby Show*, Black Americans seem to be more acceptable to look at on television. Additionally, with the NAACP lobbying for the hiring of Blacks, Hispanics, and Orientals, there has definitely been a difference in the business' casting patterns and, ultimately, who is being featured.

Change is a slow process. At a seminar on non-traditional casting that I attended a few years ago at Actor's Equity, I heard my fellow Afro-Americans complain of not getting a fair shake in terms of job availability. Indeed, the Broadway scene seemed to bear them out, with all of its British imports that don't hire many minority actors.

The only exceptions were *Starlight Express* and *La Cage Aux Folles*. In the latter production, the part of the maid was played by a Black man. I remember hearing complaints that not enough Black actors were showing up to audition for the role. The part calls for the actor to play a very effeminate and flighty man. Can you blame us for wanting something better? If you realize that for years this was the only major Black role in a Broadway musical, you can certainly understand why it didn't warrant rejoicing.

As I stated, I see more Black faces in ads since *The Cosby Show* and I realize that much of this phenomenon is the result of the success of that show. There's now a certain kind of Black look that's "in." B.C., Before Cosby, and even A.C., the favorite expression most producers stuck to when they're afraid of trying something new was, "It's not what the American public wants to see." How do they know? I've heard stories about producers who, when approached with projects that have a Black slant to them, respond with, "We're not doing Black projects right now." The racism in our business — in America

— is so overt that it's enough to whittle down anyone who's ever been a victim of it.

Among the minority groups in America, Black actors get the lion's share of the jobs. Hispanic actors do have their outlet, but, unfortunately, it's not always in this country. For them, there's more of a chance at film in Puerto Rico, Mexico, and South America. For Orientals, there are even fewer opportunities. I'm delighted that Dr. Haing S. Ngor, the actor I cast in *The Killing Fields*, still works even after his Academy Award. But his story is a rarity.

There's a small group in power that's rather afraid of taking chances. They'll dictate what they think the rest of the public wants to see and will, in turn, spoon it out to us with lots of sweetener. One week you hear how "Black doesn't sell" and the next week film makers Spike Lee and Robert Townsend do very well and make money on their pictures. That's the bottom line, because money talks. There is no moral commitment to changing the plight of Black actors. There's no commitment to affirmative action. If Robert Townsend hadn't taken it upon himself to finance and direct *Hollywood Shuffle*, he'd still be waiting for Hollywood to call.

The unfortunate reality is that if a concept hasn't already made a million dollars, or hasn't experienced some popularity on one front or another, then no one takes a chance. This includes casting minority actors in what might otherwise be considered "white" roles. Television, in particular, doesn't present the real look of America — white, Black, Hispanic, Oriental, and Native American faces. On the contrary, it is completely one-dimensional.

My position as a casting director affords me the opportunity to do something about non-traditional casting and affirmative action. Regardless of my role, however, I have a mission. There are things that I need to do in this lifetime and one of those is to improve the lot of minority performers. This will happen as we change the image of how we, "the minority," are perceived.

Which brings me to the kids. I love working with children. They're at an age in which they're not jaded, in which they're waiting to find out what's up. They have so much energy, particularly teenagers. I appreciate the energy. But unless my kid had an extraordinary amount of talent, I'd encourage him or her to do something else, such as go to law school. Then, if he or she wanted to act, I'd say go ahead. But I'd rather see my child become a studio head. That's where the power lies.

The message

I say to the children: Look at role models like directors Stan Lathan, Robert Townsend, Spike Lee, and Georg Stanford Brown. Look at such management types as record producer Quincy Jones and movie executive George Jackson; respect such people as Richard Pryor, Bill Cosby, Eddie Murphy, and Diana Ross, who run their own companies. These are men and women who didn't sit around waiting for someone else to give them their chance. The business respects people who turn out quality, who take the initiative, and who make money in the process.

Many of the children whose parents are reading this book are dreaming of going into show business and may know nothing about what the business is really like. If they're dreaming of success, my advice to them is to put *work* into that dream. By this I mean don't stop dreaming, but do understand what it means to work. Work can be fun. Work doesn't have to be a drag. On the contrary, work should be synonymous with gaining practical experience and doing things.

Study your craft, learn your skills. Become quite good at being an actor if that's what you want to do. Some people have an innate gift for acting, that's true, but not most people. Be aware that at times you might have to take jobs that you might not want to take, but in the end you may benefit because you'll learn something and you'll have had the chance to exercise your craft. The more experiences you have, the better you'll be at performing.

To kids like Malcolm-Jamal Warner or Tempestt Bledsoe or Keshia Pulliam, I say something different. You folks are already there. To you I say, branch out. Don't get locked into the overly comfortable little niche that you're in on television. Put yourself in a position in which sooner or later you can create a lifestyle in which you can grow and expand, as performers and as people.

And when you do, I hope you'll be able to take a few deserving people along with you. It will be real good to see that happen.

Pat Golden and her associate, John McCabe, have cast the films The Killing Fields, Blue Velvet, Krush Groove, Beat Street, The Handmaid's Tale, *and* New Jack City. *Ms. Golden was recently awarded an Artios Award from the Casting Society of America for her work on the film* Platoon.

JINGLE JUNGLE: HEARD BUT NOT SEEN
Ari Gold

Another normal day. My mother picks me up from school at 3:00, giving me time to warm up my voice on the way to the studio. I arrive at the pre-planned time, as dictated by the producer. Once in the studio, I can't help wonder what kind of voice I'll have today in the "background." First they play the jingle. I listen to it a few times until I know it, and then, PRESTO! It's showtime, folks.

I sing jingles on commercials, the catchy songs that are used to sell the product.

The producers know me as the "prince of voice-overs." That's because my voice is versatile. I can do many different characters. Once, I had a commercial for Zest Soap and I sang the jingle as Ari. Then they wanted it to be different so they told me to do it younger. I did it as a five-year-old. Then they told me to do it as a five-year-old *girl*! That's not uncommon. I've been on a cartoon series for Jem in which I'm a Chinese girl. For Burger King, I was a two-year-old black boy. Once my agent asked if I could do a Russian boy for the now defunct TV series *The Equalizer*.

The job I did for *The Equalizer* was a voice-over. Voice-overs are when you talk behind the screen. Sometimes, for a commercial, you can be the announcer, and other times it's just one of the characters. One of the first voice-overs I had took exactly one and one-half minutes. I walked into the studio, the producers played the commercial, told me what to say and where to say it. When the time was right, I said, "Delicious," and from that one take I made $4000.

Another time, I went for an audition for Tronalane, and all I had to say was "Aw, Grandpa." In the commercial, my grandpa couldn't take me to the zoo because he had constipation, so I, of course, was disappointed. When I went in for the audition, they told me to say it disappointedly, but *not to whine*. So I said, "Aw, Grandpa," just as I was told. After speaking my lines, the casting director just said, "Thank you, bye," common words casting directors use when they mean to say, "Don't call us, we'll call you." However, I got the job because I didn't whine — and the job proved to be a big radio spot.

Sometimes voice-overs or jingles require lip-synching. Commercial lip-synching is not as easy as mouthing words to a rock song — far from it! It's one of the hardest things to do in a commercial. For Toys 'R Us, I had to see how the child on the screen was mouthing the words. I then had to put my voice to the timing of his silent voice.

Hi Pro Glo had a jingle that I did lip-synching on, too. The client wanted it to look like the person on the screen was really singing or talking these words. Don't fool yourself when you see a three-year-old with a good singing voice.

For jingles, you don't need a great voice that has vibrato. A producer wants a sweet, cute voice that can carry a tune, catch on to a melody quickly, and is also able to do harmony. If the client or producer is doing a commercial and is looking for a six- to eight-year-old and they see a 12- to 14-year-old, they tend not to believe that he or she can sing that young.

Another interesting aspect of the business is when the client gives different words to a jingle to several producers. Each makes up a different jingle for the client. The producers then call me and I do the demo for them. That demo is sent to the client and they pick the one they like best. For each producer, I do a different jingle. Once the final one is picked, it goes on TV. Every time it's aired, the singers, actors, and musicians get paid residuals.

I've been in shows and in some on-camera commercials and TV movies, but I'm mostly heard. At this stage, I'd also like to be seen, and I hope that's what the future holds.

Ari Gold has done over 350 jingles and voice-overs in the last nine years. He is currently performing throughout the New York tri-state area with the band, The Misconceptions, and has recently recorded his first album as a solo artist. In addition, Ari has been on camera in soap operas such as One Life To Live *and* All My Children *and in numerous television movies and commercials.*

THE ROLE OF THE PRODUCER
Karen Schaeffer

When you watch a TV show or commercial or a VCR tape, the credits always name a producer. Just what is a producer? Have you ever thought about what goes into one of these productions? There are many questions to answer and details to attend to before somebody's big idea ever makes it to your TV screen.

First, you need a marketable idea: a concept that someone — a broadcast or cable network, or a financial investor — will pay you to produce. Then, a script. Then, well, what to shoot? How large a cast? Principals? Extras? Union or non-union? Voice-overs? Male or Female? Where to shoot? Indoors or outdoors? On location or build a set? How to shoot? Film or video? What will we see? Set design? Props? What will we hear? Natural sound? Sound effects? Original music? Canned music? Can we buy the rights? How will graphics enhance the production? Slides? Paint box? 3-D? Animation? How will we package it? How will we market it? Promote it? Should we bring in sponsors? How will we stay under budget?

Each of these elements must be addressed separately, yet with the intention of bringing all of them together to achieve the desired effect of the complete production. An orchestra works the same way. The conductor draws out the sound he wants from the violins, violas, cellos, basses, the woodwinds, brass, and percussion, then fuses the ensemble so each section's voice complements the others and works *in concert*. The person who pulls all of the elements together, who orchestrates the production, is the producer.

Production is broken into three stages: pre-production is all the preparatory work before shooting; production is the actual shooting of the action; post-production is the stage in which the footage is edited, and the music, sound effects, and graphics are added to finish the program.

Although each stage demands dozens of decisions, there is one unifying element that dictates the answer to almost any question: the budget. The budget is the amount of money provided to cover the cost of the entire production. The producer must work within the budget to see that appropriate funds are allocated for each part of the production, and keep an eye on the spending to see that the total amount spent does not exceed the available funds. In production, if the sets cost more than expected, then the producer may have to scrimp on props to break even.

In pre-production, the producer prepares for the production day, called "the shoot." The key in pre-production is to know what's going to be shot, and to recognize everything that could conceivably go wrong, and to be ready for it. I produced a program that involved children from four months to five years old. Anyone who has worked with very young children will tell you that shooting isn't scheduled by the director; it's scheduled by the babies. Babies are generally happy to cooperate — that is, until they're hungry or tired. One particular scene featured the star (the star was not easy to get) with a 10-month-old (the babies were easy to get). In the middle of the scene the baby started crying. No amount of cajoling or cooing could stop him. In this situation, having no back-up baby would have cost the production time and money plus the cast's and crew's good spirits. But in pre-production, arrangements had been made for plenty of stand-in babies, and we didn't miss a beat.

During the actual production, the producer continues to orchestrate the elements to keep the production running smoothly. I was on an all-night shoot in which we had an extremely difficult goal of shooting three commercials, the last of which required rain, in three locations between sundown and sunup. I don't have a direct line to controlling the weather, but I do realize what I can control, and we had the local Harbor Patrol at the ready to provide our own "rain." Our allotted time got shorter and shorter as dawn approached, and if we were still going to complete the third spot before sunrise, we wouldn't have time to get the artificial rain "just right." We had no choice but to let the Harbor Patrol and our rain go. The crew continued setting up. Soon everything was in place and we started the cameras rolling. Just at that moment the sky opened up, and as if to say, "Action!," released a drenching rain all over us. Now, I couldn't take credit for supplying the rain at the right time, but I like to think that my connections had something to do with it.

Post-production is like cooking and the producer is the chef. You mix your separate ingredients in different amounts until your product has the perfect blend of tastes. The same production elements used in different combinations can give you a program that's sweet and sour or hot and spicy. That's how one movie can have two different ratings. An R-rated, adult film can have some of its ingredients edited out to make a PG version of the same film.

There's great satisfaction that comes from following a production from creation to completion. It's challenging to become totally immersed in a project, learn all about the subject matter, and then move on to something brand new. And it's also rewarding to consider that your work may help someone you'll never know learn something new, appreciate an issue better, or simply entertain.

There's no established career path that leads to becoming a producer. But there's a way to see if a job in production suits your talents: take a job, any job at all, in a creative environment. There you'll learn the business, the nuances, and the subtleties that go into any type of production, and see where you and your talents best fit and can grow. Find your niche and take it from there. Maybe someday, the rain will start just at the right moment for *you*.

Karen Schaeffer is an award-winning televi-sion producer and member of New York Women In Film.

PRODUCTION OFFICE COORDINATOR
Eileen Eichenstein

I wish that I could invite every reader to visit me at my production office, the central point from which the films we produce are coordinated. Watching me work would help you understand what I do, but you'd have to stand in a corner, because if you stood anywhere else, you'd be in my way. There's no place for you to sit because every chair at every desk is in use. You could munch on a piece of cheese that the craft services provide for us and you could have a cup of coffee — that we've got plenty of. I don't want to seem like an ungracious host, but I hope you'll make your visit short and sweet. And don't be offended if I don't acknowledge your comings and goings. I can't. I'm *that* busy.

Seeing me at work is like watching someone in the middle of a war zone. The enemies include lack of time; inordinate amounts of pressure; demands, both reasonable and unreason-able, from everybody and their mothers; short shooting sched-ules, and sometimes long shooting schedules. I'm at the center of everything that happens on the film.

If the camera breaks down, guess who has to line up a new one? If the assistant director gets sick, guess who canvasses the files to come up with a replacement? If an actor loses a tooth during a 3 AM shoot, guess who has to find an all-night dentist? If someone hurts his back on the set, guess who's going to find a doctor? If a supporting actor is flying in for the film, guess who's the only one who knows what happens to him from the moment his plane lands? A production office coordinator — POC for short — has to learn to do it all, and to juggle many similar efforts at the same time.

I started in this business 10 years ago, after leaving a job in the distribution end of production. I wanted to be more creative and more involved in every aspect of filmmaking. When I got my first real POC job, I began to learn it all. From typing the actors' contracts, to scheduling the work day, to getting permits for minors, to making sure that the more important actors were covered by cast insurance, to making appointments with the doctors who had to give the actors their physicals — I learned to do it! I found myself working one night until 4 AM typing the next day's schedule — the call sheet — in a little hotel room in Connecticut, and I smiled to myself. I was happy. I had the fever! I said to myself, "This is my life now."

When I say that if you visit me you'll have to stay out of my way, it has more to do with my being able to keep my concentration than it has to do with being rude. I can work for 17 or 18 hours at a stretch and even though I love my work, the long hours are more a result of job design than of dedication. I can't take a lunch break because when the crew is on lunch, they call the office and I have to be there to handle the problems that arise. Your priorities revolve around the needs of the crew at a given moment. When the guys are out there shooting on the set, the POC's job is to get them what they need, and to do it in the most expedient way.

I learned a long time ago that money can't buy knowledge. At this point in my career, I'm a wealth of information that any production manager (PM) would find indispensable, and so are the many other POCs who work in the film business. Whether my boss is the producer or the head of the studio, he knows that all he has to say to me is "Handle it!" and it's done. We, my colleagues and I, are experts at preparing crew lists, coordinating contact sheets, locating various vendors, acquiring permits from the Mayor's Office for Film, Theatre, and Broadcasting, dealing with film and sound labs, reporting to the studios how much footage was shot and whether things are behind or ahead of schedule, and knowing all the unions' regulations. All this just touches the surface of what I do in a given day.

The major part of a POC's job is getting along with a multitude of personalities. An important quality is a sense of humor. Perseverance is important, too. Patience — what patience? — is essential, especially when you deal with personalities (I refer to them as "artistic types") who need you to understand their needs but rarely, if ever, understand yours. Maybe the most important quality of all is an energy level that could leave a football player breathless. The POC's energy is what makes the office come together and function.

To those interested in becoming a POC, I recommend a visit to a production office. Call and say who you are and what you'd like to do. Be prepared to work as a production assistant (PA), which, although low-paying, will afford you the opportunity to learn whether this life-style is for you. If you're good, you'll learn to absorb every bit of information that comes your way. Although a college degree is not essential, I recommend that any young person hoping to become a POC learn basic typing skills and become computer literate.

Local 161 of the International Alliance of Theatrical Stage Employees (IATSE) is the union to which production office coordinators belong, and it recognizes a category known as assistant production office coordinator, or APOC, which is an entry-level position that interested candidates can apply for. The union is looking for people with one to two years of experience in the film business, with good references, who have many of the basic skills and qualities described above. Breaking into the business isn't easy on any level, but interested applicants should send their résumés to Local 161 at 1515 Broadway, Suite 601, New York, NY 10036, where they will be screened by a committee that will test selected candidates with an entrance exam designed to determine the most capable. Once admitted as an APOC, and after working for 40 weeks, an APOC can apply for an upgrade to the production office coordinator category. The good ones, the ones who learn and listen, have the best shot of going on to the better paying and more prestigious position.

While I was working on a film in Atlantic City, a reporter from a local newspaper was waiting his turn to visit the set and was told to sit in the corner of the production office, like everyone else, until a production representative was ready for him. He was genuinely surprised at all the hubbub in the office, and I found myself one of the featured players in his subsequent article. He referred to me as someone "whose epithets could shame a sailor, but a woman you would want to have on your side of the war."

I bring this up to point out to those who may see a POC's job as that of a glorified secretary that our job really is a specialty unto itself. We do what we do, well over and above the call of our job description, because we're devoted and we care about the people and the projects we work with. Sometimes we're not acknowledged as being important, and that hurts, because I know what we give. We give blood, and that's got to be worth something.

> *Eileen Eichenstein has been the production coordinator for many major motion picture and television projects including* The Fan, The Verdict, Alamo Bay, Wise Guys, *and the television series,* Tattinger's. *She has also worked as production supervisor on the films* Dirty Dancing, Teenage Mutant Ninja Turtles, *and the soon to be released* Black Rainbow.

PLAYWRITING FOR CHILDREN
Ellen Norman Melamed

Where can young people learn to write full-length scripts for theater? Why is it that aspiring professionals in the fields of dance, music, performance, and visual arts can locate a variety of workshops throughout the New York area, regardless of their ages, while they would be hard-pressed to find even one school devoted to training the next generation of playwrights?

One could argue that public schools should be responsible for providing playwriting workshops, and, thanks to organizations such as The Playwriting Project and Playwriting in the Schools, professional writers do visit classrooms on occasion. But what about the student not fortunate enough to have a playwright conduct a class? What about the student who wants — and requires — more than 50 minutes a week devoted to intensive training? Is she forced to wait until college, or to attend a summer camp that specializes in acting? Should she assume that playwriting is too difficult, that it's reserved for the adult writer?

Writing plays *is* hard work. It's also incredibly exciting to see your words come to life and to know that what you've said will reach and affect a diversity of people who find theater a vitalizing and moving experience. The script is at the heart of theater, and we've been creating theater since we were small.

Our first experience as "dramatists" probably occurred when we were dressing up in our parents' clothing, or when we prepared our Halloween costumes, or when we played "house" with our friends. It didn't matter that there was no stage; the moment we donned an ornamental hat or oversized slippers, we took on new personas. We had no scripts; our words tumbled from us, complete with expressions and without self-consciousness, as though we had rehearsed for days. Theater was part of our everyday lives. If only we had known it then and kept a supply of sharpened pencils within our reach!

We can pick up those pencils now and profit from our early experiences. Producers are eager to obtain the rights to plays catering to and created by young people. Some of our current movie makers, Steven Spielberg and Susan Seidelman, for example, were college-aged when their works were first produced, as were many well-known playwrights. It's likely that most professionals started writing long before they became successful. Creating any art involves a process, and young playwrights have an advantage over established writers: time is definitely on their side.

So you want to be a playwright

So you're ready to write a play. You've made a wise decision and you're about to embark on a rewarding journey that requires patience and persistence. You've got the idea. You've heard about a contest for young playwrights and you've decided that the next deadline — only six weeks away — will be a cinch to meet. After all, you've got this *great* idea. You're on your way.

Not so fast. You can probably count on both hands the number of playwrights who wrote their first plays, and revised, edited, and submitted them, within six weeks. And they were adults.

An idea needs to germinate. An idea is not a play. A script is not even a play; it's the tool for the actors and the director. A script has a particular format and must speak for itself. It's the inexperienced playwright who, unfortunately, ends up having to "explain" the script, and it's the rare script that needs no explanation. You're hoping to create the latter.

You'll need to plan, to devote enough time to writing and revising, to trying one ending and giving it up for a better one if the first, or for that matter, the fifth, cannot come to life. As is the case with any skill worth developing, the process of writing the play is not magical; the magic comes when the actors take your script, interpret it, nurture it, and give it a life of its own.

Start with reading

Read ancient drama and comedy; you'll be surprised at the relevance and universality of the plays of Shakespeare and Aristophanes. Read contemporary drama and find role models whose plays you love to read and reread. Familiarize yourself with the elements of dramatic literature: plot, characterization, conflict and resolution, dialogue, and stage directions. Most importantly, don't be intimidated by what you don't know about the theater. Read voraciously and take yourself seriously as a writer — and as a reader.

Play around with the plays you read. Change endings, create new characters, add conflicts. Act plays out. Whenever possible see plays performed. Theater is available everywhere; you don't need to go to Broadway. There are student discounts and matinee performances that cost a few dollars more than a movie. Read theater reviews in newspapers and magazines. Write your own reviews for school and community papers.

Carry a notebook with you

Write short scenes in it. When you're on a bus or waiting on a line jot down conversations you overhear. Some of the most dramatic and comedic material is based on everyday interactions. The screenplay of Woody Allen's *Annie Hall* and the staged play of Neil Simon's *Broadway Bound* exemplify well the drama inherent in daily life. Pay attention to detail, to movement, to silence. A play, like a poem or a dance, has its own choreography, and as the choreographer it is your job to place your characters in an environment and to determine their fate. Speak for your characters, but listen to what they have to say, too. Write scenes frequently and eventually you will be ready to turn that great idea into a viable and marketable script.

If you're interested in playwriting and think you'll fare better without classroom or private instruction, you might begin by reading Carol Korty's *Writing Your Own Play*. If you prefer to work with a theater family, TADA! may be right. If you've written for a while and want to enter a contest, there's the Young Playwright's Foundation. If you want private instruction or would like to have playwrights visit your school, read on. For the sheer pleasure of broadening your horizons in the area of children's theater, look into what's available at the 52nd Street Project.

TADA!
120 West 28th Street, 2nd Floor
New York, NY 10001
(212) 627-1732

The Theatre and Dance Alliance (TADA!), created in 1984, provides young performers with an opportunity to explore their craft. The ensemble has grown from a core group of 15 to more than 70 between the ages of six and 17. They come from the metropolitan New York area and are selected for their talent, creativity, and willingness to learn. Professional experience is not essential, and training is offered in voice, dance, performance, and stage technique. Rehearsals and performances are after school and on weekends and are conducted in a supportive and professional environment.

The company has produced 225 performances of 12 original works by contemporary and established artists. Three or four productions are added to the repertoire annually and some are remounted during later seasons. Some are adaptations of children's literature, such as the Spring 1985 *How to Eat Like a Child*, based on the book by Delia Ephron.

A variety of workshops that concentrate more on training and collaboration than on stardom is offered by the company. In addition to after-school and summer training, TADA! provides in-school workshops for grades 2 through 8. High school and college students have the opportunity to gain experience as stage managers, directors, and assistants in the Internship Program. Although TADA! does not currently offer playwriting classes, the possibility of workshops beginning soon is promising. The company does, however, accept scripts by young writers, and seeks submissions that require child actors but are appropriate for adult as well as young audiences. There is no minimum or maximum number of characters required in the script. Writers should submit their works with a self-addressed stamped envelope if return of the script is expected. You can expect a response within three months after submission.

The Foundation of The Dramatists Guild
234 W. 44th St.
New York, NY 10036
(212) 575-7796

When composer Stephen Sondheim visited the Royal Court's Young Writers' Festival in London, he was impressed with the professionalism of the young English playwrights. Returning to the U.S. determined to create a similar program, he proposed that the Dramatists Guild, Inc., America's professional organization of playwrights and composers, be the sponsor. In 1981 the Foundation of the Dramatists Guild was formed.

The Foundation is known for two annual playwriting contests, but offers much more. The *Playwrights in Residence* program enables professional writers to work in New York City schools. Classes receive 12 to 15 hours of instruction, and teachers work with playwrights in a program offered during the summer. The Foundation sponsors the annual *Young Playwrights Festival*, which includes two contests, and if you're a New York City high school student, you may enter both.

The *New York City High School Playwriting Contest* is held in June each year. There are approximately 300 entrants annually and each receives a certificate from the Dramatists Guild. Cash awards are granted. The grand prize is $250 and there are several smaller awards.

The *National Playwriting Contest*, in conjunction with Playwrights Horizons, accepts submissions. Playwrights must be under the age of 19. Those whose works are selected will participate in rehearsals of their plays prior to production. In 1987, 12 plays were selected; in a given year, about a dozen may be given staged readings and three or four may be fully produced at Playwrights Horizons. The plays will tour 10 New York City schools and the winners are invited to join the Guild. All entrants receive detailed evaluations, so even if your script isn't selected, you stand to benefit from a professional critique.

If you want to enter the contest ...

Submit a script about any subject and of any length. You may collaborate, but all writers must have been under the age of 19 on July 1. You may submit more than one play. You may not submit screenplays, musicals, or adaptations of other authors' works. Type and securely fasten the pages of the script. Include your name, birthdate, home address, and telephone number on the title page. Keep a copy of the script; the original won't be returned, but you will be notified when your script is received. Submit the script yourself; parents and teachers may not submit for you. Mail scripts to: Young Playwrights Festival at The Foundation of The Dramatists Guild.

Here are some hints to help polish your work: Avoid the use of a narrator. Include stage directions, but convey appropriate information through dialogue whenever possible. Try to limit the number of actors to no more than 10. Keep in mind that your play will be performed on a stage, so elaborate settings should be avoided. Check a printed script for correct format and page layout.

The Foundation will accept telephone calls from those with questions about the Festival.

The 52nd Street Project

c/o The Ensemble Studio Theatre
549 W. 52nd Street
New York, NY 10019
(212) 247-4982

It is obvious to young and old alike that The 52nd Street Project is not exclusively for children. A joint creation of the Police Athletic League and the Ensemble Studio Theatre, the Project was founded in 1979 to produce original plays and musicals written by adults for a company of children from the economically depressed Times Square and Clinton areas of New York City. The emphasis shifted from adult-created plays to plays written by children, when playwright Daniel Judah Sklar introduced his *Playmaking Program* to the Project in 1987.

"Daniel shows us how to write about the characters we make up in our plays, who they are, what they're afraid of, where they live, and what they want in life," says Artiba Fortune, young author of *Lovers*. Written in 1987, it was Artiba's first play. He came up with the idea when Willie Reale, Artistic Director of the Project, suggested that the playwrights create something for Valentine's Day. "I was so excited to finish it, but when we all went to the country, Willie reminded me that I really wasn't finished at all."

"Going to the country" refers to the One-on-One Program, in which a child is matched with a professional playwright to spend a summer week in upstate New York to work intensely developing a two- or three-character script for future production. Playwrights have included Thomas Babe and Jose Rivera; actors who have participated include Kate Nelligan, Treat Williams, and Kathy Bates.

"In class, children learn theater games and character development. They really enjoy watching their scripts come out of class improvisations," says Sklar. "This year they're particularly excited because Teachers and Writers Press will be publishing an anthology of their plays."

Playwrights and actors between the ages of seven and 12 who live in the Clinton or Times Square areas can call the Project for membership information. High school students who need not live in the neighborhood, can also call to apply for technical internship positions. Call or write for a schedule or for information. Performances are free to the public.

In-school playwriting programs

The Playwriting Project
PO Box 20217
Cathedral Finance Station
New York, NY 10025
(212) 662-7217

For the last five years, students in grades 3 through 12 have been creating their own "Playwriting Packets" as members of the Project. During the 10- or 15-session classroom residency, they learn topic selection, character development, conflict and resolution, improvisation, and dramatic structure. Each completes a play and it's reviewed, edited, and revised. Plays are anthologized, produced, and videotaped by the class. Teacher-training, advanced playwriting, and across-the-curriculum workshops are available. The Project is directed by this writer, Ellen Norman Melamed.

Playwriting in the Schools
425 Lafayette Street
New York, NY 10003
(212) 598-7184

Since 1985, Joseph Papp, through the New York Shakespeare Festival, has offered playwriting workshops for students in grades 6 through 9. Playwrights and teachers work together, using techniques of acting, directing, improvisation, and script writing. Workshops include performances given by the Shakespeare Festival. Other activities include readers' theater, visits from theater professionals to classrooms, Public Theater Programs, an annual compilation of short plays written by New York City students, and intensive teacher training. Contact Arthur Wilson for further information.

> *Ellen Norman Melamed has an MA in theater education from Columbia University and is the creator of The Playwriting Project. A former actress and English teacher, she is a playwriting consultant in New York, and is writing a book about The Playwriting Project. In addition, Ellen has received the National Centers of Teaching Excellence Award from 1989 through 1991 and she is currently listed in the* Who's Who of American Education.

LOOK MA — NO HANDS!
CIRCUS OF THE KIDS
Alan Simon

"It looks easy," I say to Michelle Treistman, as we watch a talented young man named Jude Kleila execute a perfect move from one trapeze to the next. I even try to believe it.

We're both attending a class in trapeze skills that Bruce Pfeffer, director of Circus of the Kids (COTK), is teaching. We're at the group's summer home, French Woods Festival of the Performing Arts, a performing arts camp, where Michelle and Jude are campers, and Pfeffer's Circus is something of an in-house institution.

"Remember," warns Michelle, "you'll be 32 feet off the ground, with nothing but a net between you and another eight feet of air!"

"It's something I have to do," I tell her. The kids in Pfeffer's program *know* their skills, and many of them are part of his performing troupe. Not just anyone can be a part of the troupe, only those who exhibit strong technique — and a certain amount of fearlessness. There was no better way to get to know how COTK takes the fear out of the youngsters and instills in them a feeling of self-confidence than to be a part of the group for an afternoon and experience the act myself.

Michelle Treistman is trying to encourage me for my eventual Tarzan swing. I listen to her talk about her trapeze experiences so that I can build up my self-confidence. When she first attempted the trapeze several summers before, she says, she was as daring as anyone. "But," confesses Michelle, "although I'm not exactly scared of heights, I don't like them much.

"The first time I encountered the flying trapeze, I remember climbing up, then being lifted to the bar, and then, eventually, being coerced to let myself off the pedestal board. After awhile, when I got used to it, I took the safety lines off. This year, I'm doing the act. It's been a lot of work, but I can't tell you just how much being part of Circus of the Kids means to me," she asserts.

Most of the youngsters who partake in COTK classes feel the same way as Michelle does about the traveling Tallahassee-based circus. Indeed, many of them said that COTK fulfilled their childhood fantasy of running away and joining the circus.

Flying Trapeze: Brad Verebay (coach) catching a plange.
Photo courtesy of Circus of the Kids

Bruce Pfeffer giving instructions to the Ring Master.
Photo courtesy of Circus of the Kids

For Bruce Pfeffer, Circus of the Kids is his fantasy come true. As a boy, Pfeffer fell in love with the big top after seeing a circus group from Florida State University perform. "From that moment on," he says, "I had already run away and joined up. It was just a question of time before I had my own circus to run away with."

Until establishing his own circus, Pfeffer honed his considerable skills with a local city-sponsored recreation circus in Florida called the Little Big Top Circus. He worked around the country as a performer, juggler, and teacher of circus skills. It was at a Club Med in the Bahamas, where he was working as the circus skills teacher of the children's mini-club, that he hit upon the idea of a circus of the kids.

Says Bruce, "The idea was to build a fantasy world for the kids during their week's vacation. We'd set up the equipment, then teach the kids how to use it. After learning it, they'd get into costumes and perform for an audience." The idea was a good one, and Pfeffer incorporated it into a year-round operation. Its purpose is to bring in a group of circus-trained professionals to work with kids on everything from trapeze to juggling, from trampoline to clowning, from mini-tramp to the five-man-bike, where five kids sit atop each other's shoulders while riding a bicycle.

To have a Circus of the Kids program in your community requires a sponsoring organization, such as a camp like French Woods Festival, or a school system, such as several in Florida, Canada, and Massachusetts. COTK is often hired by local recreation departments to teach the community children. Sometimes they're hired by resorts like Grossinger's in upstate New York to do a show with their more seasoned youngsters.

Tammy Lutter, associate director of COTK, explains, "We're hired for one or two weeks, which is the sponsoring organization's prerogative. We'll provide a group with four distinct programs to choose from when they contract with our company. If we're going into a school, for example, we'll first offer that school a physical education program that will incorporate circus skills. Instead of playing kickball and volleyball, we'll teach flying trapeze, mini-tramp, and other trapeze acts."

She continues, "In the evening, we'll offer a full-fledged program, much more show-oriented. The kids treat it as if it's a varsity club or any other after-school activity. It's like performing the class play: you have to be there every day to rehearse and improve. Those who work hard get the chance to perform in the show that's put on at the end of the contractual period.

"In this way," Lutter concludes, "we can give the kids a bit of circus during the day, while at night we can delve into the details of circus performance. So beginners and advanced performers alike get a taste of it."

In addition to teaching circus skills, Bruce Pfeffer takes COTK into the classroom, as a learning adjunct to regular academic studies. In association with Jim Carter, a flying trapeze buff who is the assistant dean of the College of Arts and Sciences of the University of Louisville, and Carter's wife Elizabeth, Pfeffer offers "Circus Across the Curriculum," a comprehensive syllabus that teaches the basic subjects amid a circus motif.

There are separate curricula for reading and literature, expository and creative writing, mathematics and science, history and geography, and performing and fine arts. Each one of the curricula is broken into sections that would be appropriate for children from kindergarten through 12th grade. In math, for example, an elementary school student might be asked to figure how much is spent if a family buys three tickets of admission to the circus at $5 per ticket. A high school student, on the other hand, might have to find the length of a piece of wire given the height of the pole to which it's attached and the angles it makes with the pole and the ground.

By placing academics at the core of its offerings, Circus of the Kids has lasting value for the children it works with, long after the circus has left town.

Meanwhile, Jude Kleila's executing some brilliant spins overhead, just as I'm assessing what it is I've gotten myself into. It seems to me that before you can climb up and let go, you have to get yourself past the point of approaching the trapeze. So I ask Michelle Treistman, perhaps stalling for time, "What are those movements that Jude is doing?"

"Bruce teaches us the good-looking, simple tricks," Michelle says. "When Jude hangs upside down, he's doing a *kneehang*, which is just what it says it is." The young man is hanging upside down from his knees even as we speak. So is my stomach.

"Eventually," she continues, "one person from that trapeze (she points left) will fly over to another person from that trapeze (she points right). They may even do a *catch*, which is when the flier on the left, holding onto the bar, meets the catcher at the top of the swing on the right, and grabs on to his hands, and they both swing together. Then, if he's good, the guy holding on will turn around in the air and catch the bar from which he just flew off, which should be there waiting for him.

"That's a *plange*," she says, pointing to Jude who's in an inverted hang position, and being supported by the small of his back." With my heart in my mouth, I wonder aloud how anyone gets over the fear.

"It just happens," Michelle assures me. "Bruce teaches us that if you fall the right way — on your back — you'll be all right. If you fall on your stomach or on your side, you risk whiplash, or worse. I conquered my fear by falling the wrong way and not getting hurt. After that, I learned how to control my fall."

Jude Kleila finally finishes his workout, and it's my turn, if I want to take it. I'm not quite ready, so I try a diversionary tactic and ask Jude what Circus of the Kids means to him. "It has taken over my life," he says matter-of-factly.

"I've learned to trust my fellow performers and to work with them. I've learned self-discipline; I've gained self-esteem. Learning circus skills has helped me build up my body. I care about what I eat and what I look like. Learning circus skills has made me do better in school."

Jude explains that he was having difficulty with algebra at the beginning of the school year. Midway through the first semester, he remembered something Bruce had taught him in camp, which was to do what the teacher said and to let it work for him. "I ended up second in the class by the end of the year," Jude says smiling.

As an afterthought, almost as if he's reading my mind, he says, "You have nothing to fear when Bruce is around. He's the greatest!"

With that vote of confidence, and an encouraging pat on the back from Michelle and Jude, I'm ready to try to fly. Jude scurries up the ladder that hangs down from the pedestal board to the net, and waits there to coach me through my first session.

It's no small matter getting up that ladder, and I dare not look down. I suddenly realize I'm scared of heights. No matter, there's no turning back, and once I'm on the pedestal board, the only way out is down.

Jude puts the safety lines onto my belt, which Bruce controls from below. "Nothing can go wrong, Alan," Pfeffer insists. Sure, sure, I'm thinking to myself cynically. What choice do I have now but to trust the guy?

I can't reach the bar, even standing on the pedestal board. Never did I curse being a short man as much as I did at that moment. Jude had to lift me in the air just to help me hold onto the trapeze. "I hate not being in control," I think, but this is no time to curse nature, especially when I'm about to defy it.

"Just let your feet slip out from under you," Bruce shouts. It's not my feet I'm worrying about, it's my hands slipping off the bar, it's a fear of falling *off* the net, it's the fear of looking foolish in front of the kids, it's ... I can feel my heart pounding.

I let go. I hear a comic book sound, something like "Aaaaaaeeeee." It's coming from *my* throat. I'm holding on. I'm flying! The kids are clapping!

"Now, just drop," says the calm and collected Pfeffer, as I hang in midair. I do as I'm told, and, with Bruce holding the reins, I land standing up.

"How was it?" asks Michelle.

"I survived it fine," I say, my pulse returning to its normal pace.

"It's addicting, isn't it?" yells Jude from above.

I look at Bruce Pfeffer and smile. "It sure is," I answer truthfully.

✪

THE ARTS RECOGNITION AND TALENT SEARCH
Suzette L. Harvey

Many organizations and agencies manage searches and competitions of all kinds for talented young performers. However, few, if any, can match the opportunities and continuing support of the National Foundation for Advancement in the Arts (NFAA).

The Arts Recognition and Talent Search (ARTS) program is the primary activity of NFAA, a Miami-based non-profit organization established in 1981 to identify, encourage, and support young artists. It is the only organization in the country that recognizes talent in all the art disciplines: dance, music, theater, visual arts, and writing.

The nationwide ARTS program provides high school age actors, dancers, musicians, visual artists, and writers with cash awards totaling up to $400,000 and $3 million in scholarship opportunities each year. ARTS has been described as one of the largest sources of private funding for young people in the country. Equally important, ARTS gives young artists the chance to be evaluated and coached by prominent artists and educators.

ARTS dance and music awardees have found successful careers with the New York City Ballet, American Ballet Theatre, and Dance Theatre of Harlem, and the symphony orchestras of Chicago, Philadelphia, Detroit, and Cleveland, respectively. Theater awardees have performed in Broadway productions including *Brighton Beach Memoirs, Tap Dance Kid, A Chorus Line*, and *Cats*. Visual arts awardees have exhibited in renowned galleries such as Daniel Maher in Los Angeles. Writing awardees have been published in *The New Yorker, The Village Voice*, and major newspapers around the country.

Each year between 5,000 and 7,000 17- and 18-year-old writers and performing and visual artists apply to the ARTS program in hopes of making it to the final adjudications of the program, which are held each January in Miami.

NFAA conducts a national media campaign to promote the program, including announcements on network and cable television stations, such as MTV and the Arts & Entertainment Network. It also distributes ARTS applications to every public and private high school in the nation.

Deadlines for applying to each year's ARTS contest are June 1 (for regular registration) and October 1 (for late registration). The regular application deadline carries a $25 fee; the late registration a $35 fee. Once the ARTS office receives the application form and fee, each applicant is sent a packet which describes to the artist how his/her work should be presented. Dance and theater applicants submit videotapes of themselves, musicians submit audiotapes, visual artists submit portfolios of slides, and writers submit samples of their manuscripts.

All ARTS applications are screened by panels of prominent artists and educators in the five disciplines. After two rounds of judging, the number of young artists invited to participate in the third and final adjudications of the program, called ARTS

Week, is reduced to about 150. During ARTS Week, the ARTS award candidates can anticipate a vigorous schedule of auditions, master classes, workshops, and interviews.

David Burge, Professor of Piano, Eastman School of Music, University of Rochester; Luis Avalos, actor and screenwriter; Bill Jay, Professor of Photography, Arizona State University and John Rothchild, acclaimed author, University of Illinois; are among the distinguished list of judges for ARTS 89-90.

Virtually all ARTS award candidates who come to Miami for ARTS Week earn unrestricted cash awards. These cash awards are allotted as follows: $3,000 for Level I, $1,500 for Level II, and $500 for Level III. NFAA also awards non-cash Honorable Mention certificates. Most of the Honorable Mention award winners — those not invited to Miami but still deemed deserving of recognition — are selected after the second round of judging.

Of the 92 talented high school seniors who were invited to ARTS Week '88, 81 shared $136,000 in cash awards. A total of 275 applicants earned Honorable Mention awards.

Since the ARTS award candidates are not judged against one another, but against a standard of excellence appropriate for their age and art field, any number of top awards can be awarded in a particular discipline. For example, of the 20 musicians who participated in ARTS Week '88, five were Level I, six Level II, and nine Level III.

For young artists interested in attending universities or arts institutions before pursuing professional careers, applying to ARTS can let them get a jump on available scholarships. Through NFAA's Scholarship List Service, more than 150 top universities and art institutions across the country receive the authorized names of the ARTS applicants for recruiting purposes. These premier institutions actively recruit ARTS applicants by providing them with scholarship opportunities and other encouragements.

A total of approximately $3 million has been put aside specifically for ARTS applicants by these institutions, which include Carnegie Mellon University, Cornell University, Manhattan School of Music, Parsons School of Design, New York University, University of Texas at Austin, and the University of Southern California.

For the top ARTS awardees, their involvement in NFAA is only a beginning. Not only do they earn unrestricted cash awards and receive scholarship assistance from prominent colleges and universities nationwide, but also from these awardees NFAA nominates up to 50 to be named Presidential Scholars in the Arts by the White House Commission on Presidential Scholars, the highest honor a high school senior can receive. The White House Commission selects up to 20 of the 50 nominees for this high honor, along with 121 seniors chosen nationally for their academic achievements.

All Presidential Scholars are honored in Washington, DC in June during Presidential Scholars National Recognition Week. While in Washington, the artistic and academic scholars participate in a full slate of activities, including a private ceremony with the President at the White House. The dance, music, and theater Presidential Scholars in the Arts are presented in performance at the John F. Kennedy Center for the Performing Arts, and the visual artists and writers have their works exhibited at a prominent Washington, DC gallery. Each Presidential Scholar receives a Presidential Medallion and a $1,000 cash award in addition to the ARTS award presented by NFAA.

For further information about the ARTS program or for an application, write or call: ARTS, 300 N.E. 2nd Avenue, Miami, FL 33132-9990, (305) 347-3416.

National Foundation for Advancement in the Arts, 3915 Biscayne Blvd., Miami, FL 33137, (305) 573-0490 (day), (305) 437-2248 (evening).

Suzette Harvey is Communications Associate at the National Foundation for Advancement in the Arts.

6
Health

In general, people want you to fail, people want you to mess up. People love to talk, first of all. It's a hard lesson to learn. Whether you're successful or not, people talk. But people are generally interested in you messing up, to not succeed. I mean, aside from, maybe, your mother. If you're successful, people can't wait to see you not successful. They'll try to set you up. And you can use that for or against yourself. It can affect you, or you can use it to be more effective.

Anthony Michael Hall, featured on Saturday Night Live, *and in* The Breakfast Club

Being healthy is more than just being free of disease.

Young performers stay healthy by balancing their life-style. Having a supportive family environment, a positive outlook on school and career, and the ability to keep the ever-changing business in perspective, are key to any performers physical and mental well-being.

It can't hurt to eat well, to ensure a mind that's alert and a body that's prepared for the rigors of a day of production. And eating well, i.e., in a nutritionally sound manner, may be simpler than you think.

Dr. Ibrahim Abdul-Malik is a health counselor/fitness consultant, who is also an international educator. He has taught at all grade levels, from kindergarten through college. His tutoring experiences with performing youngsters include several tours with *The Tap Dance Kid* and four seasons with *The Cosby Show*.

This is an open letter to one of his students:

Dear Mark:

I can almost see the broad smile on
your face when you realized that this
letter is from me. I'll bet that you
muttered something like: "Dr. Ibrahim
is up to his old tricks again." And why
not? The fact that I do not see you as
regularly as when you were my student
does not make me any less interested in
you and your eating habits.

I remember the pizzas with double
cheese and pepperoni, washed down with
copious quantities of Pepsi, and the almost daily lunch orders of McDonald's
quarter pounders with extra fries and a
large milk shake. Oh, you occasionally
varied your orders, getting Burger King
or White Castle, but when you really
wanted to feast it was Kentucky Fried
Chicken with the works.

Most young people have insatiable
appetites, and you were no different.
That's why your morning snack was always substantial. Typically it would
consist of a bagel with so much cream
cheese, that when the two halves of the
bagel came together, the sandwich was
about twice as thick as the bagel by itself. And what is breakfast without coffee? You always insisted on plenty of
milk and sugar.

I often marveled at how you would
carefully avoid the fruits on the
table. And I can't remember a single instance when you picked up a green or
yellow vegetable. In fact, if one of
your sandwiches came with lettuce or to-
mato, you would remove it before you
took your first bite. But you could be
counted on to take your share, and

more, of the cookies and cake — the
gooier, the better.

Let me give you credit for being re-
spectfully tolerant of my "strange" behavior when it came to food. I suspect
that for a long time you really did
not understand why I consistently refused to accept your invitation to
join you, even though you wanted me to
believe you did.

And then one day you finally asked
me to explain to you why I did not eat
meat. You may recall how careful I was
to point out that my decision to become a vegetarian was entirely for personal reasons that have no bearing
whatsoever on your choices and/or pref-
erences. I wanted to be very clear so
that you would not perceive my explanation as an automatic recommendation
for you to do the same.

You had convinced me that you were
genuinely interested in foods and how
they affect our bodies, so I was happy
to answer your questions. You listened
very intently. Though you did not say
it at the time, I could see that you
were wondering about possible connections between your present eating habits and later problems.

This puzzlement lasted only a few
minutes, however, for like all teenagers, you believe (or used to) that you
are indestructible. Accordingly, you
will see little reason to pay attention to the harmful effects of a diet
high in animal fats and refined sug-
ars. From your perspective, these warnings are for "old" folks.

Well, the truth is that even at
your age, you can be adversely affected, if you continue to ignore the

warnings, and select your foods only on
the basis of taste, with no regard for
their nutritional value.

In one sense, though, you are correct in your belief that youth is a powerful ally, working to protect you from
the abuses which are an inevitable part
of growing up. But understand two
things:

1. Even at the height of its powers, youth (and that includes yours)
can be overwhelmed, if the abuses are
serious enough.

2. Youth gradually gives way to increasing age. As it does so, it slowly
loses some of its recuperative magic.
This means that your body will begin to
show the cumulative evidences of the
years of thoughtless eating habits.

I have heard the arguments that attempt to demonstrate why a life-style
like yours (hard-working actor with
full-time academic responsibilities)
simply does not leave enough time to
eat right, or exercise regularly.

Yes, you are busy, in effect carry-
ing two full-time jobs, and for this
you deserve a lot of credit. But the
same commitment and determination that
are enabling you to succeed in these
two major areas can provide the where-
withal to make the changes that will result in your improved health.

"Ah," you say, "but I'm not sick,
I'm healthy." Well, how do I respond to
that? From all appearances, you are
healthy. But health is much more than
the absence of disease. So when I talk
about "improving your health" I am not
saying that you are now sick. Rather, I
am urging that you give your body both
the quality of nutrients and the level

of activity it needs to perform with
greater efficiency.

When you are on stage, or in front
of the camera, are you satisfied with
a mediocre performance, especially
when you know that you are capable of
giving an outstanding one?

Health is like that, in a way. Most
people are quite content to live in a
body whose daily performance is only
substandard, when it is entirely
within their control to enjoy a much
more vigorous existence.

The choice is yours, therefore. You
can continue on your present pathway,
or you can make the kinds of changes
that will confer on you the benefits
of a more efficiently functioning
body. And do you know something? When
the body is really working well, the
mind is sharp, sharp.

Let's begin with the most common ex-
cuse for failure to make these changes
— lack of time. I am sure that you,
too, believe that your heavy professional and academic demands leave you
no time to choose the foods that support a healthy life-style.

But if truth be told, you also know
deep down that the far more likely reason is that you really don't want to
change. Thus, even though one part of
you may be giving lip service to the
value of eating a healthful diet, so
strong is your attachment to your present foods, that you find it difficult
to make a commitment to change.

Indeed, this scenario is more wide-
spread than you might imagine. Some,
teenagers and adults alike, go so far
as to declare their intention to eat
more healthfully, and then end up

right back where they started. Most of
the time, the reason is that they never
really committed themselves to the task.

If my sense is correct, and I think
it is, you are ready for some specific
information about what you can do to
begin making changes in your pattern of
eating.

Accordingly, I shall set down a few
suggestions which can be easily incorporated in your schedule, provided you really want to include them.

But I urge you not to begin until
you have in your head a clear picture
of precisely what you want to accom-
plish by these changes, and why. Short
of this, you, too, are likely to fall
by the wayside, like so many who undertake the changes without the proper mental preparation.

First, I strongly suggest that you
drink more water. Almost any set will
be equipped with bottled waters in a variety of sizes. Keep one with you constantly, and drink, drink, drink. By
the way, it does not have to be cold.
In fact, you may be better off drinking
it at room temperature.

Secondly, eat fresh fruit — the
more the better. There are so many opportunities during the day to pick up a
piece of fruit rather than a cookie, or
a bag of potato chips.

A good plan might be to think of
fruit as a legitimate food, containing
a rich supply of nutrients that are easily accessible to the body. Try eating
only fruit for breakfast once or twice
a week. It may seem odd at first. But
if you do it for a while, you will be
pleasantly surprised by the differences
you will observe.

Third, eat green salads. Any fast food place worth its salt has a salad bar. So when you order your hamburgers, you can certainly include a serving of green salad.

Fourth, a steady diet of hamburgers provides much more animal fat than you need. You would do yourself a big favor, then, if you limited the number of times you eat them in a week. My advice? Eat fewer hamburgers.

"Easy enough for you to say," you think, "but what do I eat? I just don't have the time to go to restaurants." Take heart. With a little thought and planning, you can significantly improve your diet and your health.

For example, have you thought to bring lunch from home? You or your mom can prepare it the night before, and in the morning when you are rushing, all you have to do is open the refrigerator and grab it.

Fifth, drink more juice. Every time you want to reach for a soda, reach for natural juice, instead. It could be apple, orange, or pineapple, or any other kind you prefer. It will satisfy your craving for the sweet taste, without filling your body with refined sugar, or artificial sweetener, or whatever else they put in sodas.

Finally, let's talk a little about exercise. The occasional basketball game does not fill the bill. What you need is some kind of regular activity — swimming, jogging, vigorous walking, bicycling, dancing, at least three times a week.

Think of a healthy life-style as a coin with two faces. (Have you ever

met one with only one face?) That is,
proper diet and exercise are two sides
of the same coin. To do one without the
other is like rehearsing without ever
performing.

These are my suggestions that will
get you started. If you make an honest
attempt to follow them, I promise that
the rewards will more than make up for
any inconvenience.

Let me hear from you.

Very sincerely,

Dr. Ibrahim

✪

One of the biggest health concerns for young performers is
stress. Linda Washburn examines ways for parents to recognize signs of their children's stress, an all too common symptom
of the pressures encountered in the business.

STRESS AND THE YOUNG PERFORMER
Linda Washburn, MSW, CSW

It's an understatement to say that show business is stressful.
We know from adults who have worked as young performers
that the more successful they became, the more stress they felt.
They've cited specifically the pressure, the competition, the
need to maintain peak performance, the sense of being in
constant overdrive, and the insecurity caused by being constantly watched and judged.

Since children handle stress differently at different ages,
it's important for a parent to realize when a child is under too
much tension and to recognize what the changing signs of
stress are for children as they mature. A parent should also
keep in mind that the younger the child, the less the child will
be able to verbalize the problem.

One symptom of stress, similar in children of all ages, is
sleeping disorders, in which kids will not be able to fall asleep,
wake up during the night, or will get up very early in the

morning. Since this can happen without any apparent external stress, it's important to be aware of your child's habits and to note any glaring changes in sleeping, or even eating, patterns.

In very young children, stress might manifest itself either physically or emotionally. They'll complain of stomach cramps, headaches, or they'll have skin rashes and develop hives. There's no point getting upset when a symptom of stress occurs, but if a prolonged pattern develops, and as you notice that whenever rehearsal begins there's an onset of a stomach ache, or that the child throws up each time before taping, or that a healthy appetite suddenly disappears, then it might be time to take some action.

Children who can't verbalize their feelings, or who don't understand that what they're feeling is pressure, should be watched for non-verbal signs: changes in behavior, irritability, not wanting to see friends, not getting pleasure from the things they normally enjoy. Another reaction to stress in young children is extreme cling-iness. If the child becomes increasingly dependent, it might reflect his inability to cope with his professional situation.

It should be emphasized that all symptoms have to be looked at in the context of childhood development, since all young children go through periods when they are more or less dependent on the parent, and they alternate between this independence and dependence. Look very carefully at your child's work life and judge for yourself if it's the cause of increased dependency. The importance of having a strong understanding of your child can't be overemphasized.

Some kids thrive on competition and do well in a high-pressure school. In the same environment, other children are more susceptible to feeling pushed or pressured and like a failure. Those kids might not be ready for show business and should wait a year or two before pursuing a career, especially if they're not thriving and not having any fun.

Signs of stress in the older child

Stress manifests itself differently once a child enters the junior high school years. At this age, the child can more easily verbalize his feelings. Still, a parent should also be on the lookout for signs of increased irritability, as well as prolonged or frequent illness. This is especially true in pre-adolescents, 11–13, who can suffer, among other things, from strep throat and bronchitis. Frequent and prolonged illness is usually a sign of psychological stress.

During the pubescent years, parents should note whether there is an increase in the amount of friction between the child and his or her peer group. It's not unusual for youngsters to take out their anxieties on the people closest to them, especially siblings and parents, even if the tension is coming from elsewhere. The young performer can't get angry at the director or the stage manager and just blow off steam. But if there's a lot of anger occurring elsewhere, and you feel that the anger is displaced, then you might want to find a quiet time to sit down and talk — parent to child — about what's happening at work, about who's bothering the child, about who she feels she isn't pleasing, and about what problems she's struggling with. Children who are unable to have fun, who aren't able to "hang out," go to the movies and enjoy themselves, are working too hard.

You might think that high schoolers, with their more developed verbal abilities, would be the group least likely to show any external signs of not being able to cope. But that's not true and, as in every other age group, it depends on the individual child's make-up. It's a confusing and intense time since kids are required to handle the normal stress of adolescence, in addition to their career commitments.

In teenagers, look for many of the same symptoms of stress that apply to the younger groups, such as insomnia and a refusal to eat. You might also look for constant nail biting, weight gain, and nervous tics. Additionally, this is the age in which drug and alcohol abuse are prevalent. If your child stays away from home for long periods with her friends and returns home with a glazed and far away look, then she might be abusing drugs.

Parents should also be aware of signs of anorexia (which is rare in males), bulimia, or other eating disorders. These develop from the need to be perfect, and to be "on" all the time.

When a child sets impossibly high standards for herself, it is usually an indication of emotional difficulties. Sometimes that difficulty expresses itself in inability to get along with peers or with parents, although the latter conflict is typical of this age group's kids who tend to be rebellious and to defy authority.

If you're not always clear as to whether it's the performance tension that's causing your child's stress as opposed to "normal" adolescence, puberty, or maturation, then keep two rules in mind. First, know your child. How well does she understand what's going on around her and how does she handle herself when things go wrong? As mentioned earlier, some kids have no problem letting things roll off their backs, while others seem to absorb problems. Second, watch for changes in your child's mood. A kid who's ordinarily happy-go-lucky and who becomes tense and irritable and withdrawn is definitely going through severe changes. Look at the circumstances under which she's working — the location, the personnel, the time pressure — and see for yourself how your child is being spoken to and how she's being treated. See if she's given enough breaks or rest periods. Determine whether there's enough sensitivity to the fact that your child is a *child* and not a grown-up.

It may require that you interfere on your kid's behalf and say, "My child is working too many hours. There aren't enough breaks." Older children may want to speak up on their own and may need your encouragement to do so. Discuss with your child what plan of action is preferable and who should initiate the contact with the production crew.

To understand your child's stress, you must get a clear picture of what your child is dealing with. It's very important for you to convey that you're on the child's side, rather than implying that it's the child's fault. And then you have to be willing, if you don't like what you see, to pull him or her out of the stress-causing environment. I think the major issue for parents is to realize that the child is dealing with a very different world in which a lot is expected of her. While there are rewards, there are also many difficulties to overcome.

It's also very important for parents to be sensitive listeners. Make it clear to your child that you're not just there for the good news, and that you're willing to hear that she's over-tired or upset or doesn't feel well. She should know that she has a place to air her feelings. Too often children have to tell their parents only the good news and are left alone to struggle with the bad. In this business, it's great to talk about the good things, especially when someone praises you. But it's important for the child to know that she has somebody to go to about things that she didn't do well and that cause feelings of fear or worry.

To be attentive to those feelings takes a lot of courage on the part of the parents, even more than they may realize. For some parents, it is difficult to hear that their child is scared. If parents place too many expectations on their child, then they must examine their own expectations. Perhaps after each project, the family should sit down and reassess its situation. Under all circumstances, the parents should ultimately send their child a message that says, "I'm on your side, whether you're in this business or not."

> *Linda Washburn is a New York City-based psychotherapist who has an extensive private practice in which she works with children, adolescents, and adults. In addition to her MSW, Ms. Washburn has a background in theater.*

Braces may be the bane of adolescence, but they don't necessarily have to put the whammy on the young performer's career. A noted orthodontist explains the options.

BRACES AND THE YOUNG PERFORMER
Melvyn M. Leifert, D.D.S

There's a lot of fear and trepidation associated — unjustly — with the work I do. The worst thing I can be accused of when working with a child who is in the entertainment business is that I can make him or her look funny. But contrary to common belief, braces don't cause speech impediments except during the initial few days needed to get acclimated to them.

Braces come in many styles, shapes, varieties, and colors. The best way to define the basic categories is to classify them as fixed versus removable.

Fixed braces are nothing more than handles with which the orthodontist can push or pull or put pressure on the teeth. Fixed braces are the "railroad tracks" type and most will not interfere with speech.

In the past, we couldn't affix handles directly to the teeth so we put a band or ring around each tooth. The rings were jammed between the teeth and were very uncomfortable. We can now take a handle and glue or bond it to the front of each tooth so there's nothing between the teeth and nothing on the backs of the teeth. If the cement fails, the piece breaks away, and, after proper polishing, there are no marks and there's no trapped food.

As long as we're bonding things, we can bond a clear plastic handle or a sapphire brace, as well as a metal one. We try to improve the wire on the brace by putting a Teflon coating on it, camouflaging it even further. But I won't kid you. A camera may indeed pick this up. It won't look like a headlight from a block away: while not invisible, it won't be as obvious as braces.

One solution to the cosmetic problem is to make braces from less obvious material, trying to find the least visible. The most common variation from the standard stainless steel railroad track braces has been a transparent plastic brace. Plastic isn't as strong as metal and tends to break. You may say, "Give up strength to get better appearance." However, an orthodontist's aim is to be done with the treatment as soon as possible. The more frequent the breakage, the longer the treatment takes.

Plastic requires an optimally cooperative patient. That means no crushed ice in sodas, no corn on the cob, no chicken bones, and no spareribs. Not only does plastic break, but because plastic isn't as dense as metal, braces made from it tend to stain more. Over a period of time, they'll tend to yellow. Initially, they look terrific, but they're not color-stable and may make the patient look funny later on.

These days, we use a sapphire brace. It's a synthetic sapphire that is completely transparent, very solid and dense, doesn't stain, and is stronger than metal. Sapphire is the second strongest naturally occurring substance known to man.

Orthodontics is a mechanical process in which teeth are moved around. We treat growing patients — adolescents — with more than just orthodontics. The reason we treat patients while they're still growing is that if we treat teeth before growth of the jaw is completed, we can actually correct problems rather than hide them.

Orthodontics has gotten a bad reputation because 20 years ago doctors used to wait until all the second teeth came into the mouth. Growth was then almost completed and they'd be treating everyone as an adult. By treating early, we not only reposition teeth, but prior to, or in conjunction with, rendering that service, we try to correct the basic problem causing the teeth to be crooked. If there's an overbite or an underbite, it's because one jaw is too big or too small for the other, or one jaw is poorly situated relative to the other. By treating early, with interceptive orthopedic procedures (moving an entire bone, as opposed to orthodontic, which is moving teeth through bone), we can stimulate or retard growth or reposition a jaw. By treating early, we try to correct the underlying problem, and use the braces to finesse, rather than just camouflage, the problem.

Orthopedic braces — night braces, bite plates, wideners — do slip on and off and are removable. That's why young people shouldn't put off treatment, but get a bona fide orthodontic consultation. Then the basic, underlying problem can be corrected, and the railroad track stage can be deferred until it's more convenient.

The initial consultation should take place when the child is between nine and 12 years of age. Since girls develop more quickly, we'd like to see them closer to the age of nine or 10; boys between 10 and 11. Too early is better than too late. It's sad to have a doctor say, "It's a shame you weren't in two years ago."

Unsightly railroad tracks don't interfere with speech. Most of the procedures in orthodontics that might affect speech or cause the patient to look funny are removable, like the night brace, which is a common early treatment we offer for home use. These and bite plates, because they're removable, allow patients to feel totally unencumbered in public. Another type of early treatment is a cemented palatal expansion appliance, used to widen the upper jaw. Although this does interfere with speech, it's visible only to a dentist and only if you tilt your head way back. But since it's transient, it does its job in three months, and then it's removed. Even though an expander is cumbersome, if the patient can take this short period off from work, we can speed up treatment to get him back and employed again.

Orthodontists work with the child and family so that braces don't become the center of their lives. There are certain kinds of removable braces that we use instead of the railroad tracks, but it should be stressed that braces, removable or otherwise, work only if they're worn.

We also use inside braces: they look terrific, but speech may become impaired appreciably, and the wearer may experience discomfort. But, if you're modeling, they may be perfect.

Confide in a professional. Let the professional determine what your problems are. Many performers get roles because of a unique appearance. We find frequently that these adorable appearances can be caused by developmental deformities.

David Letterman has an adorable space between his teeth and an overbite, both of which have made millions for him. From a professional point of view, however, he's got a strike against him in the dental ball game. His teeth aren't going to last as long nor be as stable as they'd be if he'd had the corrective work done.

If correcting the problem diagnosed by a professional isn't important to you because it stands in the way of a potential achievement, you can make your own choices accordingly. You can defer treatment or avoid it altogether. First, though, know the problems you have. Know the time frame you have to work in. Can this wait until after puberty? If you discuss your particular requirements as a singer, an actor, or a performer of any sort, the doctor should let you know if corrective measures will compromise your performance. There are trumpeters who wear braces, and the sounds they make are based on the ways in which they hold their mouths and how the musical instrument is positioned. Sometimes we can't treat orthodontic problems because of a person's profession, and accommodations have to be made.

Braces *can* be removed for the big role. It's costly, and not recommended in the regular course of events, but it can be done for a special opportunity.

> *Dr. Melvyn M. Leifert has practiced orthodontics for 20 years in New York City. He is a professor of orthodontics at Columbia University.*

Teenage girls often perceive themselves to be overweight and will starve rather than risk putting on another pound. Just as often, they will binge on food to the point of suffocating, and then purge their bodies through forced vomiting. The former is anorexia, the latter is bulimia.

If your child suffers from either you must first recognize the illness and then treat it as such. Dance editor Jacqueline Kolmes describes her personal battle with an eating disorder.

EATING DISORDERS AND
THE YOUNG PERFORMER
Jacqueline Kolmes

Anorexia is systematic self-starvation; the anorexic severely limits food intake and lives in fear of overeating and gaining weight. Anorexia's close relative, *bulimia*, is the practice of "purging" food from the body through forced vomiting and the use of diuretics and laxatives. While someone with anorexia may eat only a few hundred calories a day, an individual suffering from bulimia may consume 20,000 calories during a binge, and then proceed to throw everything up. Bulimics know how to time their "purges" so that calories consumed are not absorbed. Some people alternate between anorectic behavior and bulimic behavior, or start out with anorexia and develop bulimia as a solution to the problem of limiting food intake.

Anorexia tends to be chronic, sustained over long periods of time. Some individuals live with anorexia for 10, 20, or even 40 years. It's an illness that dominates a person's life on a daily basis. It tends to draw a person's focus inward; few people with anorexia lead normal social lives.

Bulimia can be a chronic illness or an episodic illness. Some people with bulimia lead relatively normal lives, maintain normal weight, and participate in athletic activities. In fact, in some cases, they've learned their bulimic behavior from coaches or teachers who have suggested it as a form of weight maintenance.

A person with anorexia will be very particular about food; the focus will be on finding the "right" food, food which is in some way beneficial to the body, despite the fact that adequate quantities to maintain health will not be eaten. Bulimia, on the other hand, involves eating whatever is craved, particularly foods which can be regurgitated easily. Sweets and carbohydrates are popular elements of binge menus.

The physical repercussions of anorexia and bulimia can be very serious, especially for physically active people such as dancers. At the very least, a dancer's health and immunity will be compromised by severe eating disorders. Injuries can become more frequent as muscle tissue breaks down. Sufferers of both disorders are at risk of death from heart attack, as we learned from the death of singer Karen Carpenter. People who are anorectic may die from the effects of long-term malnutrition, while bulimics occasionally die from rupturing of the esophagus.

A severe case of anorexia is fairly easy to identify, as the sufferer is visibly emaciated. The skin of an anorexic may become dry and flaky, the hair may thin out and be in poor condition. Nature will supply a growth of downy hair all over the person's body to provide some warmth. The process of starvation slows down all body processes. A medical examination of the anorectic patient will reveal low blood pressure, low body temperature, and a slow pulse rate.

Bulimia may or may not cause a person to be emaciated; some bulimic individuals are normal weight. However, internally, this ailment is also risky business. Laxative use, diuretic use, and vomiting all throw off the body's potassium and electrolyte levels. This can contribute to heart failure. The bulimic person may become very dehydrated. Repeated episodes of vomiting may cause the esophagus to bleed or rupture, or the throat to herniate. Tooth enamel wears away from the acidic condition that vomiting creates in the mouth. Individuals with either eating disorder may have chronically swollen glands. Few people are aware that the body which has learned to function on very few calories will gain weight more easily than had been the case prior to the onset of the eating disorder. This metabolic "backfire" may take quite some time to reverse.

Someone who reads about the effects of eating disorders may well wonder how a problem like this gets started. Eating problems nearly always begin with a diet that goes too far. Dancers are often told by teachers and company directors to go on diets. Some dance companies weigh members regularly. As dancers lose weight, they are steadily congratulated by teachers, directors, and their peer group. Thus begins an eating disorder.

A number of years ago, this writer had a bout with a borderline case of anorexia. I had auditioned for a ballet company, and had won a demi-soloist role. One catch: I was told to lose at least 10 pounds before performances started, although I was of average weight. Going on a diet was a new experience for me. I bought a calorie counter, and went at the project with zeal. My new-found skinniness assured my role in the production. Weight came off easily at first, and my fellow dancers congratulated me steadily on my achievement. I made it through a winter season with relative ease, except for catching a bad cold that lasted a month.

Winter ended. With no performances in the immediate offing, I continued my diet. I came up with the concept of living on 900 calories a day for the rest of my life, although I was very active. My calorie counter became a constant companion; I couldn't imagine going anywhere without it. My fellow dancers continued to congratulate me. One person even suggested that I lose 10 more pounds and move to New York to dance and model. My non-dancer friends made jokes about my eating habits when I socialized with them, but only one person voiced real concern. I was living far away from my parents, so they never even saw the effects of my strenuous dieting. I was afraid to pay them a visit, since I knew that they would try to feed me.

I've always been a fairly energetic person, but continuous dieting sapped my energy. I often took naps between class and work. Walking a few blocks became something of a challenge, and rehearsals were becoming increasingly difficult. I was generally depressed or very emotional. I took extra 7:30 AM ballet classes before work in order to burn off more calories. Sometimes I went out dancing at clubs at night to burn off any calories that dance class hadn't. No matter how thin I was, I never was fully able to enjoy my thinness, since I conceived of myself as being naturally heavy. My energy level continued to go downhill. I was frequently ill, catching any ailment I came in contact with. Finally, I went to a doctor I trusted. He took one look at me, weighed me, and said, "You're too thin for that sturdy frame of yours." That was the night that I went home, had a big dinner, and threw my bathroom scale in the garbage. My roles in the dance company dwindled as I gained weight, but I knew I couldn't diet like that again. Unfortunately, the story doesn't end at this point for many of my fellow dancers with eating disorders.

Who's at high risk for an eating disorder? The incidence of these diseases is on the rise, according to all authorities on the subject. If the statistic that one out of every 250 adolescent girls has an eating disorder is correct, then the situation in the dance community must be many times worse. Although most people with eating disorders are females, more and more males are joining the ranks. Dancers, models, and other performing artists are all at high risk for eating disorders; such disorders become an occupational hazard for many in the public eye.

The person with an eating disorder is someone with a perfectionist streak, and is often a genuine achiever. Young people with eating disorders frequently are the good kids who give their parents very little trouble. Someone suffering from an eating disorder isn't necessarily someone with no knowledge of nutrition; this kind of knowledge becomes irrelevant as the disease takes hold.

Clearly a very advanced case of anorexia or bulimia is easy to recognize. But how can you spot the disease before it becomes a health hazard?

Eating disorders produce numerous clues that can tip the observer off to the problem. Sufferers have a strong sense of privacy about food and eating. A young person living at home may help plan the family's menu, buy groceries, and cook, but won't eat full portions of food. However, food will be a favorite topic of conversation, and the person may exhibit concern about the diets of those around her. Social situations involving eating will generally be avoided. The afflicted person will develop certain food rituals, particularly concerning hours at which food may be eaten, ways of serving and cutting it, and quantities to be eaten at any one time. These rules will be abided by strictly, regardless of a person's varying needs on a particular day. Underweight bulimics and anorexics often wear clothes in layers, both to keep the secret of their thinness from the outside world, and to keep themselves warm in cool weather.

Exercise is an important factor in the lives of both bulimics and anorexics. Anorexics tend to exercise to burn calories and "fat," while bulimics may exercise as part of the purging process. Some people with anorexia have what they describe as excess energy; most have trouble sleeping.

Bulimia can be more difficult to spot than anorexia, since a normal weight person can be bulimic. One signal of bulimia is that the person spends a lot of time in the bathroom, particularly after meals. Laxative use in increasing quantities will sometimes be evident. Bulimia can be an expensive problem, since major binges require a lot of food. The parent or roommate of someone with bulimia may notice that grocery bills are increasingly high, or that food is disappearing without explanation. People with bulimia sometimes shoplift to supply food for binges; this is especially true for those too young to pay their own grocery bills.

How can the uninitiated fathom the mindset of the anorectic or bulimic individual? Imagine traveling to another country
in which thinness is valued as much as wealth, power, and
beauty are valued in Western society. Food and weight are life's
central issues, and everything else is arranged to accommodate
a certain way of eating, or not eating.

Physical reality may be distorted in the anorexic's world.
The anorexic may look in the mirror and see someone overweight. Hedy Diamond, MSW, a social worker in private practice and a graduate of the Gestalt Therapy Institute, specializes
in treating those with eating disorders. She stresses the fact
that the anorexic dissociates from his or her own body. Someone
with bulimia, on the other hand, will generally be able to see
her own weight more realistically. An anorexic or bulimic
aware that thinness has indeed been attained will feel that her
thinness is fraudulent, rather than a natural condition. However, she'll still regard her ability to diet as a major achievement, one which she won't want to be stripped of by a therapist
or a hospital stay. Control is a very important issue. These
people continue to want to maintain control over food intake
even when they go into therapy; this control is often relin-
quished slowly and reluctantly.

Hedy Diamond points out a special part of the bulimic
mindset. Individuals with bulimia often become extremely
excited about the planning and execution of their binges.

In spite of pride in maintaining low weight, there are also
elements of embarrassment, shame, and fear of disclosure
operating in afflicted individuals. People with eating problems
will deny the existence of their problems for as long as possible,
even when directly confronted.

Anorexia and bulimia are lonely journeys; the traveler
along these paths believes that she is misunderstood. People
with eating problems often feel cut off from their own emotions
concerning issues other than food; sometimes other emotions
are only expressed in the form of tantrums. A therapist dealing
with an anorectic or bulimic individual will have to work hard
to move the conversation away from food, to emotional issues.

Extreme anxiety about weight and obsession with weight
are norms in the dance world; delicate appetites are objects of
respect. Dancers who live and socialize with other dancers are
unlikely to comment negatively on low weight, and are likely
to comment on weight gain. I have vivid memories of the period

during which I gained weight after being very thin. My fellow dancers went so far as to prod my thighs and comment on their growth. My company director expressed something akin to horror as the pounds jumped back on to me; I was eventually cut from the company altogether. Only the steadfast friend who had expressed concern that I was too thin told me that I was looking much better.

A code of silence concerning eating disorders still prevails in the dance world. Mild anorexia is tolerated very well, as long as the dancer doesn't become too weak to function, or too unsightly to be displayed on stage. Company directors who suggest weight loss very rarely give directions on how to achieve good results in a healthy manner, nor is the issue of proper nutrition addressed. There are some teachers who will tell dancers that they're becoming too thin; they are the exceptional teachers.

Fran Hamburg, CSW, associated with the Center for the Study of Anorexia and Bulimia in New York City, was once a professional dancer herself. She is now a therapist specializing in eating disorders. She suggests that dancers and their families realize that the trend toward thinness in dancers hasn't abated, and to consider whether pursuing a dance career is realistically worthwhile if it entails enforcing serious restraints on the body.

Various types of families produce offspring with eating problems; there isn't one exclusive type. Often the family is one in which a parent is concerned with weight, and passes this concern on to the child, or even instructs the child to diet. Sometimes people with eating disorders come from families in which food consumption is chaotic, and overweight predominates. The person with an eating disorder responds by trying to control the chaos surrounding food.

Different kinds of families also have different reactions to members with eating disorders. One reaction is to deny that a problem exists, another is to go along with the child's denial of the problem. Some people try to threaten their children with being force-fed in a hospital; others attempt to do the force-feeding themselves. None of this tends to improve the situation. Both therapists with whom we discussed the matter emphasize the importance of taking eating disorders out of the hands of the family, and seeking professional help.

What role can a family take in resolving eating problems? First, openness about the problem should be encouraged. A child's denial can't be accepted when something is obviously wrong. Fran Hamburg emphasizes that parents can't afford to be afraid to confront their children, and that friends should also feel that they have a right to say something to an individual who's in need of help. The concern of a friend may be especially important to a person who's living away from relatives. Ms. Hamburg warns us that the person with the eating problem may initially be hostile to confrontation. However, on another level, this may be just the help that she's been waiting for. Families and friends need to try not to be immobilized by the anorexic's or bulimic's problem, nor should they blame themselves for the situation.

Teachers who see that a student has a visible eating problem should try to speak to the student or parent about the situation. It's important to make the student feel that the teacher's concern has to do with her health and welfare. A student might need to be assured of the concern that she could pass out in class, or become too weak to dance.

If a person with an eating disorder is still living at home, family therapy would be the best way to begin professional treatment. If necessary, the person with the problem may initially have to be taken to therapy on an involuntary basis, and, let's hope she'd continue voluntarily. A therapist should work closely with a medical doctor. Any matters relating to hospitalization or intravenous feeding must be decided by this team of practitioners, not by the family.

There is help for people with eating disorders once the decision is made to make use of it. The Yellow Pages identifies organizations, listed under *Anorexia and Bulimia,* which can point you toward practitioners skilled in caring for people with eating disorders. The medical doctor who works with the therapist should be able to explain the workings of the body and the dangers to the patient inherent in eating disorders. Hospitals such as Gracie Square, with which Fran Hamburg is associated, often have meetings and discussion groups for people with eating problems. Overeaters Anonymous can be helpful to those who either overeat or undereat. Numerous excellent books have been published dealing with eating disorders, from perspectives varying from medical to psychological to feminist to purely practical. Many cities have 800 numbers or hotlines for people with eating problems.

Hedy Diamond stresses that the person recovering from an eating disorder will have to learn to trust his or her body again. It's important to realize that this may take a while, and to be patient. Once food-related problems begin to clear up, the time will come to figure out what real emotional issues are lurking in the background, and to try to resolve them.

For a young person suffering from an eating disorder, the prognosis for recovery is very good, especially if the problem is spotted early. Bulimics tend to respond quickly to treatment. Once they begin to discuss their binges, the behavior often curtails itself in three to six months. Anorexia is quite curable, but the time involved often extends to a few years for complete recovery. As long as changes in the person's thinking take place, there's no reason that the rest of one's life should be overshadowed by the specter of an eating disorder.

As for our society in general, the prognosis isn't nearly as good. Although the media is bringing the problem of eating disorders to the public's attention, the problem is still on the upswing. As long as the image of only one kind of perfect, fit body is blasted at us from magazines, television shows, and movie screens, we are going to try to remodel ourselves. As long as we fail to see that bodies can be fit and beautiful without fitting the current media image, we will continue to hurt ourselves with eating disorders.

The following stories are inspirational. They tell of two young people who overcame severe handicaps to follow their dreams. Their goal wasn't to be rich and famous. It was to make a difference in their art ... and they succeeded.

BARRY MARTIN AND DÉJÀ VU
Terré West

Barry Martin and I first met at the State University of New York at Purchase, where we were both students of dance. During those years we were very close friends, and shared many experiences, including dance classes and serving as

Resident Assistants. In many ways we were like brother and sister.

The last time I saw Barry perform was in the early spring of 1983, in the dance department's theater. That was the peak time for seniors to present their final dance projects, a prerequisite for graduating.

The house lights dimmed. A spotlight shifted to upstage right. The music began. I became acutely aware of the presence his well-toned body commanded as he walked downstage left. His movements were self-assured, steady, and limber. The stage increasingly became filled with pirouettes, battements, jumps, and layouts, all generated by this single dancer. The energy became riveting and seemed to reach out to everyone in the audience. When the curtain closed, the spectators were instantly drawn to their feet, applauding. I had seen Barry perform before, but it was *this* performance which convinced me that he had a special talent; he had the ability to draw the audience into his world and make them part of the movement, participants in the art of performing.

By graduation, Barry had decided that after four years of working within the confines of institutionalized dance, he was ready for something different and more challenging. He was graduating from SUNY under the Bachelor Arts/Liberal Arts (BALA) program, with a double major in dance and sociology. Now he was ready to allow dance to provide him with the experience of having "his own wings."

Anxious to get his career launched in the right direction, Barry went to live in London for a while, to find his roots and to look for work. Things seemed promising when Barry was able to secure a job at his second audition. Arlene Philips, best known for her choreography in the film version of *Annie,* Tina Turner's music video *Private Dancer,* and Broadway's *Starlight Express,* offered Barry the opportunity to become a member of her dance troupe, Hot Gossip. Barry considered the troupe to be a theatrical dance company; a company of principal performers ... it was like being cast for a show ... nine principal members who were paid very well; it was a major job ... television appearances and tours in many cities ... it was his first job after graduating!

Shortly thereafter, Hot Gossip embarked on a world tour which was to take them to South Africa, Australia, and Hong Kong. But eight weeks into the engagement, while in Sun City,

South Africa, the first stop on the tour, the car in which Barry was a passenger skidded off the road and rolled over several times before landing on its roof. Barry, lying by the wrecked car, was left behind, while the driver, a white Englishman, was rushed to the hospital. Barry, who is Black, lay there until a passerby assisted him to the hospital. At the hospital, he was denied treatment in accordance with the segregation policies practiced in South Africa's apartheid regime.

When the Sun City management became aware of the accident and Barry's difficulty in receiving treatment, they used their influence to have him transferred to another hospital in Pretoria, 75 miles away. The transfer was done without taking exams or securing his damaged neck. Barry, with a broken neck, was transferred in a passenger car without having any medical attention at all. It was not until 17 hours later, after suffering two cardiac arrests, that he received white honorary status, and was admitted into an all-white spinal unit. Although Barry remembered walking, with some assistance, into the first hospital, when he finally gained consciousness, he was told that he would never be able to dance again. He was quadriplegic.

What becomes of a dancer who can no longer dance? What happens to a dancer who, at the brink of success, becomes quadriplegic, loses his independence, and must depend for his mobility on a wheelchair?

Four years after the accident, Barry obtained his Masters Degree in Dance Development and Arts Administration from New York University. He successfully incorporated a dance company, Déjà Vu, of which he is founder and artistic director. The transition during that four-year period consisted of many different kinds of struggle.

As a performing artist, Barry had been through one struggle, submitting his body to the strenuous and rigorous exercises necessary to perform positions and movements which are innately unnatural. Now he had a struggle with another meaning and another dimension — a dimension which is not immediately associated with the life of a dancer.

Barry recalls a year of rehabilitation at Stoke Mandeville Hospital in England, and the struggle during that period of convalescence. And then, "coming back to what was once your life, but being no longer able to get around the same way, having to deal in the world of disability and not having things accessible, and going to places that you used to go and took for granted, and to know that those five or 10 stairs are the obstacles that will prevent you from getting back to what was known before ... all of this reinforces the struggle and also the vulnerability that one day you're like this and the next day you could be like that. You never know what to expect but the beat has to go on."

The beat has gone on remarkably well for Barry. As can easily be imagined, there were moments when he experienced doubt. "When I had my accident I had no thoughts of developing dance. I did not know how I felt about dance, or what direction my life was going toward. I didn't know what difference it made whether or not I would be dancing." But with the tenacious help and support of family and friends, and even people who had been strangers but who nonetheless gave enormous amounts of assistance and words of encouragement, he was able to overcome this way of thinking. It wasn't long before he came to a different realization: "I know that I am as passionate about dance now as I was before ... my desire has probably increased because I'm not taking the movement and the physicality for granted." That Barry has been able to create Déjà Vu has helped decrease the tendency to feel despondent. For him, "Déjà Vu goes against that. It says that it [dancing] just does not stop here; it's only just begun ... when dance continues to go past the studio and past the stage and past the audience, it starts to have more value."

The life of dance has been resurrected for Barry through Déjà Vu. The company is the center of his being and embraces a significant part of what he is about. For Barry, Déjà Vu is the essence of dance and how it was a part of his life before the tragedy and how it continues to be a part of his life now. "Now it's part of my destiny, and no matter what changes take place in my life, dance will be a vehicle that will continue to let my spirit grow and develop."

Déjà Vu is an ethnically-mixed eight-member dance company which has an impressive board of directors from the art and business communities. As Artistic Director, Barry has been attentive to all aspects of running the company. He admits freely that his ability to maintain a sense of control stems from the tremendous efforts of those who work with him. Although there have been guest choreographers, such as Robert North and Blondell Cummings, most of the Déjà Vu choreography is done by Barry himself.

Barry's circumstances have not impaired his creative instincts in the least, nor has he allowed them to limit his ability to manipulate, model, and direct the art form at his discretion. He considers himself fortunate in that he had "enough foundation to pull from, as far as having a strong and diverse background of techniques and styles." Besides, choreographing wasn't foreign to him at the time of the accident. "When I first started choreographing, I was still able to walk; I was not disabled. I hadn't experienced this tragedy. I was choreographing from another perspective, where I was definitely interested in the craft and I was exploring movement from an able-bodied perspective. I am now on the other side of the fence. Now I am choreographing as a person who can no longer move, but who once knew how to move and who experienced the pain and pleasure. When choreographing, I use sense-memory to recreate those feelings. I cannot physically demonstrate. This brings the creative process to another plateau. It has allowed me to grow, develop, and mature."

Because of the way in which Barry choreographs, a special relationship and understanding develops between him and his dancers. The art of creating becomes one of interaction and sharing. As Barry describes it, "My movement and choreography develop between me and the dancer and that is a lot of what the beauty is about, because I'm not showing them how to do the steps this way or that way, so they don't have a fixed image of how I described it. This avoids ego problems and that's important."

Although Déjà Vu is a young company, it has received national acclaim in *Life* magazine, on CBS, NBC, ABC, and CNN. It's been praised by leading critics, including Jennifer Dunning of *The New York Times*, who wrote after its debut that Déjà Vu's performance was "vividly enacted by a cast that seemed to number several dancers, but consisted of nine."

Julinda Lewis, in the November 1987 issue of *Dance Magazine* wrote, "Martin had a raw edge that was effectively tempered by serious-minded yet exciting choreography."

Barry says the "positive effects of this ordeal are that people see that life goes on and that rainbows do exist and there's always something good waiting for you," providing you're willing to go forth and maintain a sense of your own self-worth and ability. When asked for the words with which he'd like to end the interview, Barry offered a "note of aware- ness to everyone that we are all vulnerable and anything could happen, but you must learn through the experience, as I have through my own."

> *Terré West is a performing artist with her sights set on art school as well as law.*

CONNECTING WITH MONIQUE HOLT
Roberta Frost

It wasn't Broadway yet, but when Monique Holt won the role of Kate in the New York University-Washington Square Players' production of *Taming of the Shrew*, it was a personal triumph of momentous importance. She had captured the cov- eted role by presenting Petronius' spirited bride in body move- ment, rhythm, and mime, winning out over a competitor whose lovely delivery was well-suited to the flow of Shakespeare's lines. In addition, she had successfully conveyed another per- spective to a character whose relevance to modern womanhood had been open to question.

If anything distinguishes this winsome 22-year-old Tisch School of the Arts student from the plentiful talent that radi- ates from the NYU-Greenwich Village campus, it's her innova- tive approach to whatever she's expressing, whether she's on stage communicating through dance or drama, or off stage teaching sign language, or counseling at a mental health cen- ter.

It's an intellectual search for something deeper and more meaningful, she explains.

At first, answers were sought through dance. Indeed, her lengthy list of credentials includes a two-month European tour with *Godspell* while still in high school; a scholarship at the Merce Cunningham Dance Studio; performances with Jacques d'Amboise, the American Dance Theater of the Deaf, and the American Dance Institute; and her own dance company — she doesn't hesitate to create opportunities. But dance alone wasn't totally satisfying. Now she experiments boundlessly with other forms of theater, always in search of greater preciseness in conveying an idea.

Whether this yearning for meaningful communication is the outcome of her early abandonment or whether it comes from the isolation that sometimes accompanies a hearing loss is open to question. Perhaps it is the way Monique Holt would have handled the material of her life under any circumstance.

She was found by an American adoption agency in a South Korean orphanage, apparently left there because she was deaf. The gratitude she still feels toward her rescuers permeates her conversations, and she continues to question the circumstances that could have allowed this to occur.

At age three, she was brought to the U.S. and to a totally different environment — a Lancaster, PA home, where she became little sister in a family that included two nonhearing parents and another South Korean, a boy who not only was deaf, but who had been untutored until age six because of which he was misdiagnosed as being retarded. Despite the difference in their ages, the two children were trained together.

Communicating at home was a lively affair; however, being mainstreamed into the local primary school was a lonely experience. "It was an abstract relationship, " she recalls, leaving her with memories of being disconnected from classmates. She could watch her teachers talk, talk, talk, but communicating with appointed translators was difficult. Mainstreaming did teach her to be observant, though. "If I closed my eyes for one minute I'd miss something."

The teenager pictured in the March 1989 **CallBack** article on visual language is Monique, animatedly talking in sign language at the Model Secondary School for the Deaf at Gallaudet University, where the feelings of isolation subsided, and she blossomed into a star pupil. Bright, articulate, and talented are the terms offered by one of her former instructors, Tim McCarty, who directed Monique in several productions there and who is unabashedly proud of having nurtured this talent.

Her feelings of estrangement were muted as she developed the knack of insisting on feedback. Sometimes these encounters were painful, but when a breakthrough occurred, she would be exhilarated.

Today she is equally at ease communicating with the hearing and the nonhearing. Often this has meant teaching others how to communicate with her before information can be shared. She doesn't often try speech, preferring to use sign language, writing, and her own artistry.

It was on McCarty's recommendation that she came to New York and the Merce Cunningham Dance Studio, arriving alone and without contacts. Not long afterward, she met her creative collaborator, Tim Chamberlin.

The Studio — where she was studying and he was already a professional dancer — had offered her a secretary-receptionist's job, and Chamberlin was asked to train her. It wasn't long before they both became impatient with the slowness of communicating in writing. So, once again, Monique found herself teaching the person assigned to teach her. Besides his qualification as a professional dancer, Tim Chamberlin today is a certified translator of sign language, and much more: not only can he voice her words, he gives character to their every nuance. They are two people in creative harmony.

Walk along a low-numbered street in New York City, east to the alphabet avenues, or down to the formerly seedy warehouse sections of NoHo and SoHo that now vibrate with art and theatrical activities. Listen to the sounds on a warm night: guitars, New Age music, the rhythmic thumping of piano accompaniment to a dance session in practice. Look up and zoom in! There in silhouette you might catch a glimpse of two persons seemingly synchronized to perfection. She: slight, bouncy, open, and possibly in pigtails. He: tall, slim, with finely chiseled features and welcoming gestures. You'll notice the hands — always the hands — graceful, animated.

Monique Holt and Tim Chamberlin are capturing the dream of so many creative young people who gravitate to the New York scene. They are performing, studying, experimenting — totally immersed in the artistic richness that the city offers.

Two Diamonds and a Blur, the collaborative vehicle with which they perform and package their artistic energies, is a venture with strong imagery, the Diamonds being themselves, the Blur being an expression in sign done with a strikingly beautiful shimmering motion. The outcome of their collaborations have included off- and off-off Broadway performances as well as a memorial production that eased the loss of a close friend, and experimental works designed for the nonhearing.

While such harmony may be a delightful achievement, for Monique it can challenge her independence. Not in reality, of course, but in the perceptions of others. Tim is acutely attuned to this possibility and goes overboard to assure everyone that Monique is very much her own woman. When he translates for her, he always speaks in the first person. "I have to be careful of this," he says. "One time when I was accompanying Monique to a class, I told the instructor that I had to leave early. The instructor was so accustomed to my using the first person to express Monique's thoughts that he indicated, well, as long as she was going, I might as well go, too. He was surprised later when I left and she stayed."

There was apprehension at Tisch when Monique applied for admission as a full-time student. The school wasn't accustomed to translating grade-scores from a secondary institution for the deaf into potential for success in work requiring excellent verbal skills and an aptitude for theater production. Thus greater weight was given to her ability to communicate and to her reputation for creativity established in drama classes already taken there. She was to become the first nonhearing student to matriculate in the school's education and experimental theater programs.

The challenge was thereby tossed to the academic community to be open to the imaginative possibilities Monique's talents offered. Since both Monique and Tim were already committed to looking at people and ideas innovatively, the results have been remarkable. One professor accepted the challenge by asking her to begin each session of his class with a two-minute lesson in sign language. He then incorporated the sense of her instructions into his own lecture, thereby providing a learning experience that everyone could share. A classmate was having trouble connecting when doing voice for her characterization in a scene from *The Maids,* Jean Genet's difficult, abstract play. "It was impossible for me to be completely deaf and for her to be completely hearing, " Monique says. "We figured out that I would teach her some signing. She would still talk, but she would know sign language. That really helped us connect."

Sometimes she can bring a unique realism to a role by capturing the tensions that develop when trying to connect, as in scenes between the frustrated teacher, Annie Sullivan, and her equally frustrated pupil, Helen Keller, in *The Miracle Worker.*

Having selected her for the role of Kate in *Taming of the Shrew*, the professor-casting director then had to figure out how to handle Shakespeare's words. He decided to award her competitor a part as her alter ego. She was to project Kate's feelings in voice! "It was a struggle for both of us, " she admits. They resolved their tensions by first coming to grips with their competitiveness, and then agreeing to be supportive of each other.

The unique interpretation was stunning theater. It gave depth to Kate's character and predicament, and sparked much discussion over whether the shrew's taming represented the reining-in of a typically submissive medieval woman or a savvy feminist in a no-win situation.

What's next for Monique Holt?

Besides the steady round of auditions and obligations already undertaken by Two Diamonds and a Blur in New York and Washington, D.C., she'll be continuing her experiments in theater with Tisch faculties both in New York and in Europe for another two years.

Already she has been accepted into the classes of Ryszard Bielak, the Polish actor-director whose U.S. reputation was earned with the Peter Brooks production of the Indian classic, *Mahabarata*. She expects that her work with Bielak will provide her with insights into the traditions of European theater, rich in ritual and myth.

Soon Monique and Tim will carry their dreams to Paris, where she not only will study, but will work with theaters of the deaf in Europe, bringing the fullness of theatrical expression to deaf audiences.

She is hopeful, too, there will be more Shakespeare.

7
Babies

There are so many parents who are struggling to pay the bills and who figure that their kid is as good or as cute as the next kid out there, and he or she could make them a few bucks. And they may be right. But there are a lot of kids and parents out there who don't know what they're getting themselves into. Often times they're unrealistic about the work that the business entails. There may be a lot of rejection. I've seen mothers and kids cry at not getting the part. Mothers will do what they want to do anyway, but I think they should listen to their children and take the cue from them as to whether or not this is the right business to go into. My main regret is that my childhood was sped up more than I would've liked. I'd want to see other kids go through normal maturation and hold on to childhood for as long as possible.

Mason Reese, featured in many commercials

Babies are big business. Toddlers and infants are used to sell products from radial tires and life insurance to cereals and no-stain carpets. Children as young as 15 days can work if they have the proper permit. Babies with easygoing personalities, who listen and pay attention to adults, and who are not afraid to leave their parents to go to another room with a stranger, may have a long career to look forward to. The following article serves as an overview for parents who are considering their child's first move into show business.

BABIES IN SHOW BUSINESS
John Attanas

There's an old adage that warns a performer never to work with children or animals for fear that they'll steal the show.

These days, following that advice can be difficult. Not only is it common to see children in theater, film, and television, but in the past few years more and more babies have been showing up in TV commercials and print ads. Wherever you look, there seems to be a baby staring back at you. Sometimes they're advertising tried and trues such as diapers and baby food, but often babies can be seen advertising tires, carpets, automobiles, or other products that babies rarely use.

More parents are wondering whether they should try to get their babies into show business. Unless a parent is well versed in the ways of the business, there is a lot of work to be done and many questions to be answered before deciding to take the plunge.

Whether a person is one year old or 20 years old, getting work as a performer is no easy task. However, breaking into show business is easier for a baby than for an adult. First, although the baby business is quite large and still growing, it's a comparatively new side of the entertainment industry. In years past, demand for babies was not as strong as it is today. Many parents interested in having their children in show business waited until they turned four or five before trying to get work for them. In addition, there is a high turnover rate for professional babies, because babies do not remain babies for very long. Moreover, since many parents get their children into the business to make quick money, and are not interested in a long-term career, they often take their babies out of the business if they experience a long period without a booking. According to Elaine Gordon, a former agent with Kronick, Kelly, and Lauren, a dry spell usually occurs between the ages of two and three years. "Babies are no longer in the diaper age for commercials, yet they're too young for a preschool toy."

This combination of growing up and moving on leaves room for new babies to break into the business. That's not to say, however, that the field is wide open, and that any baby who comes along can get work. According to Gordon, she received between eight and 20 inquiries a day containing pictures of babies. Few of these babies will get work on TV or in print ads, and fewer will work steadily. However, as a result of the baby boom of the '80s, and Madison Avenue's desire to sell products to people in their 20s and 30s by appealing to their parental instincts, there are more opportunities for babies than ever before. For the lucky baby who gets national commercials, the business can be extremely lucrative. With the cost of four years at a private college estimated at over $100,000 by the time a baby turns 18, the money made from one or two national commercials, invested wisely, will probably cover that cost completely.

Things to consider

If parents decide to try to get their child involved in show business, they first should consider a number of things. Any effort to get work for the baby will be a team effort between the baby and whichever parent is at home most often. According to Jan Jarrett of the Jan J. Agency, a parent of a professional baby must be prepared to drop everything and take the child to a call, sometimes at a moment's notice. Although agents and managers usually give parents one or two days notice for an upcoming call, this is not always the case. A parent must have a flexible schedule and a secure means of transportation to get the baby where he or she needs to be at the appointed time. For parents who live in or near New York City, this might not present much of a problem. For parents in the suburbs, the time and money spent coming into the city might outweigh the possible rewards of the call, especially if it is for print work (since the going rate is from $65 to $125 per hour). If the parent is unable to use public transportation, the cost of driving into the city and parking in a garage, where rates can run anywhere from $5 to $10 per hour, must certainly be considered.

If a parent feels that the possible rewards are worth the sacrifice and is ready to make the effort, the first thing is to take pictures of the baby and send them to reputable agents and managers. Although it's becoming common to see babies with professionally-shot 8 X 10s, most agents and managers prefer simple snapshots taken by a parent.

"It is a waste of money to have an 8 X 10 of a baby, because in a few months it will not look like that picture," says Elaine Gordon. Jan Jarrett recommends that a parent simply put the baby on a rug or on the lawn, with no other person or thing in the picture, and then take a snapshot.

While there are photographers who will not only take your baby's picture but also provide you with a list of reputable agents and managers, Denise Dunayer of Fox/Albert Management suggests simply going to a theatrical bookstore and buying a copy of the *Ross Reports*, which lists agents. Then start calling agents to see whether they have a baby department. If they do, send out your snapshots and follow up the mailing with a call.

Meeting an agent or manager

What does an agent or manager look for in a baby picture? Good looks, of course. But not only good looks. A sense of vitality is important, as is the baby's coloring. A strong character look might also interest an agent, and get him or her to make an appointment with the parent and child. What a parent must remember is that in show business everyone has a different opinion of what will sell, and no one idea is entirely correct. If you think your baby is not sufficiently good looking to get work, you may well be wrong.

Once you have an appointment with an agent or a manager, you must remember that not only is your baby being interviewed, but you are being interviewed also. Most agents first meet with the parent and the child together, and then with the child alone to see how he or she reacts to being with a stranger. If the baby is happy and active and doesn't mind being away from his mother, then that's a baby most agents or managers will want to work with. If the baby begins crying as soon as the mother is gone, or is cranky, or difficult to control, most agents probably will think twice about taking the child on.

"The ones that are laughing, smiling, and responding well to you: those are the terrific babies," says Dunayer. While most agents and managers will take a second look at a baby whose first interview went badly, if they see a repeat performance of the crying, clinging, or disruptiveness, they'll pass on the child, recommending that the parents wait until the child is older before trying to get him or her involved in show business.

The personality of the parent is also important, for while it is the baby who gets the job, the agent must deal with the parent. An overbearing, pushy parent is not one that an agent will most likely want to work with. According to Jan Jarrett, the best parents are "extremely mellow people" who are realistic about the nature of the business, yet are also able to enjoy the work that is involved.

Denise Dunayer agrees, adding that the minute the parent stops enjoying it, or sees the child is no longer enjoying it, the family should get out of the business.

One thing a parent must consider when sending out pictures is whether to contact agents or managers. Although the differences between them are subtle, it's important that a parent know them when trying to get representation for a child. According to Dunayer, a manager, there are two times in a performer's life when he or she needs a manager: when very young, and when very successful.

"Managers basically cultivate careers," says Dunayer. They take on fewer clients then agents do, and are able to give those clients close attention. Also, since managers get calls from many agents, a baby who works with a manager will have more auditions and theoretically a greater chance of working. In exchange for the greater number of auditions, a client pays a 15% commission to the manager, along with a 10% commission to the agent from whom the call came.

Agents are a different breed. They have numerous clients and don't have time to give much individual attention to every one, although many attempt to do so. If your child works with one agent, he or she will only go out on calls that originate in that agent's office. In exchange, the agent receives a 10% commission on all money earned. While it is common for babies to freelance among agents, the nature of free-lancing entails a great deal of work for the parent. In some cases difficulties can arise, such as two calls scheduled at the same time. Free-lancing, however, allows the child the luxury of getting calls from many agents and only paying 10% on money earned. While most agents still do not sign babies to contracts, the practice is becoming more common, as one agent after another has seen his best client-babies signed by managers or other agents with whom the child was free-lancing. While a contract strengthens the bond between agent and child, it limits the child to going out only on calls from that agent.

If your child is fortunate enough to get work in TV commercials or a feature film, he or she is not required to join a union until age four. In addition, a nurse is required to be on any set where babies are working, and the baby is allowed to work only four hours at a time. On all shoots there is a back-up baby in case the principal baby has a problem.

Show business is not for everyone. To some, it's cold and cruel; to others it's exciting, enjoyable, and a great way to earn a living. For babies, who don't know what's going on, and aren't affected by rejection or the cruder personalities who show up every now and then, show business is merely a strange version of play time that they later discover they were paid to be involved in. If you have the time, the desire, the cash to invest, and have a happy, outgoing child, you may want to give show business a try. For the right team there is a great deal of money to be made; for those whose children do not make much money, they'll still have an experience like no other.

This is a list of agents and managers in the New York City area who handle children and babies.

Agents

Abrams Artists & Associates Ltd.
420 Madison Ave., Suite 1300
New York, NY 10017
(212) 684-5223

Agents For The Arts, Inc.
1650 Broadway, Suite 306
New York, NY 10019
(212) 247-3220

American International Talent Agency
303 West 42 St., Suite 608
New York, NY 10036
(212) 245-8888

Andreadis Talent Agency   DO NOT HANDLE BABIES
119 West 57 St., Suite 711
New York, NY 10019
(212) 315-0303

The Bethel Agencies   DO NOT HANDLE BABIES
513 West 54 St., Suite 1
New York, NY 10019
(212) 664-0455

J. Michael Bloom & Associates   KIDS 3 YRS. AND UP
233 Park Ave. So.

New York, NY 10003
(212) 529-6500

Bonnie Kid, Inc. — BKA   DO NOT HANDLE BABIES
19 West 44 St., Suite 1500
New York, NY 10036
(212) 764-1100

Bookers, Inc.
150 Fifth Ave., Suite 834
New York, NY 10011
(212) 645-9706

Don Buchwald & Associates
10 East 44 St.
New York, NY 10017
(212) 867-1200

Carson-Adler Agency, Inc.
250 West 57 St., Suite 808
New York, NY 10107
(212) 307-1882

Cunningham, Escott, Dipene & Associates
118 East 25 St., 6th floor
New York, NY 10010
(212) 477-1666

FTA Talent Agency, Inc.
401 Park Ave. So., Penthouse
New York, NY 10016
(212) 686-7010

Marje Fields, Inc.
165 West 46 St., Room 1205
New York, NY 10036
(212) 764-5740

Frontier Booking International, Inc.
1776 Broadway, 6th floor
New York, NY 10019
(212) 265-0822

Funny Face
440 East 62 St., Suite 1B
New York, NY 10021
(212) 752-4450

The Gilchrist Talent Group, Inc.   DO NOT PHONE
310 Madison Ave.
New York, NY 10117
(212) 692-9166

Veronica Goodman Agency
1288 Route 73, Suite 201
Mt. Laurel, NJ 08054
(609) 727-7803

Henderson/Hogan Agency, Inc. DO NOT HANDLE BABIES
405 West 44 St.
New York, NY 10036
(212) 765-5190

Eddy Howard Agency
91 Monmouth St.
Red Bank, NJ 07701
(201) 747-8228

International Creative Management
40 West 57 St.
New York, NY 10019
(212) 556-5600

Jan J. Agency, Inc.
213 East 38 St., Suite 3F
New York, NY 10016
(212) 682-0202

Kronick & Kelly Agency Ltd.
220 Fifth Ave.
New York, NY 10001
(212) 684-5223

Marge McDermott
216 East 39 St., 2nd floor
New York, NY 10016
(212) 889-1583

Phoenix Artists, Inc.
311 West 43 St., Suite 1401
New York, NY 10036
(212) 586-9110

Rascals Unlimited Agency
135 East 65 St., 5th floor
New York, NY 10021
(212) 517-6500

Gilla Roos Ltd.
16 West 22 St., Suite 7
New York, NY 10010
(212) 727-7820

Schuller Talent/New York Kids
276 Fifth Ave.
New York, NY 10001
(212) 532-6005

Managers

Closeups
250 West 57 St., Suite 1632
New York, NY 10019
(212) 757-8590

Renee Courtney Talent, Inc.
688 6th Ave., Suite 201
New York, NY 10107
(212) 645-0505

Cuzzins Management
250 West 57 St., Suite 1632
New York, NY 10019
(212) 586-1573

Debbie's Kids
14 Tamara Lane
Cornwall, NY 12518
(914) 534-3485

Discovery Theatrical Management
72 Moriches Rd.

Lake Grove, NY 11755
(212) 877-6670

Michele Donay Talent Management
236 East 74 St.
New York, NY 10021
(212) 744-9406

Scott Eden Creative Management KIDS 3 YRS. AND UP
4 Vails Lane
Millwood, NY 10546
(212) 953-1379

Fox, Albert/Kids & Co.
1697 Broadway, Room 1210
New York, NY 10019
(212) 581-1011

Betty A. Geffen   DO NOT HANDLE BABIES
17 West 71 St., #7A
New York, NY 10023
(212) 874-6374

Goldstar Talent Management, Inc.
246 Fifth Ave., Suite 202
New York, NY 10001
(212) 213-1707

Elaine Gordon Model Management
1926 Helen Court
Merrick, NY 11566
(212) 936-1001

Goodwin & McGovern Theatrical Management, Inc.
9 Layton Ave.
Hicksville, NY 11801
(212) 860-7400

Shirley Grant Management
PO Box 866
Teaneck, NJ 07666
(212) 926-9082

Jarrett Management, Inc.
220 East 63 St., PH-G
New York, NY 10021
(212) 355-7500

Li'l Stars
33 Rupert Ave.
Staten Island, NY 10314
(718) 494-4000

Madison Avenue Management CHILD ATHLETES 3 YRS. UP
248 East 90 St., Suite 1C
New York, NY 10128
(212) 410-1650

Miller/Silver Management, Inc.
27 West 20 St., #302
New York, NY 10011
(212) 243-0024

J. Mitchell Management
88 Bleeker St.
New York, NY 10012
(212) 777-6686

Mollo Management
1143 W. Broadway
Hewlett, NY 11557
(516) 569-3253

Moore Entertainment Group
11 Possum Trail
Upper Saddle River, NJ 07458
(201) 327-3698

Nani/Saperstein Management
160 West 72 St.
New York, NY 10023
(212) 769-9180

New Personalities
272-60 Grand Central Parkway
Floral Park, NY 11005
(718) 631-3636

New Talent Management
590 Route 70, # 1C
Bricktown, NJ 08723
(201) 477-3355

Niederlitz & Steele Ltd.   KIDS 3 YRS. AND UP
250 West 57 St., Suite 1309
New York, NY 10107
(212) 765-3828

Our Gang Management, Inc.
44 West 62 St., #29C
New York, NY 10023
(212) 246-8621

Cathy Parker Management
PO Box 716
Vorhess, NJ 08043
(609) 354-2020

Podesoir International Management
211 West 56 St., Suite 3L
New York, NY 10019
(212) 767-0520

Edie Robb Talent Works
301 West 53rd St. #4K
New York, NY 10019
(212) 245-3250

Rosenberg & Associates, Ltd.
145-B Allen Blvd.
Farmingdale, NY 11735
(516) 249-9878

SEA-MAN Management   DO NOT HANDLE BABIES
51 East 42 St., Suite 1601
New York, NY 10017
(212) 697-9840

Selma Rubin Talent Management
104-60 Queens Blvd., 10C
Queens, NY
(718) 896-6051

Sam's Kids
901 Old Marlton Pike
Marlton, NJ 08053
(609) 596-9797

Edie F. Schur, Inc.
176 East 71 St.
New York, NY 10021
(212) 734-5100

Suzelle Enterprises
182-06 Midland Pkwy.
Jamaica Estates, NY 11432
(718) 380-0585

TLC Management
10 Bay St. Landing A4L
Saint George, SI, NY 10301
(718) 816-1532

Terrific Talent Assoc.
419 Park Ave. So., Suite 1009
New York, NY 10016
(212) 689-2800

Young At Heart
63 Drake Road
Scarsdale, NY 10583
(212) 893-6470

YTI-Young Talent Inc.   KIDS 3 YRS. AND UP
301 East 62 St., Suite 2C
New York, NY 10021
(212) 308-0930

Patricia Griffith is the mother of Julia Claire Bonaccolta, now three years old. When Ms. Griffith began introducing her daughter to the industry at the age of 10 months, she had very little to guide her on how to make contacts for infants since very little had been written on the subject. *CallBack* asked Ms.

Griffith to put her experiences on paper, and what resulted was one mother's diary, covering two and a half years.

A MOTHER'S DIARY: A BABE IN AGENTLAND
Patricia Griffith

Part 1: Julia, 10 months

Photo courtesy of Patricia Bonnacolta

How many mothers have watched the chortling infant "weatherman," "beauty pageant winner," or "rock 'n' roller" in diaper commercials, or oohed and ahhed over the dimpled, cooing babies, apparently pleased with their parents' choice of wet wipes, and thought, "My Jennifer/Joshua is just as cute and can do that! Wouldn't it be terrific if Grandma could see him/her on TV!" What exactly is it that motivates us Moms to take the first step toward making this fantasy a reality?

For me, it went back to the old actors' joke, "What's my motivation?" Answer: "Your paycheck." *My* reply is, "College costs of $94,876 in the year 2001." I also think I have a pretty and personable daughter who "can do that," and, at age 10 months, is a healthy, happy, baby. Like most healthy, happy, babies, Julia craves attention and approval, and will "perform" at the drop of a hat, or rattle, as the case may be. How about at the drop of a camera lens? Of course, making the initial decision to introduce your infant to the rigors and pressures of the business is not so simple.

First and foremost is your baby's well-being: how does she react to other people, mainly strangers, who will be talking to her, touching her, and holding her? Is she comfortable in a room without you there? How easily does she tire and, when she reaches that fatigued "point of no return," how long are her hysterics and how soon does she fall asleep? Will the two of you be able to arrive on time to appointments without much fuss and wear and tear on baby? Are you willing to take her out in inclement weather? Does the idea of any of these concepts ruffle your maternal feathers, that is to say, rub your motherly instincts the wrong way?

I must confess that I am not entering the wonderful world of kids in show business as a complete novice. I was a child actress/model and began visiting agents with my father and working at the age of four. Although my daughter Julia is much younger, some of my memories helped me to determine that my child is interesting and well-adjusted enough to give it a try and to set guidelines for her welfare. Since I fondly remember my own experiences and jobs as an exciting and fun time, I decided to take my father's lead and follow some of his boundaries. I don't recall ever feeling the pressure of being "not as good" as the last little girl in line, and I believe that a parent's cool and calm attitude can only translate to the child, particularly to an infant.

Julia will wear no ruffles or giant hairbows, will not be admonished to "smile, baby, for the nice lady," and will take no blame or personal effrontery when an interview, audition, or job doesn't work out. In other words, the reputation of *Gypsy*'s Mama Rose as the quintessential stage mother is safe. I have no intention of pressuring my baby into becoming a parody of a normal child. In a recent interview, film director John Boorman said that when he casts a child, he, in a sense, casts the mother as well. It is most definitely the parent's responsibility to keep the whole experience in perspective. I think the competition factor, especially for a toddler, should be nonexistent. As long as Julia is happy and having fun (I am lucky that my daughter enjoys meeting new people), we will continue our journey toward her Warholian 15 minutes of fame and her college tuition. As soon as it becomes a frustrating or grueling endurance test for her, we simply come home. Nothing gained and nothing lost.

So, dismissing relatives' murmured objections, I decided to see if the American advertising industry would be interested in my daughter, and vice versa.

My first step was to purchase *Ross Reports Television*. A monthly publication found at theater bookstores around town and a few select book and magazine stores, *Ross* is the definitive directory of casting agencies, independent casting directors, and television shows filmed in New York and elsewhere. Each listing includes names, addresses, phone numbers, specific representations (teens, adults, models, and commercials) and, sometimes, information on open-door policies or the stern disclaimers *DO NOT CALL* and/or *DO NOT COME*. I went through the alphabetical listings marking the agencies that specified representation of babies or children for phone calls, earmarking those with no disclaimers for visits.

I realized then and there that I had to make a second major decision; exactly how much time did I want to devote to Julia's budding career? Did I want to plunge into this full-time immediately, or take it a little slowly at first, watching cautiously to see if it would gradually snowball? I decided on the latter approach, mainly because I had an upcoming free-lance job, and I'd have more time at a later date to pursue whatever leads resulted from the initial groundwork.

I made phone calls to 12 casting agencies, resulting in eight requests for a mailed snapshot (not necessarily professional) with Julia's statistics noted on the back, two messages left on tapes (never returned), and two invitations to open baby calls during certain hours in the next two days. All of the agents responded to my questions pleasantly and were very helpful, except for one who, in a dismissive tone, advised me to obtain a manager. I crossed her off my list and prepared Julia's photos for the next day.

The first agent we visited was in the Kaufman-Astoria studios in Queens, and on the midtown jitney out, we met the casting person for "What Every Baby Knows," a cable TV show featuring this generation's Dr. Spock (and my personal baby guru), Dr. Brazelton. Having faithfully watched Dr. Brazelton's show at every possible opportunity during my pregnancy (stopping just short of taking notes and testing myself), to say that I was familiar with the show's format is an understatement. Of course I thought Julia and I were perfect for the parent/child question and answer forum with Dr. Brazelton, and apparently so did the agent, as he took our names and number for future tapings.

After this auspicious beginning, we cheerfully crowded into Agent #1's office, with about 15 other mother/baby teams. We filled out file cards with our child's statistics, then received a sheet listing advantages, disadvantages, and general information on toddlers in the business. We learned that no one was casting Shirley Temples and Lord Fauntleroys. They wanted real kids, dressed in overalls and "stretchies" to sell real products. We were briefed on pay scales, agent percentages, and residual payments (only principal — read starring — children receive them). Agent #1 assured us the working conditions, far from being blindingly-lit sweatshops, are generally excellent, with such things as nurses and cribs, and, for the most part, accommodating to meal and nap times. Then, what seemed to be the bombshell was dropped upon us: no parents are allowed on the set during shooting. At this point, discernible murmurs of "I don't think I like that" to "This is where we get off" floated above the general hubbub, and it occurred to me that this was the point that separated the mothers from the mommies. It did not worry me particularly, and when the agent explained that we would be in the next room, available immediately at each frequent break and mealtime, it bothered me even less.

We also received instructions on obtaining a model work permit and social security number, which are essential for our babies to join their tiny work force. I was most impressed with the closing note stating, "If anyone asks you to pay to get your kids in show business ... tell them to GET LOST."

After Agent #1 went over all of this and took questions, or rather shouted answers over the crying and singing, she saw us individually for a few minutes. She took Julia's picture and smiled at her; to my delight, Julia smiled prettily back and obligingly reached out to her. To my further astonishment, Agent #1 said without further ado, "We'll take her. She's on file. We'll be calling you."

We arrived at Agent #2's office early, and since we were the only ones there, she saw us immediately. She filled out the file card this time, subtly keeping an eye on Julia, who was still in the knapsack carrier. She glanced through our snapshots but did not take one. I offered to take the baby out of her pack and the agent said, "No, that's not necessary. I can tell that she's cute, photogenic, and cooperative. Get her a model work permit, drop it by my office next week, and you will be hearing from me." I thanked her, and as we were leaving, she reiterated that she would be calling and added, "Very soon". We were in and out of her office in less than 10 minutes. And yes, we did hear from her!

Part II: Julia, 1½ years

At the end of the first installment of this mother's diary, my daughter Julia, then 10 months old, had wedged her size four foot in the door at a couple of agencies and was starting to be sent out on auditions.

First we obtained a model's work permit from the Board of Education, necessary for working children under seven years of age. Her pediatrician, mumbling something about future free tickets and autographs, wrote the required statement of good health. With that step completed, it was on to the social security office.

Not surprisingly, obtaining Julia's social security number included a few absurd extra steps, such as augmenting her birth certificate. That document is only proof of *citizenship*, in the government's eye, and doesn't prove *identity*. We needed a birth announcement, too.

Finally, success! My tiny career woman was ready to pound the pavement, ready to riposte her family's tired old joke, "What, one and a half years old already? Get a job!"

All that was left was to wait for the phone to ring. Two weeks went by, and I started to consider making clandestine phone calls to more agents from my temporary corporate cubicle, whispering conspiratorially while racking up calls billable to the company. I decided that this was a bit fanatical and counter-productive, as I would not be able to bring Julia to any calls during those weeks anyway.

Also, another unforeseen fact gradually "snuck up" on us: Julia was changing, and changing rapidly. She no longer looked like the snapshots I had circulated. She was, of course, larger. Her hair darkened and grew in considerably. As teeth appeared, the shape of her mouth changed. We took more pictures to use to contact new agents, and learned that most agents, seasoned baby-watchers that they are, don't need or require updated photos until the child is no longer an infant, but a "true toddler," about two to three years old.

The first call came after two weeks. Julia was to be seen for a towel print ad. The audition was scheduled during my working hours, so the privilege of escorting the baby to her first call was bestowed upon her father. Determined to be coolly nonchalant, I nonetheless found myself staring at the phone, an unappealing habit I practiced during my own auditioning days.

My husband reported that Julia turned out to be the coolly nonchalant one, making friends and enjoying the attention. After taking several pictures of her, the photographer asked my husband if she "works a lot." Taken off-guard, he stated that this was her first audition, and the photographer replied that she was very cute and should be working shortly. It's amazing how bolstering, how motivating an off-the-cuff compliment from a professional, any professional, can be.

Julia weathered her first audition like a pro. I, for some reason, conjured up an image of her patting her daddy's hand on the way home, while making soothing sounds and calming him down.

The next audition was for a television movie. Several babies were to be cast, so obviously the odds were greater for the job than for a solo spot. I began to anticipate my role in this venture with excitement. I had never attended an audition at which I was not directly under pressure. Somehow, it's easier to cope with Julia's needs and comforts when we go on "adventures" than it ever was coping with my own pre-audition jitters. For Julia, it's still play time.

Still, we were after a job, so I looked forward to a stress-free audition, every actor's dream. I prepared clothes, pictures, and diaper bag Sunday night, and woke up Monday morning with the baby running a temperature of 103. Oh well, so much for Julia's TV debut, and for my debut as a stage mother at the audition. Actually, any disappointment at not being able to attend was eclipsed by my concern with baby's health.

The next audition was for a magazine cover, and we managed to arrive on time and in good spirits. There were quite a few babies and parents awaiting their turn, and as soon as Julia was out of her snowsuit, she became the self-appointed social director of the group, approaching to greet and pat the other babies. A sudden thought occurred to me: for those of us who don't have the Yuppie bucks to spend on Gymboree, or other baby meeting places, another advantage of auditioning is that it is a socialization process, and the price is right!

By the time Julia's turn came, she was in a terrific mood and greeted the three women in the next room with a grin and a wave. (One agent suggested that it is wise to teach your baby to wave hello and good-bye as early as possible. I now know why.) They were very sweet with her, cooing and exclaiming over her while I undressed her — the cover was to be a naked baby.

It was at this point that I suddenly found myself looking over my child as one does any marketable commodity, noticing the small birthmarks and thin hair. Then, the rush of adoration that I've felt daily since Julia was born swept in. I knew that none of that mattered, that I couldn't care less personally, and professionally, that it made me even more confident and proud of my baby. It still turns my stomach slightly when I hear mothers at auditions "assessing" their children to each other; "She just wasn't pretty enough," or "If he only had thicker hair." As an adult ex-performer I know that it can be hurtful to think a casting person finds you less than adequate. Why take a chance on devastating your own child for a few bucks?

I then sat back and the ladies waved a toy and talked to her, all the while taking pictures. I have since learned that this is the exception to the rule. For the most part, mommies must bid their babies bye-bye and leave the room. Fine with me and Julia; the only thing to which I object is the elaborate farewell most casting people seem to think is necessary to break the bond successfully. After two or three loud, rather high-pitched "Tell Mommy bye-byes," Julia is likely to eye her new "pal" suspiciously and not want me to leave. If they would just take her hand and start talking to her, after one distinct "Bye, see you in a minute" from me, I'd be out the door. Anyway, by the time Julia waved good-bye and we left, we were all hyped up into an uproarious mood, and it took an hour to calm down.

As the months went on, the auditions became more sporadic (read: dried up), and Julia's debut was stunted. I never seemed to be able to find the right block of time or to be in the right mood to sit down and begin another arduous agent phone-a-thon. Then, with perfect show-biz timing, the woman who was to become Julia's manager entered the scene.

A mutual friend had suggested that she meet Julia and, when she called for an appointment, we were able to visit her immediately. Her office is two blocks from our apartment, in "our own backyard" as it were, in midtown Manhattan. Anyway, the grass did turn out to be greener.

Meeting and subsequently working with her has turned out positively. I have completely switched from my previously-held, rather narrow-eyed suspicions that we would be slavishly, gratefully forking over a 15% chunk of salary to some faceless hack to make a few phone calls. This lady works hard, sends us out frequently, and is concerned and supportive, a true guiding light. We actually do go to quite a few more auditions, since a manager functions as a sort of Central Casting bureau. We're now sent out through many agents, as opposed to two agents, so we cover more ground.

Working with a manager has taken pressure off of me. Now all we (or occasionally Julia and her well-seasoned baby sitter) have to do is make it to the appointments. Of course, that's not *all* we have to do. Once at the audition, keeping tiny tot's energy and spirits up, nerves down, and her neatly-dressed body out of baby brawls and other's bottles and snacks can require the patience of a Peace Corps volunteer combined with the skills of a featherweight boxing referee.

As in most repetitive activities, we're getting better and better at the "meet and greet" audition process, but I know as soon as I do, tomorrow will be one of those days when I hand her to the casting director and my casual "bye-bye" will be answered by the banshee shriek, "*Mom-e-e-e*," followed by said banshee being hastily thrust back at me, and all that's left to do is to go home.

On those days her manager, bless her heart, sort of shrugs and says, "We can't really do anything about that, can we?" Nope. Just tell yourself, a tad more testily, that you're both having a good time, and if it's OK with your Shirley T. dropout for the day, try, try again. You just might succeed one of these days. We did!

Part III: Julia, 2½ years

My daughter Julia is now 2½ years old. At the conclusion of Part II of my diary of her professional career, she had become a certified member of that secret netherworld of agents, managers, casting directors, and the audition process.

Auditioning has become routine, just another activity that we get to do together, which tends to make it more relaxed and fun. When it's convenient, I find it helpful to plan to go to the park, a friend's house, or out to lunch afterward (naptime permitting), and then the audition is just part of the day's outing. Julia usually looks forward to "meeting the people" and seeing the other kids, and now strides confidently and playfully into the casting room. The operative word here is "usually" because on the rare occasions that she is tired, cranky, or perhaps has the sniffles, she makes no bones about letting me know she just isn't interested in a show biz career today. So we stay home; there'll be plenty of time for schedules and discipline when school or preschool starts. Auditions are still considered "fun time."

However, much as I ramble on about the whys and hows of auditioning, we must be doing something right, as in the past 10 months, Julia has landed six bookings. Yes, my daughter, the actress/model, now has a résumé that consists of television commercials, print ads, and two offers from television shows (including *Saturday Night Live*). Each shoot was a very different experience, of course, depending on the nature of the media (TV, magazine, etc.), the product, and the combination of personalities involved. Yet, all had one common element: a lot of waiting. Just waiting around, ready for the word to go to work.

Ever try to keep a child under three years waiting for hours at a time, then the carrot at the end of the stick is that they must appear fresh, energetic, and able to follow a stranger's orders? I (and I feel quite certain Julia agrees) find this the hardest task of all. Print work is the easiest, she usually works within the hour, but we have waited up to six hours on a commercial shoot.

This seems to be an appropriate place to describe what I call a "survival kit," without which there is simply no reason to even leave the house. A survival kit consists of many bottles or boxed juices, snacks, blankets, toys, books, extra outfits, a brush and comb, and of course, plenty of diapers and their accessories. Thus armed, you are ready to leave for the studio in time for your call, which is as likely to be at 7:30 AM as in the middle of afternoon naptime.

Her first job was a TV commercial in which she, along with 29 other toddling stars of tomorrow, ran around in biodegradable diapers. Ran amuck is actually more accurate: one by one they succumbed to the chaos (and their Mom's arms) that was created by 30 toy instruments, a loud rock music tape, bright lights, big balloons, and a crazed director jumping up and down screaming and waving her arms, mistakenly thinking that her frantic hysteria was "keeping the energy level up" (not a problem with 30 excited, noisy babies). Julia started out strong, but was one of the first to go down, plucked from the stage looking bewildered, and definitely not enjoying this jam session one bit.

The production people on this shoot (and in general, I've found) are lightning-quick in summoning, or as in this case, handing baby over to Mom when the baby looks or acts the least bit disturbed. Julia and I would return to the cramped but comfortable "backstage" area, where there were playpens, a refrigerator, a sink, and a tight playing area, to wait. Every so often we would be called back out on the set and she would gamely join in the mayhem until she could endure no more, usually about 10 minutes worth. We were released from filming after two days, and thus Julia's initiation into crowd scenes ended. We have yet to see the commercial, much less ever hear of the product again, but are watching for it, all the way to the bank.

Julia went from yin to yang on her second booking, a print ad for a bar soap, in which she was the solo, naked, lathered-up baby. Surprisingly, she took to sitting in one spot and being smeared with soapsuds and Vaseline with exuberant humor (she asked to please go to the potty in the middle of posing, and was immediately and cheerfully accommodated). The photographer, art director, and assistants were warm and supportive, and set up a little stool behind the photographer for me to sit and shout encouragements and try really hard not to be a pain in the neck. We began on time, and the total shoot lasted under an hour. Julia learned the phrase, "hit your mark," which means to stand or sit on the exact marked or taped spot on a ream of white paper, a very impressive feat for her to have mastered. She relaxed into a self-orgy of showing off and clowning for the photographer, which the camera seemed to love, and I started to worry that she was having too good a time.

However, after 45 minutes, my little starlet slowly evolved into a seasoned professional, patiently enduring yet more suds slapped on her slimy body, careful rearranging of towels around her waist, raising her arms and grinning in response to the photographer's direction. And then, as if a blue cue light popped on, Julia looked up at us all and clearly stated, "No more." And that was it. No question, *finis*. The photographer snuck a few last shots in as we prepared to go right into the conveniently placed warm shower. Everyone bade a fond farewell, and the air of "we've completed a successful project" must have been genuine because Julia's third job was another print ad (this time, a well-known clothing manufacturer), sans audition, as she was booked directly through our pal, the photographer.

Did I mention yin and yang before? Night and day ring a bell? Job #3 involved the same photographer, same studio, same "best friend" from the former crew, and Julia just refused to sit in the toy wagon with the other little boy pulling it. Wardrobe (an adorable overall set), make-up (a little rouge, powder, and lip gloss), and hair (curls with a curling iron, big bow) were a lot of fun to do in front of the mirror, but once in front of the camera, Julia decided it would be more comfortable to lie down in the wagon, and wouldn't budge from her artistic choice. After about 15 tense minutes of cajoling and panicked looks, she was whisked off the set. They gave her a second chance within an hour, but no dice. We were released, and over the next few weeks we talked casually about what was expected of us when all the fun of the audition, then preparation, was over, and it was time to combine play and the reason why we got the job to begin with.

At all jobs there has been an abundance of food and drink. Julia gets more than her fill (and probably enough for the next two kids scheduled) of cheese, fruit, cold cuts, breads (including her personal favorite, bagels with cream cheese), juice, and milk. On her first national booking, a TV commercial for cereal, by the time she was finally called on set, she had eaten and been fed a virtual deli's worth of goods, and the enthusiasm of going for a spoonful of bran had somewhat dimmed. (Red light — watch your child around lavish crew cornucopias of food.)

The day was poorly planned, with the youngest kids called in at 9:30 AM and not used until 3:00 PM, a timing *faux pas* felt by everyone participating, primarily the preschoolers. At 10:30 AM, Julia had emerged from wardrobe looking like a cuddly Dr. Seuss character, in pastel Dr. Denton's with a top-knot spout wrapped in hot pink. She rehearsed her bit with her teen-aged leading man, a gentle person (one reason he was hired, the client later confided, was his rapport with children), then settled with about five other kids in front of *Lady and the Tramp*, one of many videos rented to keep our couch potatoes happy.

It was a large backstage area, yet naptime looked like summer camp, with tuckered kids bunked all over the place, in offices, cribs, on piles of curtains, etc. No one really slept, so when "showtime" came around late afternoon, Julia, having awakened screaming from a 20-minute quasi-nap, calmed down and went on like a trouper, only to obstinately refuse to go for the cereal after the second take. She looked good and took direction well, so they gave her a new bit of business, flipping her high chair tray up and down, which she executed with a vengeance.

I was encouraged by the client (the product representative) who whispered, as we watched from behind the cameras, "Don't worry, she's beautiful and intelligent, we'll call her next year when we're in town ... she's got a future!" Well, I know that, but how nice to hear it from her employer. I later joined her in a kind of mantra in front of the video monitor, watching my daughter work, chanting in low tones, "Go Julia, it's $10,000 ... do it Julia, it's $10,000." End result was that she was edited out of the final cut, and instead of $10,000 worth of residuals, we received a day's base pay of $366.60. And so it goes.

Julia has received offers from one prime-time and one late-night show (the aforementioned *Saturday Night Live*), and was unable to do either one, the former by my choice, and the latter because of illness. A crew from one of New York's foremost "tabloid journalism" shows filmed about 10 kids including Julia in a Central Park playground one day. They then distributed model release forms to the mothers and sitters, and elicited phone numbers. I was called by the show the next day, and was told that Julia stood out on the videotape and that "everyone wanted to know who that kid was." I was flattered, and told them as much, but since I find the host's form of journalism distasteful and the subject matter generally pretty lurid, I really didn't want to sign over the legal rights to my child's likeness to the show. It was a bit of a tug to give up a prime-time job, but for my first major stage mother decision, I know I made the right one.

Saturday Night Live was a different story. Julia auditioned one day at 1:00 PM, was cast that evening at 6:30 PM with a taping scheduled for the very next afternoon. It was one of my favorite shows from 15 years back, and I excitedly confirmed all details with the production manager at midnight. At 2:30 AM, Julia awoke hot, shaking, and barking like a dog. At 6:30 AM, I learned from her pediatrician that she had spasmodic croup, a none-too-serious virus that would last a few days. So long television appearance, for now. One must keep in mind that there will always be another chance!

✪

How do the babies who work in commercials laugh, cry, and throw up their hands on cue? It isn't by luck. It's with the help of an off-screen person, known as a baby wrangler, who knows what faces, or noises, or colors elicit the necessary responses from the young charges.

BABY WRANGLERS
Cindy Hsu

When someone says he's a wrangler, images of bucking horses, corrals, and snorting cows spring forth. But Josef Schneider is no cowboy — he's a "baby wrangler."

Even though babies don't buck or snort, they do need to be wrangled to get them to "act" on commercials, advertisements, and movie sets. The job of a baby wrangler, or baby "handler," is to make faces, toss balloons, sing songs — whatever it takes to get the baby to move or laugh the way the director wants.

Schneider's been a baby wrangler ever since the term came about. He's worked with children for 40 years, has a background in child psychology, and has been photographing babies for decades. He knows children.

His assistant, Yvonne Van Orden, said, "Schneider is the father of baby wrangling. He started this whole thing. One day, when they were going to film the first Pampers ad for TV, they came to Joe to get some of the cute babies that he was photographing for one of their print ads. But once they brought the babies onto the set, they couldn't control them.

"So they called Joe over to the set, and next thing you know, he was getting the babies to do what the director wanted. From the beginning, what he did was wrangle those children."

Van Orden has been assisting Schneider — who's past 70 now — for 13 years, often leaving New York for other states or countries to handle babies. She was in Arizona to manage the quintuplets in the movie *Raising Arizona,* and she recently came back from Australia where she worked on a series of Hasbro toy commercials.

Schneider's long-time experience with babies has taught him plenty of tricks and techniques for getting them to react in certain ways. He calls these his "devices."

"The fundamental thing is to make it all a recreational activity for the baby," said Schneider. "Their span of attention is so short." One old standby he uses to get a baby to laugh is to "run up to the child and bury my head into its tummy, then run away." He said babies love to pull hair, and are delighted with this game. Schneider still has plenty of hair to grab.

To get a baby to gaze a certain way, Schneider might blow soap bubbles in that direction. Or, to catch a baby's attention, he'll light a match — the baby invariably will stare at it.

"Fire has a magic," he said. "It doesn't even have to be a match; flashlights fascinate them too."

A more challenging feat is getting babies to touch specific objects. At 10 months old, a baby will not exactly understand instructions like "touch the red car, not the blue car." Schneider said in these cases, he would take the child's hand, touch it to the object, then shout "Hooray!" and "make a big fuss." The baby then thinks it's done something wonderful, and will repeat the action.

He said some babies like toys, some prefer food, others music. He finds out what "orientation" the baby has before shooting.

Schneider's devices work for him, but other baby wranglers have their own style. Judy Kay, who's been handling babies for nine years, said that simply getting the baby to follow specific instructions is the hardest job. "On my last assignment, I had to get the baby to touch a certain knob on one of those toy busy-boxes," said Kay. "You can't tell the child which one to touch, and you can't stay and hold his hand there, because the minute you run out of the camera's view, the baby moves." Sheer repetition is often the solution.

For Sarah Herbert, baby handler and set nurse, knowing what babies are drawn to makes the job easier. For example, babies are attracted to bright red and orange colors, she said, and will usually reach for toys of those colors, not the blues and greens.

When Herbert handled babies for Michelin tire commercials, she had difficulty getting the two children — sitting inside a tire — to fight over a teddy bear, as the director requested.

"We ended up sticking a tape recorder with the mother's voice into the teddy bear to get one of the babies to like it more," said Herbert.

The commercial could have taken a different turn. "Some of the best commercials are shot by accident. Who's to say these children really want to fight over that bear? Sometimes a few moments of quiet will let you see what the child does naturally," she said. "Maybe one child will put the bear in the other child's lap and lean over and give him a kiss — then you've got a whole new idea."

Baby handlers say that most of the time on the set, they're making noises, jumping up and down, and "acting ridiculous," just to get expressions from the babies. For this the production companies pay them about $500 to $1,000 a day.

With a larger number of babies, things get more complicated. Van Orden described a Pampers commercial she worked on in Germany as "just like planning a war." For that assignment — a scene modeled after the Olympics — 30 eight-month-old babies were in the bleachers while another dozen youngsters were supposed to march past them.

"Getting them all dressed, strapped in, looking the right way, and heading in the right direction was like waging a military attack," said Van Orden. "And to add to that, neither the babies nor my assistant understood English."

Another tough task is getting the babies to cry on cue, said Van Orden. She said she'll never hit or pinch a child — instead, she knows what usually annoys babies. "They hate to have their noses wiped or their hands held together. "When they feel restrained, they get frustrated and cry."

Manipulating the children until the scene is just right can sometimes take a full day, according to Herbert. Other times, with a cooperative child or an easy scene, the director will be satisfied after just an hour of shooting.

People who infringe on the baby handler's job slow down shooting, said Herbert. "Everyone wants to play with the baby — everyone thinks they know all about children," she said. People on the set who have babies at home want to offer advice; others just love babies and won't leave the child alone.

"But the child can have only so much play and only so many people picking him up before he gets tired or someone drops him," said Herbert. "And I'm responsible."

She said babies have a funny effect on everyone from the cameramen to set hands. "Sometimes when I'm trying to get the child to laugh, you'll see these grown men start jumping up and down acting like monkeys," she laughed. "And the kid just sits there looking at them, thinking, 'What in the world is wrong with you?'" Herbert generally insists that only she and the director work with the baby, or the baby will be confused by the many different sights and sounds.

Another obstacle is the actress or actor who must hold the baby during the scene — in soap operas, for instance — but who doesn't know how to handle babies.

"I take them backstage and make sure they learn to be comfortable holding the child," said Herbert. "Some actresses get nervous, don't know how to deal with a small child — the baby might as well be a baby doll to them. That's when I make sure I'm right there the whole time."

Also troublesome are the mothers on the set who don't trust the baby handler, she said. As a rule, mothers are not allowed on the set while a scene is being shot, because babies will naturally go to their mothers.

While some mothers are overly protective of their children, others push too far, said Herbert. They bring in babies who are feverish or tired, mainly because they don't want to lose the job.

"One child was picked to be the principal player in the ad," recalled Herbert. "She looked all rosy-cheeked and drowsy that day, and then I saw her mother feeding her Tylenol backstage." Herbert told the mother the child's health was more important than being in a TV commercial and sent them both home.

Because Herbert is both a baby handler and a set nurse, her concerns center more on the safety of the baby. By law, any time a child under preschool age is on the set, a registered nurse must be there too. Herbert began working as a nurse only, then started working more with the handling side.

"I see that the child gets enough rest, eats right, and stays out of danger," she said. She looks out for things like metal toy cars getting too hot under the lights for the baby to touch, or scenes that require the baby to crawl on a high platform, or directors who work through a baby's naptime.

"I make rules like 'no caffeine'," she said. "Mothers sometimes sneak kids caffeine or chocolate to make them look alert. It's a false high. When they come down they feel funny and their eyes look tired." Instead, Herbert gives children grapes or Cheerios. Food is used often as a lure or reward device.

Mothers who are nervous or upset when they bring their children in, make the babies upset, too. Children instinctively pick up on the mothers emotions, said Herbert.

Because of the major role a mother plays during a job, Schneider says he takes the mother's attitude and personality into consideration whenever he picks a baby for a role.

Casting is an important part of any ad or movie. Baby casting is just as crucial. For Schneider, who casts most of the babies he works with, picking the right baby makes the wrangler's job 10 times easier.

"If you need four babies for a commercial, you need to see about 100 babies to find the right ones," said Schneider. Since he knows from his many years in the business what ages and personalities are optimal for what the director wants, he is adept at spotting the "right" baby for the ad.

"For a diaper ad where the child just has to sit still, I'd look for a more phlegmatic child," he said. Endomorphic — or more active — children may be needed for an ad that calls for the child to hammer or spin around or pull a wagon.

Schneider can place a child's development to the month. "At four months, they can barely sit up. At one and a half years, they're walking. And by the time they're two, they're giving you directions." He said he tries to find children who are older than they look, because they will take directions better.

Over the years, babies have begun to "mature earlier," said Schneider; they're crawling, standing, walking, and talking at earlier ages than when he began this line of work. Parents are focusing more on getting their child to be active, and pushing their kids to "achieve" from the very beginning.

As for trends, using babies in commercials and movies waxes and wanes. According to Schneider, "The past year directors seemed to use babies in any commercials, not just when the product was related to babies. Pizza Hut, for example, just threw a baby in there for interest."

The "look" that directors want has not changed over the years, continued Schneider. The all-American baby is still the most in demand: fair hair, blue eyes, fair skin. "On TV they don't want kids who look very ethnic unless there's some reason connected to the product."

It doesn't make a difference if a baby wrangler has experience as a parent or not, Schneider said. He's the father of three and grandfather of two. Yvonne Van Orden has a son — she adopted her nephew, "after hearing all the good and bad stuff from the mothers." Judy Kay is the mother of three. Sarah Herbert has no children. All are successful and happy as wranglers.

"The poet is both born and made," Schneider said. That is, one half is knack, the other is practice. The same holds for cowboys ... and baby wranglers.

Cindy Hsu is a research assistant at California Magazine *and is a freelance writer.*

GLOSSIES

AFM: Stands for *American Federation of Musicians*, the union which represents musicians who play classical and popular music. At a Broadway musical, the musicians in the orchestra are members of the AFM. In New York, the local branch is 802 and its phone number is (212) 239-4802. In Los Angeles, the local branch is 47 and its phone number is (213) 462-2161.

AFTRA: Stands for *American Federation of Television and Radio Artists*, the union which represents performers who work on live television, radio programs, radio commercials, and musical recordings. Performers covered under AFTRA's jurisdiction include actors, announcers, disc jockeys, and news persons. Its New York phone number is (212) 532-0800; in California, (213) 461-8111.

Agent: Your agent functions as a salesperson and "sells" *you*—your talent, your look, your personality, your sense of discipline, and your ability to learn your lines quickly—to the people who need a performer like you. In exchange for finding you work, you pay your agent an agreed-upon commission, usually 10% of your earnings, as his or her fee.

Arabesque: An arabesque is a pose in ballet in which a dancer stands on one leg with one arm extended in front and the other arm and leg extended behind.

Audition: A "try-out," or chance to meet the people who are in a position to hire you for a job. At an audition, you have your most important chance to display your talents and give your very best performance. Auditions are highly competitive.

Ballet: A classical dance form that demands grace and precision, it uses formalized steps and gestures set in flowing patterns to create expression, and frequently to tell stories, through music. The word, which is French, came into use in the mid-1600s.

Barre: A handrail that's attached to a wall at hip height, used by a dancer to maintain balance during practice and to assist in stretches and other exercises.

Blocking: During the early stages of a rehearsal period, the director will work with the actors to plan their specific onstage movements and positioning. This process, done with painstaking attention to detail, and worked slowly from line to line, sometimes from word to word, is called blocking.

Call sheet: This is the sheet prepared every day by the assistant director of a film and then typed up by the production office coordinator. It lists the schedule of scenes to be shot, the length of each scene, the cast members who need to report to work that day, and the time that each member of the crew needs to report to the set.

Callback: Assuming you've done your very best, and the people doing the hiring think you might be what they're looking for, they'll ask you to audition again. Maybe you'll be asked to repeat what you did in the first audition, or maybe they'll ask you to do something else. They might ask to see you many times before they're really sure that you're the one they want. A callback is something you want, and often. As long as you keep getting called back, you're still in the running.

Carnegie Hall: The old joke goes: An out-of-towner lost in New York stops a passerby and asks, "How do I get to Carnegie Hall?" The passerby answers, "Practice!" Carnegie Hall is one of the foremost performance spaces in the world for musicians. A performer who's had a recital in the Hall has logged a milestone worthy of attention.

Casting director: This is one of the people who does the hiring, and is usually the one you have to impress first. Assuming the casting director grants a callback, he or she will have you audition for other people involved in the casting process, such as the producer, director, or financial backer of the project.

Cattle call: An audition in which hundreds of people try out for a part that doesn't require talent as much as it requires the right look is colloquially called a cattle call. The cattle call gives the non-union actor a chance to be seen, which explains, in part, why it's such a crowded audition.

Clio: The Clio Awards are the largest of the awards competitions, recognizing national and international achievements in the advertising industry. They were founded in 1960, honoring 1959's work; thus, they're 30 years old. Awards are given in the areas of radio, television, print, package design, and other categories.

Cold reading: At an audition, an actor may be asked to act out a script without having had ample time to prepare character nuances. These cold readings are common in commercial auditions, and they usually require the actor to make bold, immediate choices regarding characterization.

Conflict: If you appear in a commercial for one yogurt company, you may be contractually bound not to accept employment extolling the virtues of a competitor's brand. To do so would create a conflict.

Conservatory: A conservatory is a school that provides instruction in music. New York has many fine music conservatories, such as the Manhattan School of Music, the Juilliard School, and the Mannes College of Music.

Crew: The people who work other than in front of the camera on a film and who are actually responsible for *making* the movie are called the "crew." This includes all technicians, production assistants, DGA trainees, prop people, costume designers, Teamsters, assistant directors, tutors, nurses, gaffers, best boys, carpenters, electricians, and engineers.

DGA: Stands for *Directors Guild of America*, the organization which represents directors and assistant directors who work in film, television, and commercial production. The DGA also sponsors an Assistant Directors Training Program. The New York phone number is (212) 581-0370; in California, (213) 656-1220; and in Chicago, (312) 644-5050.

Emmy: The Emmy award recognizes excellence in the television industry. Founded in 1958 by the National Academy of Television Arts and Sciences, the Emmy Awards are presented to individuals and programs in recognition of their outstanding achievements in the television field. Categories include best comedy series, best dramatic series, best news show, best documentary, and best soap opera, among others.

Ensemble: A music ensemble is a group of musicians or singers who unite for a performance. When an ensemble performs, it's considered a unit, with each instrument or voice evaluated according to how well it blends into the group as a whole.

Golden Globe: These awards are presented yearly by the Hollywood Foreign Press Association. Now in their 47th year, they recognize achievement in both the TV and movie industries. There are 11 TV awards and 13 movie awards presented each year, in such categories as best score, song, screenplay, and director, as well as outstanding musical, comedy, and drama achievements.

Grammy: The Grammy Awards, established in 1958 by the National Academy of Recording Arts and Sciences, recognize excellence in the area of recorded music in such categories as rock, classical, country and western, children's recordings, and comedy.

Green room: The green room is the lounge area in a theater or a broadcasting studio that's used by the performers when they're not onstage or on camera. In some cases, the green room is the space used to seat auditioners and their families as they wait their turns to audition. Guess what color the green room was originally painted!

Headshot: The "head" is yours and it's "shot" by the camera. This is a photograph of the performer or artist, usually 8" by 10", and is considered to be an actor's business card. You present it at the audition and the callback, and when you meet the agent or casting director for the first time. It serves as a visual aid so they can remember who you are. Headshots can be mailed out with resumes to agents, managers, producers, and casting directors with whom you'd like to work.

IATSE: Stands for *International Alliance of Theatrical Stage Employees*, the union that represents employees who work behind the scenes such as camera operators, make-up and wardrobe artists, stagehands, grips, gaffers, electricians, and ushers. There are many individual locals of IATSE, but the main New York phone number is (212) 730-1770; in California, (818) 905-8999.

Improvisation: In music, anything played, recited, or sung without having been previously composed or rehearsed is an improvisation. Of the major musical forms, jazz leaves a lot of room for improvisation, particularly for a solo performer; whereas classical music, much more tightly defined, allows for little, if any, improvisation.

Industrial: Some companies put on shows promoting their product or service. These shows, called industrials, are not — usually — intented for the general public, but are presented to distributors, dealers, and others who actually deal with the public to sell the product or service. Performances can be taped or live and are presented at trade shows, conferences, and seminars.

Instrumental: An instrumental composition is played by one or more musical instruments, and has no voice or lyric participation.

Jazz dance: Jazz dance is performed to jazz music. It's usually characterized by lively, energetic body motions and gestures. Most dance teachers tell us that jazz dance is a style, not a technique. Ballet, on the other hand, is a technique, and those who hope to become good dancers should usually start the learning process with ballet, even though for some jazz may be much more fun.

Legit: Working "legit," in the show business sense of the word, means working in any professionally-produced stage play, as opposed to working in burlesque, vaudeville, television, radio, motion pictures, or videos. However, most agency legit departments encompass all of the above categories and omit only commercial work from this general listing. While originally derived from the word *legitimate*, no judgment is implicit anymore in the use of the word.

Limited run: A show which has specific opening and closing dates. Shows with a limited run are often revivals with renowned performers such as Dustin Hoffman in *Death of a Salesman,* or Broadway concerts such as Barry Manilow or Kenny Loggins.

Location: A location is the site of the set on a given day. If a film shoots "on location" in New York, the location may change from uptown to downtown, or from East Side to West Side, every day. Usually, the call sheet will list the exact address of each location.

Manager: A manager is a professional representative who guides a performer's career. A good manager will introduce you to the right agents, will help develop your overall image, will steer you to the right career moves, and will manage your business dealings. A manager gets paid a commission, which is usually 20% of your income, but can be as high as 25%.

Modern dance: Modern dance uses special techniques in movement to express abstract ideas. Whereas ballet is formal and jazz, like the music, is wild and funky, modern dance encompasses many different forms and styles. It developed in the early 1900s as a revolt against the formalities of ballet.

Monologue: A dramatic or comedic single-voice recitation is called a monologue. Many actors adapt monologues from established plays, which they use for appropriate auditions. An actor must learn many monologues so that he has a repertoire of audition pieces from which to choose.

Motivation: There's the old joke in which the actor has just been told by the director to cross the stage in a certain manner. The actor says to the director, "But what's my motivation?" and the director answers, "Your paycheck!" Motivation is the reason that brings you to do something, and in acting, it's the psychology behind an action or a deed.

NABET: Stands for *National Association of Broadcast Employees and Technicians*, the union which represents many behind-the-scenes employees. NABET, like IATSE, is localized around the country and there are similarities in the types of entertainment industry personnel covered under both unions. The international offices of NABET are located in Chicago at (312) 922-2462 and Bethesda, MD at (301) 657-8420.

Obie: The 35th Annual Obie Awards are presented by *The Village Voice*, which founded them in 1955 to recognize excellence in off-Broadway and off-off-Broadway theater. They're unique in that they're not limited within a category. If in a given year there are three actors, or four plays, or five writers deserving of the award, then they're all honored. Categories acknowledge innovative use of sound, music, and lighting.

Open end run: Most shows on Broadway have open ended runs. This means they stay open until they lose popularity and money, or theater politics bring down their curtain prematurely. Occasionally, it appears as though open ended runs go on indefinitely. Two prime examples are *The Fantasticks* which celebrated its 30th anniversary and *A Chorus Line,* which closed after 15 years.

Opening night: The official first performance of a show with theater critics in attendance. It is the first time the show will be officially reviewed. Unfortunately, this first performance can turn out to be the last. For highly publicized shows, such as *Phantom of the Opera* and *Les Miserables*, opening nights are black tie galas, covered by major news organizations.

Oscar: The Academy Awards have been presented by The Academy of Motion Picture Arts and Sciences since 1929. The award, currently voted on by the nearly 5000 members of The Academy, takes the form of a golden statuette commonly referred to as "Oscar." The Awards recognize outstanding technical achievement as well as excellence in the areas of best picture, screenplay, director, and leading and supporting actor and actress. The televised presentation of The Academy Awards reaches the largest live audience of any TV show.

Out of town run: Prior to opening on Broadway, shows usually go to a smaller city for a limited run in order to work through production problems. Constructive criticism from out of town critics and audience is used to enhance the show before it comes to Broadway. Favorite out of town cities are Boston, Baltimore, and Washington.

Pas de deux: A French phrase, it literally means "step of two," and so is a dance for two people. In classical ballet, a pas de deux is divided into four parts, and each of the partners, always a male and a female, has the opportunity to dance a short solo.

Plié: A plié is a movement in which a dancer's knees are bent while the back is held straight. It comes from the French verb *plier*, which means "to bend," so thinking of the word "pliable," which means bendable, should bring to mind an image of a plié.

Post production: After a movie has completed principal photography, it goes into post production. This is a period of fine tuning during which what's been shot is edited for continuity. Not only is the look of the film pieced together, but the sound is "looped" to match the actors' moving lips. If there's a musical score, it's added at this time as well.

Preview: During previews, a show is exempt from critics' discerning reviews. The show plays performances for audiences who often pay lower prices. Actors usually rehearse by day, and are expected to follow a regular evening performance schedule.

Prima ballerina: This term literally means "the first ballerina," and the prima ballerina is the principal, or starring, ballerina in a ballet company.

Production assistant: This job is an entry level position which usually involves being at the beck and call of the assistant director, production office coordinator, producer, or anybody else who needs something immediately. Although primarily a go-fer position (as in "go-fer coffee" or "go-fer lunch"), most production people agree that working as a PA will provide a realistic look at the film business and its life-style.

Production manager: A production manager is responsible for the day-to-day overseeing of the production. This person is hired by the producer to create a budget, hire the crew, and handle all of the crises that arise in seeing a film through to completion.

Production office coordinator: A person who works on a movie and whose job it is to set up and run a production office for a specific film through all stages of its production—preparatory, filming, and wrap-up.

Recital: A recital is a performance which allows a musician to perform a program designed to show him or her off to best advantage and to demonstrate achievements and progress. In a recital, a performer works alone or with one or more accompanists.

Rehearsal: The expression "practice makes perfect" aptly defines the rehearsal. It is there that the actors, technicians, dancers, musicians, and everyone else involved in the production study their lines, run through their blocking, and practice their technical cues, all in preparation for a public presentation.

Repertoire: A list of dramas, operas, roles, musical pieces, dances, or other works that a company or a performer is prepared to present is called a repertoire. A repertory company, which presents different works on a regular or alternating schedule, has an extensive repertoire, or collection of fully-rehearsed pieces.

Résumé: To the back of your headshot, you'll attach a one-page listing of all of your performances, where they took place, and what part you played. Your résumé will also itemize your special talents and physical attributes. Most performers update their résumés after each performance of significance.

SAG: Stands for *Screen Actors Guild*, the union which represents performers who work in feature motion pictures and any other type of production on film. Its New York phone number is (212) 944-1030; in California, (213) 465-4600.

Screen test: This is a filmed audition that determines whether or not the performers who are being seriously considered for a role are, in fact, suitable for it. It's reasonable, after all, to audition in the medium in which you'll be seen.

Sides: The pages of a script containing only the lines and cues of a specific performer's role are referred to as the sides. At an audition, the actor is given the sides for a particular character whose part he'll be reading. It's from these pages, containing minimal information, that he prepares.

Sign-in sheet: When you go to an audition, you're required to list some pertinent information before you actually meet the casting people. The sign-in sheet asks for your name, the name of the agent who submitted you, the time you arrived, the time you left, and, in the case of a commercial audition, whether you have any conflicts with the product you're about to pitch.

Soloist: Soloists in music are singers or instrumentalists who perform alone. Many performers solo until becoming part of an ensemble, such as a chamber group, a symphonic orchestra, or a chorus. Conversely, many members of ensembles hope for the day that they'll perform a passage, or as much as an entire composition ... alone.

SSDC: Stands for *Society of Stage Directors and Choreographers*, a union that represents theatrical directors and choreographers. All directors and choreographers working in professional theater are members of this union, with the exception of any producer who is directing his or her own play and was not previously a member of the society. The New York phone number of the SSDC is (212) 391-1070.

Stage: Stage has many meanings. In the sentence, "John is making the stage his career," John is pursuing acting as a profession. In theater, the stage is the platform on which the actors perform. In film, a sound stage is a large studio in which the movie is created.

Stage business: Once cast in a role, the actor looks for those movements, gestures, or actions that help to flesh out his character. By finding the appropriate stage business, the actor adds detail, nuance, and expressiveness to his part.

Stage direction: If an actor is told by the script or the director to go up stage, down stage, stage right, or stage left, or to enter or exit, he's being given a stage direction. A stage direction indicates actions, movements of performers, or production requirements.

Stage door Johnny: If you're a man in love with an actress, and you spend every night at the stage door, bringing her flowers and writing her notes, then you are dubbed a Stage door Johnny, an expression that dates back to the early part of the 20th century. Although women can fall in love with actors and stand at the stage door hoping to court them, there's no equivalent expression for them.

Stage door: If you want to see an actress after a show to get her autograph, you're most likely to find her if you wait by the stage door. This is the entrance to the theater that's used by the members of the cast and crew, away from the general public.

Stage manager: The person responsible for the technical details of a theatrical production is called the stage manager. This person's responsibilities include assisting the director during rehearsals, supervising the lighting, costuming, setting, prompting, sound, special effects, and all the other myriad technical aspects of the show, straight through control of the stage during a performance of a play.

Stage right: The cartoon character, Quickdraw McGraw, used a now-famous saying every time he made a getaway. He faced the audience and said, "Exit! Stage right!" This meant that it was time for him to leave the audience's view, and he was doing so by getting off the stage to his—the character's—right side, the audience's left side. If he had exited stage left, it would have been to the character's left, the audience's right.

Stage whisper: An actor can't really whisper onstage because his lines would never be heard by the audience, so he speaks in what's called a stage whisper, a whisper loud enough to project from the stage and be heard by the audience members sitting in the last rows of the upper balcony.

Stagecraft: At summer camp, those kids who didn't act, dance, or sing usually went to "stagecraft," which meant that they painted the scenery or designed props or worked on costumes. Technically, however, stagecraft is the skill in or the art of writing, adapting, or staging plays.

Stagestruck: If all you've ever wanted to be when you grow up is an actor or actress, and you live, eat, and breathe for being onstage or on screen, then you're stagestruck. However, you don't have to have only the burning desire for acting to be stagestruck. You can also have passion for and be enthralled by those people and things associated with theater, especially the customs and the traditions.

Tap dance: In tap dancing the rhythm is tapped out with the toe or the heel by a dancer wearing shoes with special hard soles or taps. Tap dancing is a standard of many Broadway shows and, as do the other types of dance, it has a vocabulary all its own.

Tech week: The period of rehearsals devoted solely to the technical aspects of the show. Although actors are not present, technical crews, designers, and stage-management staff run through the show to set lighting, sound cues, and iron out kinks with the set.

Ten out of twelves: The rehearsal period just prior to the opening of a show. Actors Equity Association permits rehearsals to last 10 hours out of a twelve hour day. The other two hours are used for meals and breaks which occur at various intervals depending on the specific contract.

Tendu: This is another dance term that comes from the French, this one from the word *tendre,* which means to stretch and extend. The tendu movement is one that is stretched and held.

Tony: Named for Antoinette Perry, the American Theatre Wing's Tony Award honors outstanding achievement on Broadway. Presented since 1947, it's given to musicals, plays, and performers, among other categories, on the basis of distinguished achievement, rather than the notions of "best" or "outstanding." As a result, twice in the Wing's history there have been two winners in a category in a specific season. In 1947, Frederick March and José Ferrer both won in the actor category, and in 1960, *The Sound of Music* and *Fiorello* were the musicals of the year.

Typecasting: A performer who's 17 and tall and muscular and has wavy blond hair is certainly different from a performer who's 42 and short and pudgy and bald. A casting director who needs an actor to play a certain "type" will immediately pass on all others during auditions. Typecasting is based on images that most people can recognize.

Up stage: As a stage direction, up stage, with the accent on the "up," is any area located at the back of the stage, and down stage means to the performer's front. Upstage, as one word with the accent on "stage," has another meaning. When an actor is upstaged, it usually means that another actor has outdone his performance and drawn audience attention.

Virtuoso: A virtuoso is a performer who has a highly special skill and can perform a musical piece in an exceptional way. A virtuoso is generally gifted with extraordinary ability on one musical instrument, as was Artur Rubinstein on the piano, and as are Jascha Heifetz on the violin and Matt Haimovitz on the cello.

Vocalizing: Vocalizing is the voice exercise performed before a singer sings. The purpose is to "warm up" the voice, practice vowel sounds, and condition the vocal cords and larynx for the stress they're about to undergo. Vocalizing can include the singing of scales, arpeggios, trills, and other simple exercises that build vocal strength.

WGA: Stands for *Writers Guild of America*, the union which represents writers who work in radio, television, and film, but not industrials or commercials. Any professional writer working in these media is a member of this union. The New York phone number of the WGA is (212) 245-6180; in California, (213) 550-1000.

Wrap: Sometimes the most glorious expression to people who work long hours on a film is, "It's a wrap!" The wrap is announced when production ends for the day or when the shooting of a project is finished in its entirety. Once production has wrapped, there's usually a period of time in which loose ends are tied up and everything gets returned to its proper place.

INDEX